Nell Stroud was born in 1973. With a degree in English Literature from Oxford University, she has worked in American, German and British circuses on and off since the age of eighteen. This is her first book.

Josser

Days and Nights in the Circus

~

Nell Stroud

virago

VIRAGO

First published in Great Britain in 1999
by Little, Brown and Company
This edition published by Virago in 2000
Reprinted 2009 (twice)

Copyright © 1999 Nell Stroud

The moral right of the author has been asserted

A CIP catalogue record for this book
is available from the British Library.

ISBN 978-1-86049-695-0

Typeset in Minion by M Rules
Printed and bound in Great Britain by Clays Ltd, St Ives plc

Papers used by Virago are natural, renewable and recyclable
products sourced from well-managed forests and certified
in accordance with the rules of the Forest Stewardship Council.

Mixed Sources
Product group from well-managed
forests and other controlled sources
www.fsc.org Cert no. SGS-COC-004081
© 1996 Forest Stewardship Council

Virago
An imprint of
Little, Brown Book Group
100 Victoria Embankment
London EC4Y 0DY

An Hachette UK Company
www.hachette.co.uk

www.virago.co.uk

This book is dedicated to Rick,
who showed me how to find the way,
and Mum, the Lionhearted Mother

Acknowledgements

~

I would like to thank everyone who has helped me along the way, but especially Clover Stroud, Emma and Matthew Rice, Sophy Bridgewater, Tom and Camilla Bridgewater, David Godwin, Sally Abbey, Joanna Weinberg, Andrew Onslow, Rex Barker, Miles Connolly, Theresa and Derwent Gibson, Gerald Balding, Yasmin Smart, and a very special thanks and love to the wise and brilliant Eva Santus, and all of the Santus family. I would also like to thank all the people in and around Minety who helped mum and my family so much during the first two years after the accident. This is an enormous list of people, but I would like to thank in particular, Paul and Dawn Greenwood, Peter and Angela Crocker and Judy Walthew.

Circus 1. *A travelling show of performing animals, acrobats, clowns etc. 2. A scene of lively action, a disturbance. A group of people in a common activity, esp. sport. 3. An open space in a town where several streets converge. 4. A circular hollow surrounded by hills. 5. Roman antiq. A rounded or oval arena with tiers of seats, for equestrian and other sports and games. A performance given there.*

Preface

The circus boy had the cheekiest twinkle in his green eyes.
The Circus Book, ENID BLYTON

~

Elaina is a trapeze artist. She is a trapeze artist in the classical circus tradition. She is not a New Age, self-taught trapeze artist: she doesn't work in state-of-the-art fabrics under black light, she doesn't wrap easy tricks in clever effects, she doesn't compromise her art to move with the times – moving with the times is not important to her. Instead, every day, twice a day, the perfectly precise movement, right up there in the roof of the tent, the circus tent, that type of movement is important. She stands on her head on the trapeze bar, and the bar is swinging and spinning at the same time. Her neck is straight and supports her spine. Her arms and legs are outstretched, at right angles to her body. As she sits on the bar, swinging backwards and forwards in this position, she looks motionless, as if her head were attached to the bar and as if her body were made of plastic. In fact, she is balancing on the bar with a thousand tiny adjustments of her body, minute, invisible adjustments. She learned the act from her father. Her father did the same act. She told me she had to practise every day. When she was a teenager that was all she did, study and practise. She is Romanian.

I asked her what it felt like, on the bar in the air on her head. We were sitting in her lorry one night after a show, eating Kentucky Fried Chicken. Her eyes were black and white in sweeping, sly streaks. She didn't look at me and bit the flesh from a chicken portion. She chewed and swallowed and licked her lips.

'It is like dancing.'

Her reply did not open up further conversation. It was a single statement with a door slamming loudly at the end of it. It was important all round that I heard the slam.

Someone said that the ring-boy who ran away last week was hiding from the police. He was hiding in the circus. People hide in the circus. The chicken was going cold. Elaina's husband, Speary, put a video on. They hide in the circus until the circus finds out when the police arrive at the ground, asking questions, and the boy or girl behaves strangely, comes and goes from the show, disappears when the police are there. It is a problem for the show when this happens.

'There are enough problems eh, for the circus. You don't need this shit.'

Elaina's hands were greasy and she stood up and washed them in the sink. 'Anybody want coffee now? I make coffee.' She lit the gas on the stove and put the kettle on. She turned round and put one hand on her hip. 'Anyway, Nellie, you are hiding in the circus. What are you running away from?'

I didn't say anything. Then I said that I was not hiding in the circus, but inevitably I felt as if I was guilty of something.

*

I worked for Santus Circus for the 1996 and 1997 season. It is a small family-run show. The Santus family are French and have been in England with their circus for the last ten years. They are a very big family. Ernest Santus is the director of the circus and he runs it with his brother Roget, but they have four other brothers and two sisters, who live in France. They also work in the circus. For circus people there are no relationships more important than ties to family. Perhaps that is why outsiders – jossers – are never really on the inside when they work for a circus. They are not family.

Santus Circus supports Ernest, his wife Eva, their teenage son, Sasha, and Roget, his wife Anne Marie, and their two small children, Lucian and Ruby. It also supports Ernest and Roget's father, Grandpère, who never speaks English and rides around on a fold-up bicycle with his little dog and a filterless Camel cigarette between his lips. Grandpère is as fit as a fiddle and as neat as a pin. He is always the first out of the caravan in the middle of the night to shine a flashlight in the eyes of midnight gypsies or vandals or animal-rights protesters. If ever a group of people fought for their freedom it is these. Eva said to me that they were like pioneers in reverse. The rest of the world is rushing forward. They are fighting to stay the same.

Santus Circus was not the first circus I had worked on. It is, however, the truest manifestation of the idea about life and art contained within the word circus. It is an abstract, idealised, non-didactic performance. It is humorous, and the humour serves to chase away, with the shout of a laugh, the problems that beset the circus every day. It is not an avant garde 'new' circus. It doesn't overtly address philosophical questions, or spin a cautionary tale – there is nothing conspicuously theoretical about Santus Circus at all. I will tell you a tale of love.

When I first joined the circus I washed the floor of a booking office, sold ice-creams and looked after horses. I was often ripped off and frequently exploited. I arrived at Santus Circus with a second-hand car, full of my possessions. Ernest took a chance. He offered me the job as ring-mistress, which I accepted immediately because it was a chance to work in the ring. Over the few years that I had worked on shows, I had harboured a desire to have my own horse in the circus. I have ridden horses all my life. Yes, I was a pony-mad schoolgirl, with names of ponies in biro on my schoolbag and rosettes on the wall. Sometimes, when I was little, my sister Clover and I had brought the ponies into the kitchen for tea. The circus ring magnifies the mythological beauty of these animals, the horse in the circus ring (nose to tail, nose to tail) encapsulates every child's notion of the possibilities of the horse. The fantasy made real, the pretty horse with the feather nodding in the light, the harness reflecting light, near enough to touch, with warm, formidable breath. I wanted to live in the circus with a horse and felt that this would seal up and end, once and for all, the scraps and shimmers of my uncompleted, rudely cut past.

But in the circus I saw other people with horse acts, and it looked difficult – the logistics of mobile pens and tents and lorries. I put it out of my mind. It was impossible to attempt alone. The idea didn't rest and I began to see, after I had been working in the ring for a few weeks – 'Ladies and gentlemen, please welcome into the ring the beautiful Miss Elaina' – that I could, perhaps, incorporate a horse into the ringmistress role. We could open the show together. I put the idea to Ernest and he agreed. He said that the horse could live with the other animals in the stable tent. Over the Christmas of 1996 I bought a Palomino stallion. He was called Prince.

Of course, nothing works out exactly as planned, and though I started the 1997 season with Prince, he did not work straight away in the ring. He came from some people who lived under a motorway in Newcastle, and as far as I knew he had no experience of the physical world of the circus – and there are a hundred strange elements of a circus show that could frighten an inexperienced horse. The public are close at hand, waiting, watching, trusting, so it is vital that the events they see in the ring offer no actual threat, no danger to them. The children sit in the front row and wave their sparkly wands.

The circus was touring East Anglia for a few months of the season. We moved every week, on Sunday nights. On the way up from the outskirts of North London, we stopped at a ground in Colchester. The circus's route is mapped out the preceding year. It is not, as people sometimes assume, a haphazard gallivant across the country putting on shows spontaneously: it is precisely organised, and the need to fill the tent as often as possible means that, for the duration of the season, the routine of the circus shows – pull-down, move night, build-up, more shows – is relentless and tightly scheduled. There is little time for sleep, for rest, for leisure of any sort. The circus cannot move very far in one night, and we had only one night for the move. Ten miles between the old ground and the new would mean an early night: the last load of lorries would be standing on the new ground by perhaps two or three in the morning. Twenty miles, and the possibility of any sleep was threatened. If the move was more than twenty miles – and it would never be more than fifty – the late-night drivers, who were Ernest, Roget, two of the boys who worked on the show and myself, would reckon on no sleep at all. In this instance we would arrive at the new ground at perhaps eight or nine in the morning, or later, have a cup of coffee, then continue straight away with the build-up of the tent.

Prince and I had practised together in the tent for about a fortnight. In the day-times the tent is quiet and empty, lit only by segments of daylight where the wallings have been lifted. Of course it smells of the circus – last night's popcorn, crushed grass and animals. In this new world Prince moved slowly, his ears turning and listening and his eyes wide, revealing the shining eyeball. The inside of the tent holds its own silence, and the outside noises, barking dogs, traffic, become unimportant. The horse concentrated on me. I told him that it was all right, he was safe in the tent, and he believed me. I led him round the ring, then took him back out into the fresh air. We did this every day and he quickly became used to the high ceiling and the shuddering plastic walls. I held him in the back of the tent during the start of the show, when the music played as the people took their seats. He became used to the electric light and the artists moving around him, arranging their costumes and warming up. After a week or so we held a dress rehearsal, after a show, and I rode him through the curtains and into the spotlight at the centre of the ring. He was quickly blasé.

Prince's first show was packed. The boys said that it was standing room only around the front. I stood at the back of the tent in my costume and held Prince's reins. I made the five-minute announcement: 'Ladies and gentlemen, no smoking in the big top, no smoking in the big top. No video recording, no flash photography, no video recording, no flash photography. Thank you.' Then I put my foot in the stirrup, pulled back my skirts and swung up into Prince's saddle. For the first time in my life I was on my own horse, in the back doors of the tent, beside the fold-up trestle table where the music system sits, among the dark curves and angles of props, the wind lightly lifting and shaking the side of the tent, waiting to start the show. Ernest appeared through the back entrance of the tent and blew his whistle. The show would not start until he was ready, and the whistle was a signal to everyone that he was. On the lighting tower at the front of the show Sasha turned off the house lights. The opening lights for the show spun multi-coloured about the tent, and the faces of the company behind the curtains were lit by running coloured lights. Ernest started the fanfare drums and brass of the opening music. Roget clapped loudly, and his nephew Robert, who had recently joined the show, started clapping too. Then the people on the other side of the curtain began to clap. Robert was smiling and laughing with his uncles. Prince tensed and widened his eyes. I kept my legs relaxed and stroked his neck. He pricked his ears and looked up into the roof of the tent as if he was trying to see over the steel bar from which the ring curtains are suspended. The first act of the show is a double rope act.

The music grew louder. The audience's claps grew more resolute. Ernest turned up the music. Any minute now we would be through the curtain – in seconds. The children in the front row waved their sparkly wands. I bit my lip then licked my teeth. Prince started to walk backwards and shake his head. Jason and Speary wear black dinner-suits in the ring. They moved nearer to the curtain, ready to open it. There is that smell in the circus. Roget said to me that he hated the circus without animals because there wasn't that smell. He says he thought there was magic in the circus, in the smell of the circus, if there were animals. If there are no animals, he said, more as a question than a statement, there is no magic. Now the clapping seemed to have grown impatient. There were some raised voices. Ernest leaves the music playing for a long time before he announces the ring-mistress. I could see his hand on the volume control, and he was listening to the drumming in the music. I was shaking with nerves, but trying to sit relaxed, as I knew that my nerves would go right through the saddle and the reins to Prince. Grandpère clapped his hands and laughed. There is one single bare light-bulb at the back, on the music table, and his face held a shadow from this, and over his hair there were stars of colour. Ernest lowered the music and spoke into the microphone.

I felt as if I was waiting for an exam to start, waiting at the edge of that moment when you open the page and the clock on the wall starts to tick. It was like the first night of last season, when I went into the ring for the very first time in my life. My stomach had doubled up inside. The curtain would go back and I would be on my own in the ring, and the people would be silent, waiting for my voice to start, waiting to be led to their first reaction, disinterested, expectant, critical. 'I'm terrified,' I had said to Roget, and he had slapped me on the back and said, 'Don't worry, darling, just smile and say whatever first comes into your head.'

Waiting now, with Prince, it was the same nerves again, excru-ciating nerves, just bearable. Ernest turned the music down. 'Ladies and gentlemen.' He glanced at me over the microphone as he spoke. 'Please welcome Nellie and Prince. *Nellie and Prince!*' I could honestly have been sick on the spot. I nodded to the boys, and on each side they swept back the curtains.

Prince leaped forward towards the ring. The spotlight threw the rest of the tent into darkness. All I could see were the run-ning lights on the edge of the ring boxes and the spiky grass sticking through the sawdust. We galloped to the edge of the ring. The children in the front row waved their sparkly wands. We swerved to the right. I tried to remember to smile, and I caught in my eyes some bright eyes in the ringside seats. We trotted round the ring once, twice, three times. This, then, was what it felt like after all that work, the long search for the right horse, the trauma of the first few days in the circus, the anxiety, doubt and error, the slow afternoons practising in the empty tent.

The crowd had roared as we came in, they had loved it, you could hear it in the inhaled breath and the murmurs and shouts, 'He's beautiful, gorgeous.' I was proud of my horse, and my eyes stung.

We didn't move very neatly: he cut across the ring, and bent his head to the outside, broke into and out of a trot. The dust from the sawdust rose into the air and we came to a halt in the entrance to the ring. There was an indistinct start of a clap, not applause, an idea of applause rising and falling. Ernest handed me the microphone. 'Stand still, Prince. Ladies and gentlemen, welcome to Santus Circus. For you this evening we have gathered together performers from all over the world.' I was out of breath. Remember to smile. Look into the white light. Don't look in any other direction but forward. Speak to the people who are listening. 'A trapeze artist from Romania, juggling from Italy, exotic animals from the Far East, and artists from as far away as Texas in the USA.' (Jason throws a flaming knife and under his cowboy hat his eyes mimic hard, and Claire stands against the board looking down, one, two, three knives, and her body is flaming orange on all sides. She steps out of the flames.) 'But now, please welcome, on the *corde lisse*, an aeriel duo, ladies and gentlemen, Claire and Elaina.'

I handed the microphone back to Ernest, and we turned to leave the ring. Robert started a drumroll on the drum-kit to the right of the curtain. Prince shied. The curtains were still shut so he had nowhere else to go. I shouted for the curtains to be opened. Somebody heard me the other side: Claire and Elaina stepped through with Jason and Speary, glinting sequins and forward eyes. Prince and I passed by them, and the starred material dropped and closed behind us.

Jubilee

There are times when one has suffered a particularly severe blow that life seems scarcely worth living. It is then that something seems to help us, and we can start again with renewed hope.

Circus Company, EDWARD SEAGO

When I was ten years old we moved from Oxford, where I was born, to the country. Mum and Rick – my father – bought a house in a village called Minety. I was ten, and my little sister Clover was seven. Clover has round soft cheeks and eyes that curl into half-moons when she smiles. On the day we arrived in Minety we found a cardboard box on the table with two kittens in it. In the stables there were two ponies. We ran around the house and got lost in the corridors. The picture in the memory comes into sharp focus when I remember the early days of life in the country, the move from Oxford to Minety; before that, life is funny, blurred, and memory and photographs overlap like loose cuttings in an old scrapbook.

Memories of early childhood are, for everyone, idiosyncratic, a personal folklore, tales from the time when we didn't seem to make decisions and when the minute fabric of the world is close up and fascinating. This is what I associate with early child-hood: crushed lime leaves on the warm pavement and the smell of the lime on the way to school; the gritty tarmac pavements, interrupted by white tiles where the cars went in and out of driveways. At bathtime Clover and I would pick flaking green paint off the walls, then animals and monsters would emerge from the shapes in the paint. The walls of the big dark hall at the bottom of the stairs were covered in murals of my older broth-ers and sisters. The walls were brown and the murals were in white, the lines of their faces picked out in the light. When my parents had parties the grown-ups danced in the hall. They didn't mind if we stayed up late and watched them through the banisters or danced with them. I remember a man with a painted white face fencing in the hall. I remember wondering if we could hang ropes from the banister and swing around in the hall like monkeys. I loved monkeys and collected them – stuffed ones. Above all, I wanted my own pet monkey.

To celebrate the Jubilee the whole street threw a party outside. Red, white and blue bunting hung between the trees and we all wore fancy dress. The photographs of this day reveal a hot, sev-enties home-made parade. Rick is dressed as the ring-master in breeches, boots and top hat. One of my big sisters is dressed as Charlie Chaplin, with a tight suit, bowler hat and a painted moustache; the other is wearing a yashmak and stripy stock-ings, and is riding a dappled horse along the pavement. Clover is a squinting peasant girl, in a tatty straw hat and little dress. I wore a red velvet Little Lord Fauntleroy costume, and my brother was a queen in a long grey evening dress and steel crown. There are other figures, a ghost in a draped sheet over fishnets and high heels, a lion, some rock stars in sweaty ban-danas. There was a man with a mini hovercraft. I hated that hovercraft as I thought that it would run me down. All this early *Blue Peter* stuff is the fabric, the music and the sensation of scores of childhoods all over the country and probably the world. But everyone likes to believe that their own experience is unique and new, and I like that, the refusal to lead a disappointed life.

The seasons are clear and easy to remember. The summers were hot and we played on the lawn, hid in nylon sleeping-bags and made dens under the bay tree. Before Clover was born I played on my own and filled the doll's teapot with gravel and tried to eat the gravel. I tried to grind it in my teeth. After Clover was born we played together. We did everything that children do outside in the summertime in the garden, like putting hand cream on sycamore leaves and stealing sweets and eating them at the end of the garden. In the child's mind the emotions of love, contempt, deceit, fear, affection, elation run true. It is just from the outside that they are hidden in play. In the wintertime the nearby water meadow flooded and froze. Clover and I had double-bladed ice skates. This meant that we could walk on the ice. We thought we were skating like the grown-ups. Mum looked so beautiful in coloured scarves and a black coat, moving over the ice to the white silence of the outlying fog.

My earlier memories of life are particularly free from fear. I am sure that there was nothing to harm or threaten us. During the summer of 1976 I heard the grown-ups talking about the drought. It had something to do with the gardens. I thought it was a cross between an insect and a worm, and that it crawled into all the gardens along the street over the walls. As children, the sun's heat didn't affect us: we were protected with sun creams and straw hats, and we had an indigo, bright plastic paddling-pool. Through the water, where shreds of grass floated, the crumples of plastic at the bottom were made solid under the weight of the water.

If there was fear, it was in the form of specific terrors. There was an old blanket hanging over a climbing frame at the end of the garden. It had become wet and started to rot. That was a certain terror, the rotting blanket. I thought there were spiders hiding under it. There was an empty house in the street that ran at right angles to ours. The house was derelict and the garden overgrown. Some people said that an old lady lived in the house on her own and that at night-time you could see a light in the upstairs window, but others said that the light was a reflection of the street-light opposite. It wasn't the house or the old lady or the thought of the old lady that was so frightening: it was the idea of the garden, which was, so I was told, an absolutely solid, impenetrable mass of brambles. The plastic grid at the back of the television was a terror, because the monsters from *Doctor Who* lived in there, and I was haunted for months by a television programme about a village where all the people died of the plague. They put crosses on the door of the houses occupied by sufferers. I lay in bed in cold, sweating fear when I remembered this programme; the plague programme is my single most terrifying memory.

On the whole, early childhood was delightful and mysterious. I had an imaginary friend called Jonathan, who lived in Toyland, and who I spoke to by whispering into a candle. I left notes for him in the paraffin lamp on the table downstairs, and by the morning he would have left notes for me. Peter Pan was as real as the postman: it was only a matter of time, Clover and I believed, before he would appear through the curtains and the light of Tinkerbell would fly around the room, and we would be able to fly just like them. I can remember hearing country music from the door of Rick's study, and the singing voices seemed to wail incoherently. I think that my ear was too young to pick out meaningful words. My dad's typewriter rattled. Rick was writing. He is a film and television director and wrote film-scripts and novels and poems. We would use the back of the thick pads of scripts for drawing, but the study was a bit frightening – it contained too many books about war, and too many Pop Art paintings of robots. My big sister and I sat on the stairs: she stretched out her long legs and said that I shouldn't scratch the midge bites on mine because I would have scarred legs and they wouldn't be beautiful like hers. When it hailed, Clover and I would sit and watch the hail through the kitchen window. Mum said that we should look carefully, because when it hailed the hail fairies appeared. That is one of the things I remember very well about being young – laughing: Mum and Rick were funny, they made jokes and we laughed.

Now I believe that Mum created the world for us. We learned the world through her and she was the essence of everything we encountered. I have lost her now so find it difficult to see her as a normal person. I can't separate her from all parts of experience. She was the world. She sat on the night storage heater in the kitchen and blow-dried my pet guinea pig with a hairdryer, when it had fleas and had to be washed. When we had flu she lit a candle in our bedroom at night-time. The candle smelt strange, close and reassuring, and the sides of the room were lit by soft, bouncing shadows. She bicycled past the school playground and I saw her from over the school wall. When I was nine I nearly died from appendicitis, and she slept in the hospital with me. This meant that when I woke in the night the lion was there, and my stirring stirred the lion, and the lion made me feel better and fall asleep again.

I rode in a baby's seat on her bicycle. A car knocked us over. She stood in the road and shouted swear words at the car. I cried. I thought that if you swore in public you went to prison. Clover and Mum and I went for a walk up a stream, in the bottom of a deep gully. Everything we saw she transformed into a fairy-tale cast, until we were moving in an ethereal, imaginary landscape. The gully was dark and the water was cold. We seemed to find crashed space-ships and goblins and fairies. She made it up for us. I realise that, though she has gone, Mum lives on in my senses. She is the smell of the marshes on summer holidays by the coast, and she is the song of the curlew and the low drone of traffic on hot evenings in Oxford; she is the tap running the bath and the hot steam from the water. She is the frayed silk of a cushion on a sunken sofa and the yellow light through a paper shade and the cold blue walls of the downstairs loo. She is the smell of the damp roses in the night-time garden. She lives inside me, because she taught me to read the world and it is a lesson I cannot forget. She spellbinds me.

We moved to the country on Clover's birthday. There was a brown pony waiting for her in the stable. Clover and I have a photograph of her sitting on this pony and she is wearing a plastic badge that says, I AM SEVEN. Mum still made up the narrative for us, and then, after a while, when we stopped being children and became teenagers, we believed we made it up for ourselves. We drove a horse and cart to a party. The cart broke. Two of our friends were with us. They lived in London. They had to walk all the rest of the way in high heels on the tarmac. Some neighbours of ours asked Clover and me to throw a party for their two young children. We borrowed a Babar the Elephant bell-top tent and painted all the children's faces like clowns and had egg-and-spoon races across the lawn with real eggs, and we gave Wild West cart rides in the field. We swam in the gravel-pits, ran through the nettles with bare legs, rode the horses naked in the fields at night, worshipped and idolised the gypsies whom we saw camped on verges around Minety. We reared orphan lambs on bottles and kept chickens in our bedroom. Never for a moment were we led to believe that we were incapable. Quietly, silently, Mum showed us that there was nothing in life to which we were subordinate, that there was nothing to which we had to bow down. Yes, we were taught sternly to be polite to old people, grown-ups, told to hush up, never to answer back. But every moment of every day was underpinned with the conviction that, if we tried, we could do anything.

I was in my second year at Oxford University when we sold our house in Minety. Clover was away travelling in Ireland. It seemed that the house had become a ghost town. Nobody wanted to live there any more. Rick was in London. Mum was in hospital. She would never be able to come home. The house was empty yet full of her presence, in the still furniture and silent landscapes of paintings. There were no horses in the stables now, and the cats and dogs had gone. Mine and Clover's bedrooms were still full of teenage clutter, which was trunks of old letters and bottles of scent and plastic makeup and photographs of ponies, and piles of coloured scarves and hardback books, and old school uniforms and gym kits, a picture of a girl with a rabbit, some cartoons of geese, a reproduction Van Gogh in a broken frame, hand-held lipstick mirrors, an old gerbil cage, dusty copies of *The Jungle Book*, drawers full of laddered black tights, piles of dressing-up clothes, broken gold stilettos and a red sequinned bra.

When we were teenagers we made our own mythology just like others. The days had passed and we had spun webs around them for our own protection, pacing along the hot tarmac, in the thick sweet nights of summer, dark roads and the grown-ups in bed, to the village beyond and pubs where the boys we knew drank. Late, and all night, too, sometimes, we swam, and smoked cigars and occasionally thought we knew of the brilliant wild closeness of a boy in the dark on a summer night. We drove to the pub on the horse and cart. The horse drank Guinness too. In the end we lost it all, but we didn't know that then.

Much later on, though, and after we had all moved away from Minety for ever, after it was all finished, cut off, broken, I went back to see some friends. I went to stay with some people who still live in their reliable farmhouse across the fields from where our house was. There is a neat parlour type of room, a hall with slidey wooden floors and a big mirror. The kitchen has a high mantelpiece from which smile happy china cows with curly tails. Usually there is a golden retriever barking, a cat curling its lips, a horse blanket drying, an older son smoking a cigarette, a younger daughter on the telephone. So far, nothing has changed.

I walked back across the fields, across the old familiar paths of a happy childhood. The children playing in the street on their bicycles had the faces of the boys in the pub on those nights far away now. I went to see an old lady who used to help Mum with the housework. I said I was sorry that we had all seemed to leave in a hurry, failed to say goodbye properly. On the way back, all the world was flowing into me and out of me. It was a beautiful summer evening. My heart was in two and I could not cry. The fields were low and rolling, and the sun shone across them. A cow stared at me through a fence. I stopped by the fence. There was a rusty bent nail sticking out of the fence post. I would never have imagined that I could be this unhappy, that my heart would hurt as it did. This was the unhappiness of profound loss, of things violently cut off, and the past a little jewel that you can stare right through and then out again and into the world.

Circus Light

Then there is the circus light; all the lights and colours are so soft in the night; the whole thing looks like some Princess had come along by the lake and thrown all her jewels down, and gone away and left them.

Circus, BETTY BOYD BELL

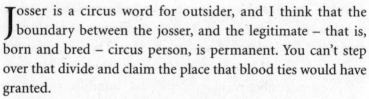

Josser is a circus word for outsider, and I think that the boundary between the josser, and the legitimate – that is, born and bred – circus person, is permanent. You can't step over that divide and claim the place that blood ties would have granted.

The circus casts a spell over some people. Jossers have chronicled their days in the circus. In 1931 Paul Eipper described the circus music as 'some alien hymn of worship'; in the 1970s Juanita Casey described the elephant as John the Baptist: 'He is looking at me with judgement written in the white in his eye.' The circus becomes a quasi-religious experience, more than a show, more than flesh and bones, more than its day-to-day secular pain. However, the josser who is blinded by the light of the circus on first encountering a show will enact an innocence to experience transformation: knowledge demystifies the original incantation. What I mean is, work in the circus will knock the romance out of you, eventually.

I first joined the circus when I was eighteen, ten months after my mother's accident. I was in my gap year between school and university, and I went to America for a month to work on a show. A good friend of mine, Gerald, had left England to join the circus, where he started as a set designer and ended up looking after the elephant, Flora. I arrived at a park at the northern end of New York State. It was very early in the morning. Gerald appeared from a motel room: he had long hair and a beard, bare feet, and his trousers were covered in paint. 'Welcome to America,' he said.

I, too, felt overwhelmed by the circus. It filled up existence – what was there to do apart from the circus? I found out that I was a good worker. I helped with the tent. I loved carrying heavy boards. My arms grew hard and strong and my hands callused. I bought an adjustable spanner and walked around with it dangling from my belt. One day I was instructed to ride one of the two broad-backed horses around the ring. The reason for this was to compact the sawdust into the ring, which was very wet. All I can remember is riding round and round the ring in the daytime, with the light coming in through the lifted wallings of the tent, and the electricians working in the coppolla, the metal frame at the top. I felt as if I was on a journey. That is what I wrote in my diary – round and round the ring on a journey where there is no distance to be covered.

During the show I worked on one of the three spotlights and listened to the gossip over the headsets. The weather was mainly hot. I bought a green Army waistcoat in an Army-surplus store, and I wore it all the time. One time I sat on the roof of the tent and watched the circus ground below. Flora was flapping her ears and the children were playing on unicycles. In the far distance, over a conifer plantation, I could see Canada. The surface of the tent roof was stretched drum-tight and it was shiny and hot. Up there, in the warm winds, with the new view below, I was overcome by the silence of the sky and the quality of circus life. My arms were brown and bitten by mosquitoes. England was far away. The problems of England were far away. I felt very happy.

On the first night of a show I walked up to the tent from the motel room. It was dark, and on the horizon there was an electric storm. At the back of the tent there were clowns with painted faces, horses with sparkly harnesses, ponies, goats, little carts, people juggling, and Flora, quiet, stepping slowly, swaying, swinging her trunk, the blue harness on her head lit by the light that came out of the back of the tent and the electric flashes of the storm. I couldn't recognise any of the people there as the people I had met in the daytime, in black clogs and shorts, around the caravans or working in the tent. This was not simply because I did not know them well. It was because I had my eyes in the lights of the circus juggernaut. The circus was doing what it always does to the first-time josser, the enchanted sentimentalist: dazzling, deceiving, bewitching.

I rode a horse called Lady Lightfoot in a circus parade through a nearby town. While I was with it the circus did one move, from Louistown, a little town on the American side of the Niagara Falls, to Cooperstown, the home of American baseball, a straight little town in the centre of New York State. There was a girl called Sky who worked on the show. She did the trapeze. She had a face like a cat and a body like a twelve-year-old boy. She painted my eyes black and found me an old trapeze costume to wear. Gerald was laughing. 'Now you will never go home.' I rode right through the town on the big strawberry roan horse. In front I could see the juggling troupe dancing, the band jamming, dancing as well, a straight street lined with people, and at the front of the parade the vast, softly swaying, silent shape of Flora the elephant. I rode the horse and waved at the crowds.

I came home to England in the autumn of 1992 and went to university. I stayed at university for three years, read some of the books, wrote essays, took the exams. When I left I had no plans except to find work in a circus in England, and pick up the thread of America. I had no idea, then, that I was a josser. I didn't anticipate any particular resistance: I just wanted to see if I could make it in the circus.

Mr Zero

. . . a fighting machine of gruelling work, of long, hard hours . . . a thing which fights constantly for its very life against the demons of adversity . . . a great, primitive determined organisation that meets defeat every day, yet will not recognise it . . . a driving, dogged, almost desperate thing which forces its way forward, through the sheer grit and determination of the men and women who can laugh in the face of fatigue, bodily discomfort, and sometimes in the leering face of death itself. That's a circus!
    The Circus Book, EDITED BY R. CROFT COOKE

I arrived at the ground of a small circus called Circus Moon late in the evening. The show had finished and the tent was being taken down. The circus was in the middle of Cheltenham. I had finished my finals and the summer was under way. It was mid-July. I was looking for Mr Zero.

I had seen a circus poster in the window of a betting-office and had called the box-office number. Mr Zero ran the show (PRESENTED BY ALBERT ZERO, in nostalgic, circus-poster typeface, EUROPE'S GREATEST CIRCUS, CIRCUS ZERO). He said on the telephone that I could join them for the back end of that season. It had been a short conversation; I could hear the music of the show behind his voice, and he had been out of breath. They couldn't pay much, times were hard, you know. He said that I would need my own accommodation, they had no spare caravans. He said that they would be in Cheltenham in the middle of July. He gave me the dates. You know the ground? Cox's meadow. Right in the centre of town. I have to go now, OK?

I went to stay with an old friend of mine called Andrew who lives on a farm at the back of an industrial rubbish tip on the northern side of Cheltenham. From his kitchen window on the first floor of the house you can see the top of the tip, a massive pile of rubbish, and along the skyline the lorries work constantly, picking up the rubbish, dumping it on the tip, dumping and compacting so that the tip, over the months, grows and changes shape. Then more fields are dug up for the rubbish, and the holes in the ground are so big they're like inverted mountains, and the machines at the bottom look like yellow toys. Andrew and I suspect that the house is haunted, and we wonder if the haunting is caused by the disturbed earth.

James Herbert is a mechanic. He services the lorries that bring the rubbish from the towns to the tip. He is known as Herbie. Herbie and his girlfriend and I drove in his open-top Land Rover to Tewkesbury car and van auctions. They both had sun-bleached hair and dark glasses. In my pocket I had six hundred pounds in cash and we bought a second-hand Bedford Midi van for five hundred and twenty. It had been used by the council as a works van. It still held a couple of concrete kerbs and an old high-visibility jacket. I built a bed in the back from a wooden board and a roll of foam. I hung a curtain on a piece of cord in the back window and bought a fold-up two-ring gas cooker in a car-boot sale. There was also a wooden bench in the van, and I painted it with bright blue gloss paint. For two weeks I stayed in Cheltenham with Andrew and prepared this makeshift camper van for the circus.

*

A tall man with glasses was unhooking the edge of the wallings from the metal cable that runs around the base of the roof of the tent. He was standing on a step-ladder. It was pitch dark and the last people were leaving the circus. There were cars turning in the rain and drops of water in the car headlights, and the sound of tyres turning in the water. The man looked at me. I asked him where Mr Zero was. He held the wallings with one hand and pushed his glasses further on to his nose. Then the rain gusted, and he pulled at the length of plastic canvas trailing behind him. He said he thought he was in the tent.

Then I heard some shouting from inside the dark walls of the tent. 'Come on, boys! You want to go to the pub tonight, eh? You stand around like girls! Come on, quick, the poles, hurry up!' This was the loudest voice but I could hear others, laughing and shouting, and the noise of metal banging from inside the tent, whose roof seemed to lose its tension. The rain ran off it in a sweep of light. The loud voice came nearer and a man burst through the entrance of the tent. 'Come on, Gary, what you doing up there, eh? Chatting with women?'

Now the rain was falling hard and my van was alone in the car park. This man looked at me and frowned. 'What you want, darling? There's no show now.'

I said I was looking for Mr Zero, I had come about work. The man stopped and put his hand to his brow. He shut his eyes and his hand looked dirty. Then he looked up. He said that I had called him a few weeks ago, in Coventry. I nodded. He shook his head and put his hand on my arm. 'I'm sorry, darling. I can't do it. The business is so bad, I have no money for more people, more wages, I can't do it. We have no more place for more people, do you understand?'

The rain fell harder. Men were dragging things from inside the tent. It was dark: there was no light save for some neon seeping through the metal railings behind the tent, and from the road beyond.

The next day I called Mr Zero again. He said that he definitely could not employ me. He said that theirs was a very hard show. They moved every two days. His voice grew emphatic. He said that he had done twenty-seven towns last month.

Mr Zero did not give me a job with his circus, and I never saw him again. However, that rainy meeting in the car park was not a full stop, a rejection. Mr Zero gave me the telephone number of another circus. He swore they needed workers and he advised me to ask for Bill Bailey. Bill was his brother-in-law. I called them and, without hesitating, they offered me a job.

It was a Chinese circus: the artists were from China though the show was run by English people. I lived in the back of the van and sold ice-creams, sticky liquid Mr Whippy, over a varnished wooden counter. It was not, in retrospect, a bad show to be working on. I had to do three hours in the box-office every morning, and sell ice-creams in the interval. I was paid ninety pounds a week, and none of the women on that show had to help with the pulling down and building up of the tent, and the show moved every week. It was a listless, boring, lonely time, defined in my memory by the constant chiming of Chinese music. The weather was very hot, a boiling August on seaside commons along the south coast of England, where the skies were bright blue and full of kites, and the landscape England's seaside landscape, which was high resort hotels, open-top double-decker buses, amusement arcades, tarmacked fun-fairs where burnt children appeared and reappeared around the sides of giant plastic ice-cream cones, and *Jurassic Park* heads roared from the sides of bingo high walls, among turning wheels and Tannoy waltzers. I sat at a wooden table one afternoon and ate a plate of chips with a girl called BJ. She was called BJ because she gave blow-jobs to the drivers. The sun was hot and there was a wind blowing. BJ tipped a salt-shaker upside down above her chips and the wind caught the salt and blew it horizontally across the table. She looked at it then up at me and laughed hysterically, only the music from the fair drowned most of her laughter.

Though I didn't appreciate it at the time, life on the Chinese circus was easy. The hours were not long and the work was not heavy. I sometimes heard a woman called Viv, who also worked there, saying that nobody knew what hard work was, these days, and that she could remember when she had had to run from the box-office to the tent in her costume, quickly ride the elephant then run back to the box-office as well as selling in the interval. 'This is nothing,' she kept saying. Her husband was the same: he kept warning me that in the real circus you had to lie down under a lorry in the wet and hook the chains on. I didn't know what they were talking about, but I wanted to know.

There were no animals in the show, and I began to realise that I wanted to work on a show where there were animals and European artists. I didn't dislike these artists, they were friendly and smiled, but I couldn't talk to them and I felt that I wasn't getting close to the circus culture that I had seen, touched briefly, in America.

One morning in the box-office I heard two of the girls gossiping about a mutual friend on another show. 'She put on weight terrible, didn't she?'

'Yes, but only when she started showing the bears. She only did it for a season after that and then they left. Her daughter works now, doesn't she?'

'Same as what happened to me, really. The last season I worked I'd just had Mark and I couldn't lose the weight. Anyway, the show went bankrupt and they sold the elephants. Still, once you put weight on . . . that's a job gone. Mind you, she did eat a lot.'

'Like a pig.'

'Three pizzas after the show, ice-cream, candy-floss.'

I was sitting by the telephone. I asked them where that was, the elephant riding. They said that the show didn't exist now. I asked them if any of the shows still had elephants. They said that Richie Richards still had elephants, and they looked at me and laughed. One of them turned her hand over and flexed her fingers. Her nails looked like purple enamel. She said that I wouldn't want to work there. Oh, no. They would have me doing everything, riding the elephant, riding the horses. The other girl nodded. And you have to watch your Ps and Qs there, don't you? They both laughed. I asked them if they could give me the number of that show, and the girl with purple nails said sure she could, she would give them a ring if I liked.

I went back to Cheltenham for a few days. I stayed again with Andrew on the farm at the back of the tip. We went to the pub and got drunk, and he bought the old caravan that was parked in the yard at the back of the pub for fifty quid from an old man sitting at the bar with vodka lines in his face. He gave it to me as a present. I needed more space for living – the van was too cramped. I couldn't even stand up in the back. The next day Herbie welded a tow-bar to the back of the van. He had just sold his Land Rover and bought an American Jeep.

'Off to the circus again, Nell?'

'That's right.'

'Whereabouts?'

'Up in Liverpool.'

The caravan was about fifteen feet long and half the insides were missing. The foam seats were rotten and the cupboards were full of mud and bottles. The woman at the circus, whom I spoke to on the telephone, said that I would be working in the stables. They could pay me a hundred pounds a week. Andrew gave me a pair of waterproof trousers, and two days later I hooked up the caravan and drove up the M5 for Liverpool.

Circus Pictures

Yet the circus people are the happiest on earth, and not one of them would change his life for any other.
The Circus Book, EILEEN MAYO AND WYNDHAM PAYNE

~

I had never towed a caravan before and I was very nervous. I was to join the show in Warrington, a small town outside Liverpool. Circus signs appeared high on the lamp-posts. I followed them around roundabouts. I turned a corner. The circus appeared: red and yellow lorries, caravans, a huge blue four-pole big top. Auntie Sheila was the wife of Richie Richards. She stood at the top of the steps of her caravan and frowned at me. She could have done with me yesterday. There was a yellow awning over the door of the huge trailer and at the bottom of the steps an Alsatian turned and growled in a red steel pen. No emptying loos in the skip, OK, no electric fires, no electric kettles. This is my daughter, Polly, she runs the stables. A short girl with long blonde hair had appeared behind me. She tossed her hair and grinned. And I can be a bitch to work for. Now look, don't doubt it. She will be a bitch to work for, and you'll be screaming and tearing your hair out within a few months, you won't take it for long, but for the moment try, carry on, see what happens.

I didn't have a loo anyway. I had to use the show loos. These were only open during show-time. I didn't have a shower either, although at that first ground there were some showers right opposite the circus, in a sort of abandoned sports club. At other grounds I used to drive around, every few days, looking for a sports centre to buy a shower for a quid, or I would just wash in a tub in the caravan, with water heated up on the gas rings. I plugged my caravan into the electric box. The hand pump on the taps didn't work, so I used to fill the sink with a plastic bottle. Occasionally I would walk through the area on the other side of the tent from the stables where the artists' caravans were parked – the Moroccan troupe, the trick rider, the ring-master and his girlfriend, a hand-balancer, a unicyclist – and I envied the big new caravans with efficient water-pipes and satellite dishes, the lorries full of gas bottles and fold-up tables, all the normal stuff of family life. The grooms and the ring-boys were parked away from the artists, at the very back of the show, behind the stables. On no account were we allowed around to the front of the show, unless we were wearing clean clothes.

The circus toured the suburbs of Manchester. I never knew, from week to week, where we were going next. After a while I stopped caring, because the location of the circus did not affect the never-broken routine of work. I asked someone once where the next ground was. They said they didn't know. I asked another person. They didn't know either. So I went and asked Auntie Sheila. She said she didn't know. I realised that it was a secret. I did not know where we were going and I was not supposed to know.

Competition for grounds between circuses and other itinerant entertainers has always been fierce. Lord George Sanger was, perhaps, the greatest showman of the nineteenth century:

Before the advent of the Showman's Guild and better organisation, it was a case of first come first served at any new ground . . . Lord George Sanger tells of a battle between Hilton and Wombell's Menagerie on the Reading to Henley Road. The Wombell drivers tried to overtake the others in their efforts to get to Henley in time to secure the best places. Caravans were overturned, beast wagons broken open and the animals allowed to escape. Sanger writes: 'We had a good day after all for business, though it was the sorriest lot of battered performers and damaged caravans that Henley had ever witnessed.'

(*Historic Fairground Scenes*, Michael E. Ware.)

We went to a different town each week, and parked on sports fields, in municipal parks, or on farmer's fields, or on sections of rough ground behind rows of terraced houses. Knutsford was a tight little *nouveau-riche* suburb, with expensive delicatessens and a toyshop/hardware store. But mainly the places where we worked showed a face of poverty. Working with a circus will reveal the spirit of a town like no other encounter. It seems that in the circus you are in permanent contact with the raw surface of day-to-day reality. Perhaps you can hide from your own problems in the circus, but you can't hide from the world through which you travel. If there is a change in the country, someone said to me, the circus will feel it first. The show was rarely full. The public were thin, pale and hard-faced. I took my clothes to the launderette once a week, and bought cheap food from cheap supermarkets, where the food is displayed in stacks of cardboard boxes, and vodka is five pounds a bottle. In one of the supermarkets there was a girl pushing a trolley about, and in the trolley there was a radio playing pop songs, and a baby. Baked beans, fourpence a tin. The girl was walking sideways almost, she looked shell-shocked, and the baby was lying sideways in the bottom of the trolley. She was nodding slowly in time to the music.

The other girl in the stables was called Anna. Every morning we had to muck out and get the horses ready for practice. There were three grey and three chestnut Arabs. They all worked together in the ring. Every moment of our day was given over to ensuring their comfort. They lived like kings, and they were nonchalant and aggressive. Practice was the most stressful part of the day. If it was cancelled, the day was like a holiday, but it rarely was. Polly's father, Richie Richards, would walk into the ring, and at that moment we had to bring the six stallions across from the stable tent to the big top, then line them up in the middle of the ring for Richie Richards to practise them. We stood in the entrance to the ring, in front of the closed curtains. This area is known throughout the circus world as the ring doors. He would finish practising the horses, and we would take them back to the stables then bring in the Shetlands, then swap them for the donkey, or the llamas, and so on. It would take the whole morning, running backwards and forwards from the stables to the tent. The objective was to make sure that the right animal was in the ring and ready for practice at the right moment, and so avoid being shouted at.

Anna had a long white face and black rings around her eyes. She told me that her mum and dad were dying, and that she had been battered by her boyfriend until she hit him on the leg with a poker and ran away. She used to work in a factory, sewing baby costumes, but she left it for the circus. She said that she had always wanted to be a groom and work with horses. We could hear the horses moving on the other side of the curtains. We were both waiting, ready to exchange the donkey for the two Shetlands who were in the ring. We could hear Mr Richie screaming at his son, Little Richie. He would be running around the edge of the ring now, Little Richie, his face twisted, running and stumbling. Little Richie was a clown and he walked like a clown all the time, both in and out of the ring. He hated the circus and he claimed to resent his family. He said he wanted to run away, but he couldn't. He had no qualifications, could barely read, and his family controlled his money and his life. They hated his girlfriend – whom he loved – and she lived shut up in the caravan all day and you never saw her, and if you did, as a rule, *you didn't talk to her.* (Polly told me that, she said, don't talk to the bitch.) Sometimes his dad made him ride the horses, and he often fell off, or cried, and he might as well have ridden the donkey backwards with a dunce's cap on, for that was his humiliating fate, to look stupid, so that he was punished for being too slow, too inept, not like a circus boy at all. Anna was shivering and so was I. We just wanted to avoid being shouted at so we did things as best we could. Anna said that the donkey was God's animal. She said her nan had taught her that. She said that it had a cross on its back. She stared at me and her eyes were circles of black and around her neck was a thread of engagement rings – they all used to batter her in the end but she kept the rings anyway. Her face was white and the curtain behind was black; the rain had started outside and was seeping under the wallings. It felt as if all the air about us, in the gloom behind the curtains, was thin and colourless and damp.

There were four Hungarian boys who worked on the show as ring-boys, and they helped with the animals in practice, changed tyres, moved the lorries, washed the tent, cleaned under the seats in the mornings. One of them, Pishti, helped to look after the three elephants. There were four people in the stables constantly, myself, Anna, Pishti, and Alfie, the old man who had looked after the elephants all his life. Alfie was very overweight. He rocked from side to side when he walked, and he cursed and muttered under his breath. On the first day I was there he came up to me, put his finger on the side of his nose and whispered to me that Anna was a lazy bitch, she never did her work properly. Then he rolled on through the tent, pushing his barrow of elephant shit. His trousers were held up by braces and string, and his caravan sat in the dark brown pond of elephant piss at the back of the tent. Alfie had used to sleep in the straw with the elephants. As he had grown older he had been given a caravan, but for years he just bedded down among the sleeping elephants. It was a tiny caravan and the radio was always playing. He had a little dog called Meg. This is what you would hear, from Richie Richards, when he came into the stable tent to shout to Alfie. 'Alfie, Alfie, ALFIE, ALFIE! Where the fuck are you, cunt? I SAID I WANTED THEM ALL READY THIS MORNING.' And Alfie would appear round the side of the wallings cursing and swearing. One day, he told me, and he had a smile in his eyes, he would win the lottery, and he would tell Mr Richie, to his face, to fuck right off, and then a helicopter would come and pick him up and take him away.

You see, a strange thing happened to you at that circus, if you stayed for a while. Mr Richie did not talk at all, he just shouted. You knew when he was near because he wore on his belt a set of keys, which jangled and shook as he walked. After a while I became like an animal. Everything I did was to avoid that shouting. I hated the sound of the jangling belt, and the shouting, the fear of his shouting dominated my thoughts.

We would see the Hungarians in the morning, when they appeared in their tank suits and sat around in the stable tent, on the grooming box and bales of hay, waiting for practice, murmuring and muttering in Hungarian. Pishti was tall and blond, with quiet eyes. He thought of Hungary, his girlfriend and the end of the season. It seemed to me that they were, more or less, slaves. Pishti worked hard, quietly. He smoked Superkings and avoided the shouting. Before practice, Pishti, Anna and I would fill haynets beside the lorry that was parked alongside the stables. Anna and I joked about who we fancied, ate custard creams, and asked Pishti questions about Hungary. He carried on filling the haynets, making sure that they were tight full, a Superking in his mouth, one eye shut against the rising curls of smoke, and sometimes he would stop and say something to us. He was very tall. Plenty of good food at home, not this cornflake shit, and then he would shake his head and turn his back on us, and we would look at each other and laugh, as we both fancied him.

It wasn't so bad to start with. There was an Indian summer at the back end of that season, and I worked in a T-shirt. The caravan had holes in the roof, but it didn't rain much and the nights were still relatively warm. Alfie looked out for me a bit. I had no idea about living in a caravan, less still about living in a caravan in public spaces. One night I was getting changed and some boys were looking in at the window. I didn't see them, but I heard a noise outside and some shouting. I looked out and saw Alfie chasing them away across the football pitch. He came to my door and I opened it. He was gesturing towards the field with his thumb. 'Those boys were looking in your window,' he said angrily, slightly out of breath, and then he leaned forwards. 'You want to be careful, Nell, there's puffs and all in that park.' He looked at me, nodded, winked conspiratorially, then rolled off back to the stable tent.

Anna and I had quite a good friendship. We didn't argue much and shared the work fairly equally. She loathed the shouting too, and we were both wary of Polly. Auntie Polly. She had an act with a troupe of little poodles, which came into the ring on a cart pulled by an Alsatian, and she had a brightly coloured African macaw. The names of the poodles seemed to me to be bound up in her fixation with luxury: Chocolate, Raspberry, Apricot. Polly loved anything sweet, or pastel-coloured, or shiny. I went to a bar with her once and she immediately noticed the brass elephants' heads holding up the bar rail, and stroked them admiringly. One day she marched into the stables and said she had bought a new bra. 'Look, girls,' she said, and lifted up her top, 'a new red bra.' She would bitch and gossip and back-stab. She had little to say about anyone, unless it was sly criticism. Despite this, though, she had an almost childlike fascination with people. When my friends came to visit, she would cross-question them about their lives, and at the end of the show, when the public paid fifty pence to look at the animals, she would wait in the stables in a red coat and talk to the people, shining and beaming into their faces. She bought me some little diamond hair-slides, made sporadic affectionate gestures, clasped a hand, locked her arm in mine. But her behaviour the rest of the time negated the friendliness. She would come into the stables and, like her father, and I'm sure her mother (Auntie Sheila, who never seemed to leave her trailer), would just shout and shout, 'I don't want my stables to look like this. You girls have been getting very, very lazy recently,' and she would shake her finger and stand in the middle of the tent and toss her hair and march about. It doesn't sound bad? After a while, shouting eats away at your morale, so we worked hard to try to avoid it. We raked up the loose hay and straw, kept the horses swept out, the haynets filled, we cleaned out the feed buckets, tied the bits correctly, trampled down the skip at the back of the tent, packed up the stables at the end of each week, rolled the horses' flooring – heavy, slippery rubber mats – on our hands and knees in the shit, but it didn't make any difference. The shouting was continuous.

On the evening of my first day with the show, I went to the pub with the Hungarians, a girl called Charmagne and her sister Josie, and another girl called Jena, who had blonde hair and blank eyes. I didn't know any of them but the boys had knocked on my door and said come to the pub. I walked along the side of the road with Charmagne and Jena. I didn't know what to say to them, so asked them something, anything, as a means of starting a conversation. But they brushed me off, giggled, crossed the road and a car passed between us.

We sat at a table in the pub. Jena said, 'Are you tough? Are you tough enough for this?' and I took her question as a warning, which it was. The Hungarians bought everyone beers, pushed back the pool table and charmed the barwoman into turning on the juke-box. They didn't sit at the table for long, but drank and danced. Jo was short and he had wide eyes with lazy irises. He loved the Army, so they called him GI Jo. He danced and danced, and tied a handkerchief around his head and sweated a lot and fell over. Pishti closed his eyes and rocked in the night to get away from it all. Jo pressed a beer into my hand. 'You feel good?' he asked. They were taking themselves out of the circus and I was losing myself in it, but I started to see what they were doing, how they felt. The shouting of the day was nearly intolerable, and the nights like this, with the curtains drawn, the music loud and the beer flowing, were a way of getting away from it, of feeling good when most of the time you felt bad.

Toddy had dirty blue eyes, a thin twisty body, and he had his eyes on Charmagne. He danced with his head tipped forward and his eyes forward. Marti, the fourth Hungarian, just looked on, cynical. He was separate from the other three. He was not exuberant, generous and passionate, but cold, and he had a mean mouth. They called him Marti Bartsi, which means Uncle Martin in Hungarian; it was a joke against the Richards family's habit of calling each other Uncle this or Auntie that. They danced properly with Charmagne and me, held us right up close, rocked the night, lost the night, forgot the circus. The morning would be harder, the shouting louder, but it didn't matter. These nights made the life worth living, antidoted the circus, kept us going, and when the boys left at the end of the season, and nights like that stopped, I realised what a necessity they were.

After the pub we went back to the Hungarians' caravan, where they had some tins of beer. They opened cans of ham and carved slices of bread. The caravan was close and very dirty. They all lived in there. The light above the table at the end of the room had a dark yellow shade and socks were hanging from strings above the table. The caravan smelt of socks and gas and cooking oil. We sat around the table. Jo split open a bag of potatoes, which scattered over the table and on to the seats; he bit into them raw. They played with knives, stabbing them between their fingers, and between Charmagne's – she was standing at the end of the table with her hand on it and her fingers outstretched, laughing. They listened to Hungarian love songs on the cassette player and sang along in Hungarian. Toddy translated the words for me, roughly, with a low voice. 'I had a good love . . . and she left me . . . when the birds left the skies . . . she left me for the seas.' He got left behind, his English dried up. He said, 'You get the idea,' and laughed. I used to love it in that caravan. It was dark and full of stuff, piled in corners and hanging from strings, and the black and white television always flickered in the corner.

Often, on a moving night, when all the work was done and the circus was ready to move, we would have to wait – perhaps for the ground to be vacated the other end or for a lorry to be driven somewhere. I didn't always know why we waited, but we often did. Then I used to go round to their caravan and wait with the Hungarians. There would be no electricity now as the cables had been taken up and the generators packed away. We were always dirty, and exhausted, and a moment of free time like this would be taken up with sleep. One time, when we were in Congleton, there was a long wait. I went round to see the boys, and Alfie was sitting in there, drinking a beer. He was telling them stories about when he was young, about stealing apples from a tree. He spoke slowly, as the boys' English was never good. They were all laughing, and Alfie was laughing too, and I couldn't work it out. Alfie, a little boy, mischievous and gleeful, and now an old man, with bright red cheeks from too much cold air, trapped in a circus with nothing of his own.

'He is a very good man, Alfie, I think,' said Pishti, 'a very good man, very funny man, yes, a very funny man.' He looked at me then sat back on the seat a bit, with his head against the curtains at the end of the table, and closed his eyes in sleep, in preparation for the long night and the long driving hours.

I was learning about the circus. Richie Richards' Mega Circus was one version of life with an English travelling show, and although it was composed of archetypal circus elements – stripy tent, elephant, generator, macaw – the life there was unique to life on the shows, because of the way the people were treated. There was something dehumanising about it. The animals were treated well; it was the human rights that were neglected.

Sometimes I used to think that the stable tent, which was a long bright red marquee, was haunted. The light was strange in there, and sometimes out of the corner of my eye I saw a man beside the llamas. Polly told me that her great-grandfather had bought the elephant man as an exhibit. She seemed quite proud of this. In low moments, I thought that it was the elephant man who lived in the stable tent, lurking around the corners. I asked someone if it was haunted, and they said it was probably Alfie, and laughed.

I became aware of circus folklore. On some shows, circus vernacular was thought quaint. On that show, however, it was adhered to more obsessively. I became friends with Little Richie. I was as unsure of his loyalties as I was about the rest of his family's. 'Me and my mum and dad think Anna is lazy and that you do all the work,' he said, and then gave the message in reverse to her. He seemed to occupy himself by playing the circus's communication system – a system based on rumour and gossip. But I was an open ear to his complaints, and in retrospect I cannot be certain that anything he said was true, or a fabrication that was, in some curious way, for my entertainment. Richie Richards was a clown and I was a josser, and the joke was perhaps always on me. But he seemed open about his own unhappiness with the situation. 'Polly and my mum are horrible to me,' he said. 'They won't let me go. I tried to run away, but didn't have anywhere to live so I came home again.' They didn't give him any money and he didn't have a driving licence. He had taught himself to read: he read Beckett and Wilde, and made Wildean quips and jokes. He was not stupid and he was not insensitive. He did little oil paintings of clowns, made wire sculptures of horses and figures, and musical instruments. He collected padlocks. Little Richie taught me about the circus, about the culture and language and people. After the shows I would stand at the end of the rows of horses, and watch as the public came in to look around the stables. On some nights there were queues of people, but mainly there were just a few, complaining about the smell of the animals.

'Nante the mozzie.'

'What do you mean?'

'What?'

'What you just said, about a mozzie or whatever.'

The public were drifting slowly past the horses.

'Please don't walk too near the horses' back legs, sir.'

It was the second show. In the dim lights their faces looked tired and the children were cross. Most showed open disgust on their faces at the thick smells of animals in the tent.

'Look at the girls. Nante is look, mozzie is girls. Chaver the mozzie – you know what that is, what the Moroccans do with the girls.' He looked at the ground and laughed and rocked on his heels.

'Scarper means run away, and Omey is the police. You're a josser – you don't belong in the circus but you live in it anyway.'

I got the idea. Look at the girls. Fuck the girls. Run away from the police. And only your own blood counts for anything.

'Josser.'

'You're a josser.'

'Watch the back legs, please, kids.'

The last of the people were leaving the stable tent. Polly was wearing her red coat and someone was asking her about the horses. She was beaming into their face in the way that she did. She could do that, all right, look someone right in the eye and draw them in. It isn't so much a trick: in the circus you see the same faces day in and day out. The public come and go, facelessly. So a new face to talk to is fascinating.

It need not have been a bad show to work for. They were professional people. The show, though reliant on the iconography of television – artists were presented in tawdry rip-offs of TV personalities, Batman, Ninja Turtles – was fast and entertaining. But the shouting drilled away at your soul. It came through the sides of the stable tent, it was a disembodied voice in the air beside the elephants, it banged on the door of the caravan and rattled the bunch of keys as its own advance warning. It was triggered by a snapped rein or a dusty hoof or a late night. The shouting got louder at night and more frequent on move nights. Going out, away from the ground, and passing out cold with drinking were the only ways to escape it.

There were two brothers working on the show that season called Phillip and Ivan. Phillip was the ring-master and he was going out with Charmagne's younger sister Josie. Charmagne and Josie were chatting together in the back of the tent. Someone introduced me to them, on that first day with the circus, and they didn't say hello or smile. What they did was open and close their eyes and tighten their lips, then laugh when I had turned my back. But Phillip and Ivan liked going out with the Hungarians, and Charmagne and Josie did too, so after a while, when we had been drunk together, had danced, and after they had wound me up a bit, watched how I reacted (I didn't react as I was too shy to retaliate), we became friends. I never carry rumour, I never gossip so, in a world where nobody is to be trusted, I became privy to much of what went on behind closed doors. The doors will remain closed. On one of my first nights out, Charmagne and I were sitting on a table outside a pub waiting for a taxi back to the circus. All the boys were there, and Josie and Jena, a few others. It was dark. I can't remember the fine detail, though the meaning is not lost. 'Don't trust anyone here,' Charmagne said, and she was not smiling. She swallowed. She was still hard and serious in her face. She had a thin face and big black eyes. 'Don't trust the boys. Don't trust Phillip, nor Polly, nor Alfie. Don't trust anyone. Don't trust me.'

I thought that that was an extraordinary thing to say to someone. Don't trust me. It shows such great confidence. It marks them out as dangerous, enigmatic, transient. Don't trust me. Her voice is ringing in my head. Don't trust me.

Phillip was wrapped up in his relationship with Josie. They had a big trailer, which was a converted mobile library. It had a tall kitchen with a black-and-white checked floor, and a sitting room with a life-size china horse. Josie loved the horse, and had made it a harness and a blanket. She had a lamp with a stained-glass shade. She loved that too. She kept the trailer spotless and she made costumes, for herself and for other people. How hard had her life been? She had slept in lay-bys often, worked in the ring all her life, beaten and stretched her body into shape at a very young age, and she had learned to reveal and conceal it high up in the roof of the tent with sequins and fishnet. She was very hard. She never complained. She was highly professional. She didn't take shit from anyone. Never take shit from anyone, especially not in the circus. She said she would like to live somewhere where there were no hassles. She wanted a hassle-free life. There were so many hassles in the circus. When we were waiting to go on to a ground Josie would come over to my van for a chat. They're used to that scenario, circus girls, it's a routine part of life, hanging about late on a Sunday night while the men shunt lorries, start generators and lay cables. She was watching Phillip, who was setting their trailer straight. Josie had her arms folded and half her face was concealed under a peaked cap. 'I hope he sets it straight this time,' she said. 'I like my bed to be straight, you know. If the groove in the middle of the bed isn't straight to the ground, I can't sleep well. You know, it has to be straight, the groove in the bed.'

She was right, I suppose. My trailer was so excruciatingly uncomfortable that it didn't seem to make much difference how straight it was. Phillip called across the ground to her. 'OK, Josie!'

She unfolded her arms and banged once on the side of the van. 'See you later, Nell. Sleep well.' She went off across the new ground to her trailer, to replace the bowl of fruit and unwrap the china horse from its protective blanket.

Ivan was Phillip's younger brother and he had a yellow Land Rover, which he loved passionately. It had a big roof-rack, a winch, a stereo, a mobile-telephone holder and a notepad on the dashboard. He lived in one end of a lorry that towed his parents' trailer. Sometimes I used to sit in there and watch videos with him. There were teenage posters on the walls, books about Land Rovers, muddy shoes in the doorway, a fan on the roof and a gas fire in the wall. Once I was seen coming out of Ivan's trailer and a bit of gossip went about the place in the morning. Polly flicked her hair and wagged her finger. 'Tired this morning, Nell? I saw you *last night*.' There was nothing going on between us but an amicable friendship.

Occasionally, Ivan took me to the cinema. We went to see *Braveheart*. In one of the scenes a large cream horse appears, walking through the crowd pulling a wooden wagon. Mel

Gibson is in the wagon and he is about to be executed. The cinema was dead quiet. It was a key dramatic moment in the film. Ivan turned towards me and he whispered, 'Look, it's Mantel.' Mantel was the name of the horse on which he did the trick riding, and in Ivan's heart Mantel was second only to the Land Rover. I laughed, and felt reassured by Ivan's affection for the horse. It was a bit of love in a hateful world. All the other horses stayed in the stables all the time, but Mantel went out on a tether, outside Ivan's lorry. Ivan fed him biscuits and the big heavy horse followed him around like a dog.

One afternoon the Richards family were all out. Mr Richie was away at the next ground and Polly and her mum had gone shopping. Anna and I had done all the morning's work and were standing behind the ground, hidden by the rows of lorries, beside a gate to a big field. It was a brilliant sunny afternoon and the grass was shining bright green. Ivan's little terrier was sniffing about in the grass and he appeared from the stables with Mantel. He opened the gate and went into the field.

'Come on, Mantel,' he said. 'Hi, girls, skiving off as usual?' and he laughed. He started to run across the grass and we watched them both. Ivan was running and stopping and Mantel was lumbering after him, shaking his head and watching Ivan all the time, out of the corner of his eye, turning and stopping and running with him, the sun on his back.

I had no idea about how to live on the road. You have to be rigorously well organised to live in a caravan, work from it and remain healthy, clean and happy. Circus families are the most fastidiously clean people. It is part of their culture, and for every circus woman a large part of the day is dedicated to cleaning the caravan. During the back end of that season Richie Richards' circus did not journey out of the north of England; no, they were heading north, for a Christmas season in Glasgow. We arrived at a high sloping field somewhere in Derbyshire. The night we got there I locked myself out of my caravan and I had to break the lock on the door to get in. Somewhere in the darkness inside was my bed and, though the door was wide open and banging in the wind, I slept heavily – the move had been long and hard, and the weather was bad, and it had taken three hours to drag each load to the ground through the mud. Anna and I had watered the horses, then I had sat in my van waiting in the stationary convoy that stretched down the empty hill road, smoking cigarettes and half sleeping. I didn't bother to change for bed any more, just pulled off my oilskins and slept in my clothes. It was too cold to take them off, and in the morning I could lie in bed for a few seconds longer as I was already dressed. I didn't know then about packing down a caravan for moving: every object in it must be put on the floor or packed away. Moving simulates a mini-earthquake as the caravan jolts along the road.

In the morning, I woke up and saw the windy fell through the caravan door, bent yellow grass and muddy tyres. There was a chiming noise, which was the boys knocking in the first stakes. The floor of my caravan was covered in smashed glass. During the journey a jar of mayonnaise had fallen out of a cupboard and broken on the floor. Glass was stuck to the bottom of my socks, and I was wearing the day before yesterday's clothes. My hands were black with dirt and I must have rubbed and scratched my face on the journey, because the pores on my face were black too and there were red scratched spots. None of these things was anybody's fault but my own: I had no idea how to live that life, and I spent a lot of time feeling uncomfortable and dirty. My hands were always dirty, every day, but especially on move day, when we had to roll up the horses' heavy rubber mats. I developed a huge cyst behind my ear. I am sure that this was because of the dirt on my face and in my mouth. I used to chew my nails on a move night, and this accounted, I think, for the burning sensation at the back of my throat that plagued me every time we moved to a new ground, in the slow convoy, in the night, when I had no idea where we were going, and even less of an idea as to how to get there without damaging my health.

I ignored the smashed glass. I was unused to the dimensions of a caravan. Every time I turned round I knocked something over, or a bottle fell out of a cupboard and smashed down into an ashtray, or I tangled my leg in the radio lead, which knocked over the rubbish and scattered it all over the kitchen at the end of the caravan. I usually ended up throwing everything out of the door in annoyance. I didn't want to think about it, or the broken lock, so I left the caravan and opened the door of my van. I found my oilskins and swapped my clogs for a pair of rigger boots. I pulled the van door shut and walked out across the ground. Pishti, GI Jo, Toddy and Marti Bartsi were unloading the llamas. The animal lorry was at the front of the ground and they appeared around the side of the tent lorry, slowly, in single file, the boys quiet and serious, accompanied by the preposterous, glancing llamas who picked through the grass with their thin hoofs, looking to the left and the right at the early-morning with their impenetrable, stupid glass eyes.

Bare-knuckle Boxing

*We called him the funny man because he was sad and
serious and said little, but gazed right into our souls, and
made us tell him just what was on our minds at the time,
and then came out with some magnificently luminous
suggestion that cleared every cloud away.*

Dream Days, KENNETH GRAHAME

~

In 1768 Phillip Astley roped off a circular piece of wasteland
called Ha'penny Hatch in Lambeth. Once a sergeant major in
the 15th Light Dragoons, he used it to show off his equestrian
expertise. Over the next ten years he added other performers to
the ring, rope walkers, clowns, musicians, dancing dogs, learned
pigs, a shadow-puppet show, ventriloquists, contortionists,
strong men. The marketplace provided the artists. In 1779 he
opened Astley's Amphitheatre Riding House. Here the public
could enjoy large-scale spectacle: the stage and the ring were
full of artists and animals – perhaps hundreds of horses in one
production. The building was lit by gas-light and many shows
contained ambitious pyrotechnics. It burned down in 1794 and
1803, and was rebuilt each time. It thrived until 1893, when it
was demolished as a result of council legislation.

Astley is often credited as the father of the modern circus, its founder. But the content of the circus, grotesque and sublime, predates the form. On 21 September 1668, Samuel Pepys recorded, '... And thence to Jacob's Hall's dancing on the ropes, where I saw such action as I never saw before, and mightily worth seeing.'

In the middle of the eighteenth century, showmen, artists and performers, players, dancers and conjurors, beastmen and clowns, horsemen and aerialists, rope-dancers and wire-walkers were making their way towards each other, drawn together without feeling the pull. They were leaving the informal arena of the marketplace to perform in the circus.

The essence of circus is showmanship, or making spectacle for entertainment. A showman loves spectacle and he is probably an advocate of big scale, technically complicated spectacle. Sometimes in circus in England, I have seen quality sacrificed for scale – a thin show but a big tent, and the big tent is a hollow proclamation of the quality of the show. Scale demonstrates power. Ptolemy II, who ruled Egypt from 330 to 323 BC made his power manifest by large-scale parades of exotic animals – he is said to have paraded ostriches in harness. The greater the technical problems overcome, the larger the scale, the more powerful the ruler. I could trace a similar logic – I think – in Richie Richards' Mega Circus. Richie Richards' spiritual father was not Astley: it was a showman in ancient Egypt, or a Stone Age man who taught a dog to walk on its hind legs then added rabbits and ponies to the fireside spectacle, and toured other caves exhibiting his animals. The instinct of circus people is formidable because it is ancient; in circus somehow you come into contact with the primeval spirit in showbusiness. It is as if circus is the core of showbusiness, of which all other forms are a version of the content of a circus performance.

Much of Richie Richards' kudos within the circus world was due to his three elephants, and his fairly large stable of horses. After the second world war, Billy Smart's circus toured with sixty horses and twenty elephants. Today, none of the shows in England compares to this in scale, and Richie Richards' Mega Circus is one of the few contemporary shows that tours with animals. Richie Richards mixed the horses with the elephants, the donkeys with the llamas, the Shetlands with the bigger horses. (Little and large: the sight of a tiny Shetland cantering into the ring behind a large horse of the same colour never failed to entertain children.) The show was glittery and traditional. The music consisted of digitalised theme tunes – West End melodies, superhero jingles, as familiar as unplaceable, and snatches of credit roll instrumentals. The artists, hired through an agent for the season, supplied their own music and costumes. Some stayed for several seasons. The Moroccan troupe, for example, had been with the show for three years – which meant literally that they knew the ropes. Their act, which included tumbling, hand-balancing and aerial work, was altered each year with a change of costumes, but their ongoing presence with the show meant that the pull-down and build-up of the tent was quick and smooth. There was also a man called Darrete, who climbed up a ladder with a huge lampshade on the end of a pole in his mouth. There was a stern, slim, professional boy, who did unicycling and juggling. Anna and I rarely saw the acts: we just heard them being announced and learned by heart the order of theme tunes that echoed out through the tent walls.

It was not a bad show, but it was not a great show. It was a small English circus where the girls on the elephants wore smelly nylon costumes, the grounds were often muddy, and the mud found its way on to the costumes. But I wonder what fantasies, of gilt, glitter and glamour, raced through Mr Richie's mind – the multitudes of girls, owned (our girls, they called them), the great swaying lines of elephants, the horses, from the best blood-stock of all Europe, too many to count. Yet in the long grass the lorries looked like a scrapyard and the ponies were from scrap-yards too. There was a tragic, brilliant discrepancy in Richie Richards, between self-image and actual image, between his notion of how his show appeared and how it actually appeared to a twentieth century audience – to people made sophisticated by television. His perception of himself was peculiar, and like-wise his perception of the show.

The act in which Mr Richie worked the horses and elephants together, amid clouds of dry ice to a Disney soundtrack, was styled on *Aladdin*. They needed another girl to ride one of the horses, a dark dapple grey called Cardeem. During showtime I had seen the artists coming and going from the back of the tent wearing dressing-gowns over their costumes, their ballet shoes pressed into wooden clogs to avoid the wet. They sparkled beneath the dressing-gowns, their faces made up under the dark shadows of hoods pulled over their heads against the rain and the wind. I wanted to find a way to work in the ring too. A couple of weeks after starting at the circus it was suggested that I could ride Cardeem in the *Aladdin* act. I wore a yashmak and sequined trousers and gave what could hardly have been called a performance; I was more a prop on the horse to dress the act. Still, I was a bit closer to the ring, a bit closer to the point where I could be on the inside and look outwards.

Polly and I waited for the act at the back doors on our horses. Jena and Josie sat on the Moroccans' wooden vaulting horse and knocked their feet on its side. They rode the elephants, with Charmagne, in yellow costumes cut away to the hip, sparkly knickers, swathed sparkly bras, and yashmaks. They chatted, pulled the material tight across their faces, leaned into each other and said things quietly, to each other only, and didn't place their eyes in any direction. If you are talking about someone, don't look at them, don't give the game away, talk indistinctly. Circus people, used to living with loud music, are good at lip-reading.

Pishti and Mr Richie brought in the elephants. They brushed and ducked under the walls of the tent, their huge shapes momentarily obscuring the night air outside. Toddy lifted the wallings for them, they lowered their heavy heads and skimmed the ground with the end of their trunks. Charmagne was just behind them: she did not look at Toddy. Jo was looking at Toddy, from the ring curtains, where he was waiting to run inside the ring to collect the hand-balancer's props. His eyes were sleepy and his arms were waiting to lift the heavy table from which the hand-balancer works. Charmagne walked over to Jena and Josie, and over the material that hid her lips her eyes were smiling, smiling but not looking, no, never looking.

To my left, down in the dark corner of the back door, beside the curtain, Mr Richie took off his purple dressing-gown. I was surprised when I first saw him do this, on my first day at the back doors, waiting while the music went up and down in the ring and the lights flickered over the top of the curtain. I hadn't expected to see the boss standing in his underpants surrounded by his artists waiting to be dressed. It's typical of circus life, though – private and, at the same time, intimate. Charmagne helped him to change into his *Aladdin* outfit, white silk trousers and shirt, gold waistband and gold turban. Charmagne was at the top of the pecking order among the girls: she helped Mr Richie to dress, which signified her status. They used to chat together, about the circus I'm sure, and for this she held every qualification: she knew everyone in the business, and most were her cousins. She knew about lorries and tents, grounds and councils, trailers, elephants, horses and costumes, good artists, bad boys, high winds, no public, buried money, scrapyards and winter yards, stakes and cables, ropes and shackles, plastic, welding and splicing, about mozzies and omeys, jossers and scarpers. Once, later on in the season, I asked her about riding an elephant, trying to find the knack.

'Look,' she said, 'it's just what I do, OK? I have ridden the bleeding cows all my life and I could sit there and pick my nose and it doesn't make any difference, all right? It's just a bleeding elephant all right. Stop panicking. Just sit there and look glamorous and don't fall off, because if you do you'll get shouted at whether the public are there or not.'

She lifted the purple cape around his shoulders and buttoned it under his chin. He said something to her over his shoulder and she nodded, her lips pressed closely together. Polly was beside me on the other horse, chatting and gossiping and bitching. She pointed to a notice she had Sellotaped to the wall of the tent: the artists were to wait until all the animals had had water before they attached their hosepipes to the taps. The pressure at that ground was low and Anna and I had had to run the water all morning to get enough water for the horses. It was a fair enough request. The clown, Marco, he had taken the mickey, and moments before we had come to the back doors with the horses he had sprayed water from his squirting hat all over the notice. Polly said that when her dad saw the notice he'd blow up; nobody sprays water on her notice, she said, and gets away with it.

Charmagne had finished helping Mr Richie and stood by Cardeem. She stroked his face, very quietly, told him things, nice things. She loved that horse, like her sister loved the china horse. The ink on the notice was running and the paper was wrinkling in the wet. Marco was saying something to Toddy and laughing. He had a high crumpled top hat, with paper flowers in the rim, and big shoes and tight trousers. I wondered that he wasn't scared. Any minute the shouting would start. Mr Richie was still in the corner, swapping his clogs for ring shoes. Charmagne put her cheek lightly against the horse's hard cheekbone. He didn't move. Polly took her feet out of her stirrups and let her legs dangle. Then she shook her head. 'I am disgusted by that,' she said. 'My dad is going to really blow up when he sees that, you watch. There is going to be a big stink.'

Mr Richie arranged his belt so that the stones were at the front. Then he walked over to the elephants. Charmagne, Jena and Josie went over to them too and swung up on to their necks, from the elephants' lifted left legs. Polly called to Mr Richie from the horse and pointed to the notice. The Hungarians hid in the folds of the curtains and looked at the ground. Mr Richie stared at the notice with small, mean eyes. He turned red. He chased Marco around the back of the tent with his stick. The shouting exploded.

MARCOYOUFUCKINGLITTLECUNTHOWDARE-YOUYOULITTLEBASTARD.

Marco's paper flowers were falling off his hat. He ran backwards and behind the elephants. The music changed and I could hear the ring-master, Phillip, announcing the next act. 'Ladies and gentlemen . . . trained and presented by Richie Richards, will you please welcome . . .' The dry-ice machine was hissing and the elephants were moving towards the curtains. Mr Richie was due in the ring. Through we went, the girls on the elephants, and Polly and I on the horses. Marco usually stood on the ring fence to clap and cheer as the animals went into the ring. But that evening there was no Marco on the ring fence and the act was tense. As we came back through the curtains Polly and I dismounted, and I had to run back to the stables with the horses so I missed what happened, though from the stable tent Anna and I could hear shouting and we could see people running in and out of the tent. Later, though, we heard about it.

Ivan was saying goodnight to Mantel. Anna and I had bedded down the lines of horses and hung their haynets. The Hungarians were in the tent, clearing rubbish, sweeping the ring boxes, and raking the sawdust. The other artists were in their trailers and over the circus ground we could smell food cooking, and see the windows of the trailers lit from the inside. Polly had gone back to her trailer. 'Good night, girls,' she had said. 'Remember to lace up the tent.' Ivan gave Mantel a biscuit and patted him, then he walked around to where we were raking up some stray bits of straw. He leaned against one of the poles in the centre of the tent.

'So did you see what happened with Marco?'

We said that we were in the stables, we didn't see anything. Alfie came round the side of the wallings with an empty wheelbarrow. He was coughing. He saw us talking and came over. 'They reckon Marco will have to leave the country now, eh, Ivan?' He was grumbling and he didn't know whose side he was on, the clown's or Mr Richie's. He put the wheelbarrow down. He said it served him right, all this shouting and that. I couldn't work out who it served right.

Anna said that Mr Richie had had it coming.

Ivan asked if anyone actually heard what Marco said to Mr Richie. I felt cold and tired and wanted to go home to my caravan.

'You know what happened, Nell?' Ivan said.

'No.'

Two of the Hungarians walked past the entrance to the stables. They were speaking urgently to each other. The events of the day were over, fact would be passed into the hands of fantasy. What occurred that afternoon in the back of the tent was mythologised, reduced and embroidered at once: it would now be impossible to determine exactly what had happened – and everyone would secretly enjoy their own rendering of the tale.

'Well, Mr Richie went for Marco and started shouting and swearing at him, and then Little Richie stepped between them as Marco lunged for Mr Richie. He hit Little Richie instead. Little Richie had an asthma attack and Auntie Sheila came running in from the trailer to try and break them all up, and then Marco hit Mr Richie.'

Ivan smiled and shook his head. Then he looked over to Mantel. He said, 'Good boy, Mantel.' Anna was staring at Ivan. She was in love with him, perhaps, and he could be very nasty to her. 'Don't stare at me Anna, I know you fancy me,' Ivan said. His voice trailed off.

'So what happened Ivan?' I asked.

'He bloody loves himself,' Anna whispered to me.

Ivan looked at the three of us. 'Well, Mr Richie shouted to Marco "You finish!" And Marco shouts back, right in front of everyone, "I'm Spanish!"'

The next day Marco and his family left the show. The rumours said that Mr Richie refused to pay his wages for that week so they took some machinery with them. The police came then went away again. The events of that day lost sequence and meaning and became momentary impressions held together by loose strings of speculation.

The next day in the pub the Hungarian boys lamented Marco's departure. He was a very good boy, they said, yes, he was a good boy. He didn't take any shit. In the stables Polly tossed her hair and said that Marco would never work in England again, her dad would make sure of that. I felt sorry for Marco's mum. After the incident I had seen her walking across the ground looking alienated and depressed. I thought of them in the lay-by down the road, on their way back to Spain.

The night of the row I didn't sleep well, and in my head and in my dreams I could hear raised voices and whispers, in other languages, but I was never sure where they came from, from outside the walls of the caravan or just from the echoing memory of the day.

The Leaving of Liverpool, November 1995

*I think it would be good to lose your own certainties . . .
don't you? Disappear into somebody else's culture?*
                                    Falling, COLIN THUBRON

~

Liverpool was the last ground of that tenting season. In
December we would move into buildings in Scotland for
Christmas. The weather had turned for winter, the Indian
summer was over.

The night we moved to Liverpool I left the jockey wheel
down on my caravan. This must have put too much strain on
the draw-bar, and as I pulled off the motorway I heard a horrible scraping, grinding noise. I stopped at the side of the road
in the dark, got out of the van and saw that the front of the caravan was scraping along the ground. The Hungarians were
behind me in their four lorries. The lights came up the road,
the drivers signalled, pulled out and drove past. Pishti was the
last in the line and stopped ahead of my load. He jumped out
of the lorry and looked at the caravan. He was wearing the red
boiler suit he always wore, a red Camel Trophy boiler suit. He

laughed and shook his head. 'I think that is scrapyard caravan, eh, Nell?'

I felt dismal.

'OK, we come back later, wait here, yes?'

I waited in the front of the van for a couple of hours, somewhere on the outskirts of Liverpool. I locked the doors. Two boys in tracksuits walked along the side of the road opposite. They had a dog with them. It was dark, it was the middle of the night, and there was no light on either side, no dusk and no dawn. I had dreaded something like this happening – it was why I chewed my fingers and scratched my face on a move night. There seemed too many things that could go wrong. The boys would be ages. Perhaps they would never come. Perhaps I should just drive off, home, anywhere. But it seemed easier to wait. I was part of the show now anyway. You can't just drive away from people that easily. The Hungarians and Ivan and Phillip, Charmagne and Josie and Anna – Anna who would not have watered the horses without me to climb about on the partitions in the lorry and risk my neck in the stamping darkness. She wasn't a bad girl but she was slow, and she couldn't really climb. She was not agile. The boys would sometimes help her with the watering. They would roll up their sleeves and hop up on to the partitions and pass the buckets along down the lorry to the stamping horses. Toddy would sit on one of the Arabs' backs and lean forward and hug it, like a little jockey in a starting-stall, and Pishti would whistle to his favourite horse, Farouk. 'Farouk, my little angel.' He loved that horse, a wild chestnut Arab with a sharp look in its eye. 'Watch Farouk,' Polly had said, 'he's a bastard,' and on my first day he attacked me, pinned me in the corner of the stall. But he was humorous, really, in the way that some horses are, and he was just trying things out. Farouk.

'Pishti loves Farouk like Ivan loves his Land Rover,' Anna and I would agree.

The boys arrived in a Land Rover with Mr Richie. I had nearly fallen asleep and was doodling inside my head. They started to pull cables and a generator out of the back of the Land Rover. Polly's boyfriend was with them and they were all talking in Hungarian, pointing to the jockey wheel and the bent broken wheel. I felt stupid. Mr Richie told me to look around for a piece of metal, so I walked up and down the side of the road kicking at bits of stick and staring at the darkness. 'You have to find a bit of metal,' he said. I was still looking. He was a voice beside me in the dark and I didn't want to do anything that would provoke shouting. 'What you need is a piece of metal. I've welded stuff up with motorway crash barrier before now.'

He lost his Rs in speech. He was a frightening man, but still he sounded funny – 'motorway cwash bawwier'. But there was no metal to be had in this street, and the boys could not get the generator started. GI Jo said, 'OK, Nell, we do like we do in Hungary. I have a garage, this is how we do it.' He took off his jacket and pulled back the oily sleeves of his sweatshirt. The caravan had to get to the ground and dawn was near. Jo found some pieces of angle iron in the back of the Land Rover and used them to brace the broken sections of the draw-bar, like a splint. He had a pocket full of the orange nylon string used to bind hay bales, and he used it to tie the angle iron to the draw-bar. Mr Richie said that they would fix it properly at the next ground. 'I knew that was going to happen. Look, the metal is all rusted anyway. Ivan should have checked there, silly bugger.'

I had bought the caravan recently, as the other had become too cold. Auntie Sheila had lent me the money, and sent Ivan with me to look at a caravan I had seen in the local *Trade It*, as I had no idea then of how a caravan should hold together. Ivan had a look at it and said that it was all right. We had towed it back with the Land Rover, and he had said that it towed well. He was travelling at fifty m.p.h. I had been so tired, and the Land Rover was warm, so I was dozing.

Ivan said, 'Should we pull over into the lay-by, you know, try it out?'

'What?'

'The new caravan, you know?'

I could never work out if he was serious or not, so I just laughed, and he turned his eyes back to the road and his thin face was in silhouette under his baseball cap.

GI Jo drove my load on to the new ground. We were in the Liverpool docks. It was a very big ground, with no grass, just acres of pebbles and concrete. I fell asleep in the caravan at about five o'clock in the morning. I could hear something humming outside. In my head I could hear Mr Richie. *I've used a motorway cwash bawwier before now.* The caravan was well and truly knackered. I stopped worrying about it, the leaking taps, the broken gas fire, the spreading patches of rust, and just listened to that noise, the humming, and the voices. I thought that these people were like blank, selfish children, taking everything they could, but at the same time unthinkingly loyal. When you were with them, they would not leave you stranded by the side of the road, not out of compassion but because you were with them, temporarily, and – extraordinary as it seemed – a member of their tribe.

The sun glared off the white concrete. The boys stamped their boots, buttoned their boiler suits to the chin and put their hands in their pockets. Just the other side of the wall at the edge of the ground, beyond steel benches, was the Mersey. It was seven

o'clock in the morning. Ivan appeared from his lorry with a bal-
aclava on. We started to work, pulling stakes from the lorries and
dragging out the wheelbarrows and hay bales. The cold sun
warmed and the boys unbuttoned their closed necks.

I climbed up on to the piles of stalls in the lorry, whose sides
were plastic curtains. Someone had to fold them back, and Anna
was standing beside the lorry with her knees slightly bent and
the corner of her mouth pointing downwards. Across the
ground, the Moroccans and the other artists were winching the
coppolla off the tent trailer. It jerked slowly upwards and the
folds of the tent hung from it. The boys were working on the
stakes. I climbed up to the top of the lorry and reached around
the roof for the lacing. I must have missed my grip, and I slipped
against the plastic, which gave way, and fell about nine feet on to
the ground. I bashed my elbow. The Hungarians turned round
and laughed. 'You learn to fly, Nell? OK? You OK?' They were
laughing and my eyes felt full of tears in the cold.

We stood in Liverpool for two weeks. The docks were ten
minutes from the centre of the town and we went out to the
Irish bars almost every night. Pishti went every night; when he
returned from town he would fall into the door of the
Hungarians' caravan with his eyes shut. 'Very very fucking good
night,' he would say, still with his eyes shut. The television played
an English film, and I was talking with Toddy, the other two fast
asleep on the bunks at the end of the room. 'Very fucking good.
I make so many plenty good friends, too many good friends. I
will live in Liverpool, eh?' and he slumped down on the seat
beside Toddy and put his head on his folded arms in front of
him, and the yellow light swung gently and the shadows moved
in his hair.

Charmagne was a hard drinker. She said her father had taught her to drink in bars in Spain when she was little. Ivan said that Charmagne could drink anyone under the table. Ivan was sharp and defensive when he went out, and didn't drink at all. He nodded and his blue eyes were cold. 'Ivan says you can drink anyone under the table,' I joked, and laughed. We were sitting in the Irish bar in Liverpool: Charmagne's head was down and her eyes were forward. The bar was starting to empty and we listened to another medley of Irish songs.

'How can you drink so much, Charmagne?'

She pulled on a cigarette and blew out the smoke, upwards. She was nodding slightly but her eyes were steady and her voice was clear. 'Balance.'

On the way home we ran along the concrete banks of the Mersey. Charmagne and I stopped to look at the dark water that was striped and metallic, with a repeating pattern moving across its surface in light. Toddy ran ahead in the dark. We walked more slowly along the edge of the water, and then we saw Toddy, in his boxer shorts, climbing down some dark slippery steps into the water.

'Swimming?'

'Let's go swimming!'

'Now, in the cold, let's go swimming – Toddy, Toddy, what are you doing?'

'It can't be that cold, the water. It's not Christmas time yet.'

'We can't go swimming now, it's too cold.'

'Why not? Let's go swimming, come on! Toddy, where are you?'

'Down the steps.'

I could hear Toddy laughing. At the bottom of the steps his eyes were glinting blue. He was so serious sometimes. I thought Toddy made life too serious half the time. We were very drunk.

'Where is the water, Toddy?'

'Is it cold?'

'It's cold in the water.'

'The wind is blowing, it's bleeding November for fuck's sake. Toddy, what are you doing at the bottom of the steps?'

'I'm going swimming.'

'I want to swim too.'

'You're bleeding mad.'

'Come on.'

'The water's fast. We can't swim in that.'

'Here, hold these clothes for a minute, so they don't get wet, Pishti. Do you mind?'

We took our clothes off and hopped about in the wind. Toddy was at the bottom of the steps. Pishti picked up the clothes and stood at the top of the steps. He looked annoyed.

'Toddy, Toddy, what are you doing.'

Charmagne and I slithered down the cold steps to the water. It was less bright than it seemed from the edge of the concrete. I couldn't see Pishti any more. Charmagne stopped on the steps. The water splashed on to them and I slipped and fell right under the water. I couldn't feel the steps any more. The water was very cold. Toddy caught my arm and pulled me out. He was freezing cold too. We climbed back up the steps and wrapped ourselves in clothes. That night Pishti stayed in my caravan the whole night, and there were late-night songs on the radio and violet light outside.

I never really knew the Hungarians. Toddy spoke quite good English but the others very little. I knew that GI Jo had lost his father, and that he loved the Army, thrived on the shouting. He was a body-builder. During the last few weeks, he had withdrawn from their company and stopped coming to the pub. He was thick with Polly's boyfriend, and the others thought he was double-crossing them. I knew that Pishti loved his girlfriend, and the food in Hungary, and that England meant only the expectation of a memory, where the bad bits outweighed the good. Toddy loved fishing in Hungary, the banks of the rivers in the summer-time, and his girlfriend, who ran a clothes shop. I didn't know Marti Bartsi at all, he never said anything apart from 'I am a bastard', and he had a mean mouth and mean eyes. But they were my good friends.

They fixed the light on my caravan. One night we were just about to leave a ground when I realised that a boy who had uncoupled the van from the caravan the week before had forgotten to unplug the electrics, and the wires had ripped out of the socket. ('You bloody bastard, Andy,' I said, 'why didn't you tell me?' He was a lanky, dishonest boy, who never looked you in the eye, and he said that it wasn't his fault, it was like that already.) I can't wire up caravan electrics and I would have just had to chance it, and hope that the convoy stayed together, the vehicle behind acting as my lights. But the boys cut their sleep short and fixed the lights, squinting into the socket in the darkness and calling to each other as the lights flicked on and off. I stood behind the caravan with Pishti, and he looked at the lights flashing red and amber as the wires connected, and he laughed and said it was a Christmas tree. I took them to the supermarket and the launderette in my van. In Liverpool we drove away from the majestic docks and into the narrow back streets, where the pavements were lined with old sofas and bicycles and the faded plastic of worn-out toys, and the air in the van was cold and all our breath was white. The launderette was beside an Army-surplus store. We all went in there. The man behind the desk looked surprised: all the boys were wearing tank suits. He asked who we were, and they nodded and smiled in Hungarian, 'From the circus, down the road, in the docks.'

In Liverpool I learned a painful lesson about circus life: that people may become the centre and meaning of your existence, for a while, the closest friends, you eat, drink, sleep, laugh, cry in their company, then they go away and you never see them again. I woke on the Sunday of the last show with a gripping hangover. I had to be in the stables for eight o'clock. Clover was staying for the weekend. She was asleep in my bed. I woke her up, and her face was crumpled and cross. I put the heater on in the caravan. The little plastic table was covered in makeup and shot glasses and cups of cold tea. I had bought a new pair of clogs that had a rainbow stripe across them and they were lying under the table. 'Come and help me in the stables, Clover.'

She put her face into the pillow. 'I'm too tired, too ill.'

'Please come and help.'

'Stop hassling me, Nell.'

'Come on, Clover, please, look, I've got to get up.'

We mucked out and harnessed the horses for practice. The *Aladdin* act was discontinued, and for the Christmas season I was to be promoted from horse to elephant: I was about to become an elephant girl. Mr Richie said that he wanted to practise the elephants that morning in preparation for Glasgow. I mean, we heard that he wanted to, because Little Richie appeared in the doorway of the stables, or Polly flicked her hair and waved her finger at us.

Charmagne could remember the routine for the three elephants and she shouted down to Mr Richie, who was standing in the middle of the ring. 'Sharon [that was the elephant's name] should turn this way, and then we stand up in the middle, while

Barbara and Beverley [the other two elephants] walk around the back.' She was sitting on her elephant easily, without holding on. She had a cold and kept blowing her nose into a white tissue. I remember it distinctly. I was sitting on Sharon, holding on to her harness, while the Hungarians, Clover and Polly waited in the entrance to the ring. I was wearing my oilskin trousers and felt as if I was going to slip off. The elephants stood on their back legs and we had to kneel up on them and point one leg in the air; we were on all fours on the elephants, one leg pointing to the unlit roof of the tent. Charmagne kept shouting at me to look glamorous. Her voice was echoing in the tent, shriller and louder than usual. She said she'd give me a hand with my airs and graces. It seemed so absurd to have a terrible Liverpool hangover and be up there clinging on to a length of chain while this huge animal lurched and ran and stood upright, with no warning, nothing between me and the crashing ground. Then we had to lie down on the ground in a row, Charmagne, Jena and I, and the elephants walked, one by one, over us, stepping between us slowly and carefully. Jena was squealing, and Charmagne told her to shut up. I didn't say anything at all, and Charmagne said, 'Sharon, don't touch my leg, you bleeding cow,' and above us the elephants moved slowly and swung their trunks.

The last show of the season, at the end of that fortnight in Liverpool, was wild. Polly was screaming as we went into the ring, and Clover stood in the corner of the back doors with her hands in the pockets of her red bomber jacket, smiling. Of all the people, the friends and the family who have been to the circus for visits, it is Clover who understands the point of it all. Clover, my sister, my confidante, my best friend, my angel, my rival. The Hungarians did their work gleefully, knowing they were leaving the next morning, that it was over, they were through and that Hungary was a few hours away. Their contract with the circus had ended when the circus finished the tenting season and moved into the buildings in Glasgow. After Liverpool they were free, and could go home. Pishti always used to bring Mantel back from the ring to the stables for Ivan. He would run into the stables with the horse trotting beside him, and I saw him doing this on that last night: he was smiling, and he wasn't swearing, where before he had been quiet and never smiled, and muttered his Hungarian swear-words. *Koravanyard*, son-of-a-bitch – and I could tell that there had been shouting in the tent. Today, though, this evening, the last show of the tenting season, he just smiled, and if there was shouting, he didn't hear it.

The night before they left, the Hungarians came round to my caravan to say goodbye. GI Jo had shaved off all his hair and was wearing a white tracksuit. He had had a shower somewhere and the circus was all washed off him. He looked like a monk. Later on in the night Pishti knocked on the door. He gave me his red Camel Trophy boiler suit. He sat down and groaned as he always did, and then he said 'goodbye, Nell,' and blinked and rubbed his eyes then leaned over and kissed me goodbye. The next morning I saw him briefly, pulling wires from the electric box. I went round the corner and into the stables. I said to Anna that I was very sad Pishti was leaving now, and she said that it was good. She adopted a motherly tone. 'You know, Nell, you can get your life back together, now that he's going.' I thought she sounded ridiculous, as if I had just ended a long-term relationship. I hadn't: a brief affair with a man to whom I could barely talk had finished with the season. And yet her words reassured me, because they explained the empty landscape – and made me feel normal.

He came into the stables to say goodbye finally. All four of them were about to leave, to drive some lorries back to the farm for the circus, their final chore, but his eyes had gone already. There was one Irish song, a few lines of it, that I kept singing over and over again. 'It's not the leaving of Liverpool that grieves me but, my darling, when I think of you.' I climbed up to the back of the horses' boards to fill the haynets. There were no boys to help us now. Farouk tossed his head and stamped and pulled at the haynet I was untying. Alfie called from beside the elephants, 'You're going to miss that Pishti now, eh, Nell? I saw him coming out of your caravan.'

'So fare thee well, my own true love, and when I return united we will be, it's not the leaving of Liverpool that grieves me but, my darling, when I think of you.' That was all I could remember of the song.

I heard the engines outside and some raised voices. I jumped down the back of the boards. My clog fell off. I caught it with my toe and ran round the back of the boards, ducking where one of the horses had its head over the top. Two seconds, Anna, two seconds. The big top was down so I could see right across the ground. A line of lorries and trailers was pulling out of the entrance. The sunlight was very bright and the Mersey was sparkling. The wind blew across the gravel. I could see Pishti driving one of the Land Rovers, and he never turned back and he never waved.

After we had done the horses I walked round to Charmagne's caravan. She was dressed for leaving, in a long wraparound skirt. She was smoking a cigarette and her long thin fingers looked red. Once she told me that when she was a child she had had to soak her hands in her own urine to harden them. I think she was sad as well that the boys were gone; she looked miserable.

'Where are you going?'

'To see my mum on the St Petersburg Circus in London.'

'All the boys have gone now.'

'I know. It hurts, doesn't it?'

Outside, through the lace curtains, I could see Ivan driving on to the ground in his Land Rover.

'See you in Glasgow, Charmagne.'

'Yes, OK, Nell, 'bye then. Take care.'

I thought that I had never felt so depressed in all my life. All my clothes were dirty. I had drunk too much recently and I had had nothing to eat. If I went to the launderette, ate a meal, and slept a good night – and there were no shows now, so there was relatively little to do – I would feel better. I went to the launderette beside the Army-surplus store. I just couldn't go in there and be surrounded by their ghosts, smiling and looking at T-shirts and joking in words I didn't understand. Pishti's boiler suit was on the passenger seat. I pulled over beside a rubbish bin and threw it away. The lights were starting to come on in the shop windows and there were already Christmas decorations for sale.

It was a dark evening. I parked the van and took my clothes to the launderette, then went to a junk shop at the end of the row of shops. I bought a little purse, and I overheard two old women talking together. One said that when a door shuts another opens. I found consolation in what she was saying. But it was true, too, it was painful, this separation, the memories of a place, walking to the bars after the show and coming back late, and swimming in the cold water, and Pishti staying in my trailer – the unexpectedness of that, all this, the night long and the radio playing love songs, and the delirium of love and desire at the same time.

I parked the van beside the animals' lorry and walked across the ground to my caravan. It was pitch dark. If I had been in Liverpool for another reason and had seen all the lorries and the dark shape of the stable tent then I would have longed to have been on the inside, part of the caravans and the lorries, whatever their mysterious purpose was. I felt cheered by this, and kept saying to myself, 'Be somebody, be something,' carried away by an ambition that burns continually, and provokes me to see another pattern in the bleak outlook – or, at least, fancy that I see one.

I tidied my caravan a bit and put away my clothes. Tomorrow I would find a shower somewhere, and that afternoon we would leave Liverpool and I would not be sad any more. Anna and I went back into the stables to bed down the horses.

'Do you think Farouk misses Pishti?' I asked Anna.

She called over from the other side, 'Does he fuck!'

The puddles outside were lit neon by the dock lights. We laced up the tent together and said goodnight.

There was a knock on my door. It was Alfie. He said that if I rang the pizza-delivery people on my telephone he would buy me a pizza. We ordered two tomato pizzas and I went round to his caravan to eat them. He had a gas fire in the corner, and the shelves were full of car-boot ornaments, tiny china figures painted in pink with gold lines, pastoral emblems, embedded in the close fabric of his small caravan. Meg, his dog, was curled up in the corner among piles of plastic plates and spanners and blankets. 'They were good boys, them lot. Shame they left, really, and that. They'll never come back, not with all that shouting that goes on.'

There was a tin of beer on the side of the table. Pishti had told me that it was Alfie's Christmas drink. 'Why you not drink it, Alfie?' he had asked him, and Alfie had whispered to him, with his old glee, the rebel inside him, cursing and swearing under his breath, 'Pishti, that is for Christmas.' Alfie made me a cup of tea, breathing heavily, slowly pouring the water from the kettle that heated on the gas. The steam rose through the makeshift wire handle, and the light from one bulb in a china lampstand caught in the rising vapour. The night was cold outside, and it was thick and warm in the caravan. The boys had gone and my heart was broken. But the move would happen tomorrow, the next place, the new place, the carpet pulled out and replaced. Be somebody. Be something. There was no time to feel sad. We ate the pizza and I went home to bed.

Scrapyard Collage

I may say that the circus fulfilled my every expectation.
'The roar of the greasepaint, the smell of the crowd', as
some joker has transposed it, had entered in to my soul.
                    Circus! An Investigation Into What Makes the
                                        Sawdust Fly, ALAN WYKES

~

We left Liverpool at five o'clock in the afternoon. The entire show was moving to Glasgow for the Christmas season. I had heard that we would spend a couple of weeks in a yard outside the city before we went into the buildings. An old schoolfriend of mine, Jackie, was at art college in Glasgow, and I was looking forward to seeing her. She lives in a big first-floor flat in the middle of the city. I could have my first bath in three months.

Just before we left Ivan and I were sitting on the last partition in the horse lorry. The ramp was down and in front of us the Mersey glittered in the November sun. It was cold, hard, bright, shiny, painful, exciting, a big night to come and the M1 and a farm outside Glasgow. Ivan was sitting beside me and for a while there was nothing to do but sit there and watch the shine on the river passing. Then Ivan looked to the river and to the lorries parked in front of us, and he looked at me and he had a smile on his lips, which are thin lips, and he had a hard face. 'Pretty wild, isn't it?'

And it was wild, but that wasn't the point, then. For a moment Ivan was giving the game away. He mustn't admit that he sees all this as strange too. Where would that leave me, running as I am and never able to keep up? It is essential that we don't know them, the circus people, too well, otherwise the function of their otherness collapses. The allure of the circus arises in part from the sense that the circus people are other, outside normal life. But this quality cannot be self-conscious, flaunted – or the allure is lost. 'Pretty wild isn't it?' That should have been my own private observation.

We stopped for a break at Carlisle Services. The Moroccans went inside and played on the fruit machines. That was when I saw the little baby through the lorry window. All the Moroccans' wives were looking at the bundle in the woman's arms. They were lit only by the dim lights in the lorry. The baby was said to be only a few days old. I was slightly spooked by this baby: I had been living in a caravan only metres away from it and had had no idea, until then, that either wife or baby existed. The Moroccans' wives never seemed to step outside the trailer.

One of the trailers had a flat tyre and was somewhere on the hard shoulder of the motorway. Mr Richie climbed up on top of the elephant lorry where he kept the spare tyres and started to unrope them, flinging them down on the tarmac. Anna and I stood a distance away and watched the tyres bouncing and rolling in the car park. Someone had opened the door of the elephant lorry and Sharon had her head out of the door, silhouetted in the dark and yellow neon of the service station.

'I must be fucking mad,' Anna was grumbling. 'My mum and

dad are only twenty minutes from here. I might as well go home.'

She sniffed and coughed. Her health had deteriorated recently. She'd become very dirty and the dirt had worn itself under the skin of her fingers. She developed a huge swelling behind the ring on her right hand, which enlarged her finger to twice its normal size. The swelling was trapped behind the confining strip of metal. She had ignored it. She showed it to me one day in the stables. I said she would lose her finger and told Polly about it, who took her off to Mr Richie's workshop, where he cut off the ring. Polly told me that pus had burst out of Anna's finger as the ring was cut. I think she had just given up washing so I took her with me to a sports centre and made her have a shower.

'I might as well go home.'

But she wouldn't go home and I knew why: she had told me before. Her mum and dad were dying. I met them once and her dad was very thin and her mum was very fat. I didn't know if they were dying but they did not look healthy.

'Standing in a bloody service station and the elephant's got its head out of its front door. I must be fucking mad.'

Later that night I was split up from the main convoy. In fact, the whole convoy fragmented. Phillip had to drive back with the spare tyres, so Josie drove their load on. I was supposed to stay behind the horse lorry, but I couldn't keep up with it. I dropped back and ended up behind Ivan, who was having to drive a very slow lorry and trailer. I had a bad problem staying awake. It was the first time I had ever done a twelve-hour tow or experienced that particular tiredness: it's like an entity that comes into the van and tries to seduce you; the tiredness is there on the seat beside you, coaxing, persuading, suffocating, until the lights on the road are dancing across the windscreen and your eyes are sliding shut, stinging, the other car lights fading, the noise of the engine distant. Then the van and the caravan start to drift over to the other side of the road, and you wake up again, alert for a few minutes, or you see some blue flashing lights and the adrenaline moves in your blood and your eyes open. I opened and closed the window, pinched myself, pulled my hair, shouted, sang, talked, just fought off the thing lurking in the cab and tempting me into delicious warm sleep. I figured out that I couldn't physically fall asleep and sing at the same time, so I sang anything, everything, for about six of the twelve hours of driving.

We pulled over into a service station. I had flashed my headlights to Ivan as I had to stop for a minute. I was afraid of blacking out. In the car park he jumped out of the cab of his lorry and ran over to my window. My mouth tasted of metal and the back of my throat was burning. I had smoked two packets of cigarettes and eaten twenty-five Pro-Plus. Ivan's face was gleaming with tiredness and excitement. I don't think he had nodded at all.

'You OK? Just keep your eyes open.'

His eyes were really sparkling. I couldn't tell if he was joking or not. I never could. He was a master of dead-pan.

It wasn't a farm, it was a scrapyard. Daylight had broken as Ivan and I arrived. Alfie's caravan had been left in Liverpool. It would be picked up later in the day. He rode in the elephant lorry with Mr Richie. I wondered if they sat there in silence, or if they talked. Mr Richie couldn't just shout at Alfie all the way. If they talked, did they sense any sort of companionship? Perhaps they gossiped about people on the show. I set my caravan and walked across the yard. The ground was deep mud and grit. There were high banks of mud on all sides and bits of discoloured plastic, broken yellow barrels, strings of white polythene, sharp twists of metal stuck out of the ground. Rotting cabs of lorries were sinking into the mud and broken, gutted caravans. In one corner, beside a brick wall (the yard belonged to a haulage company), there was a pile of silver foil stars, a set of rusty lights and split cables, some boxes painted with clowns' faces. I walked over to the elephant lorry. Alfie was filling some blue plastic barrels with water for them. Mr Richie had gone to bed and Alfie had nowhere to sleep. I asked him what he had been doing and he said that he had slept for a while with the elephants but that they needed water now. His face was bright red, his eyes were bloodshot and his lips were cracked. He shut one eye and looked quickly about him. 'That bloody Mr Richie has left my caravan in Liverpool and that. He just goes inside and everything. You'll see. He won't come in the stables once while we're here.'

I was not disappointed with this news, but I felt sorry for Alfie so I made him a cup of tea and helped him water the elephants. I stood in the lorry and he filled the buckets then passed them up to me. The three elephants were thirsty after the journey and they squabbled over the water with their trunks. The door of the lorry took up about a third of the wall. There were two elephants between me and the wall, and for a moment I was frightened. They had only to become over-impatient and lean against each other, and I would be squashed as flat as a pancake between them.

We stayed on the scrapyard for three weeks. On some nights, after work, I went to see Jackie in the flat – it was the first time I had been away from the circus since I had joined. The rooms have high walls and stuccoed ceilings. The walls are painted in bright gloss colours, egg yellow and dark green and orange and

red. The kitchen has red walls and is hung with Jackie's paintings, flyers for clubs, messages, doodles and Polaroids taken at
parties. Jackie and the two girls she lived with wore dazzlingly
bright clothes, silver jerseys and stripy tights and gold dresses.
The kitchen was hung about with paper chains. There was a
Christmas tree in the corner glowing with dark fairy-lights.
Jackie always says that everything she does is inspired by Mum
and Minety. I went to the flat with Little Richie. A girl was sitting
on a stool in the kitchen with a silver star attached to her forehead. Little Richie loved the flat. He said it was one of the first
times he had ever been into a house.

I lay in Jackie's bath and chatted to her. She had painted cher-
ries on the walls of the bathroom, and she had made cakes and
mulled wine. I sat and turned on the hot tap. I lay back again. I
felt bloated from eating too many chips. I said I was worried
about being fat, for the elephant riding, and Jackie said, 'Don't be
stupid. You don't look fat. You look fine.' I got dressed and sat on
the sofa. Little Richie was still there. He didn't say very much but
laughed at other people's jokes. We watched *Wild At Heart* on
video. Jackie's flat was warm and Christmassy and quiet. This
whole world is wild at heart and weird on top. That is one of the
lines from the film.

Beyond the mudbanks of the scrapyard a field sloped sharply
upwards to the road. The edge of that field was the horizon,
and the tops of the cars and lorries moved along the horizon,
and beyond them, just visible, burning day and night, was a
Burger King sign. As the start of the Christmas season drew
nearer, artists began to arrive at the scrapyard. I walked up to the
Burger King for some breakfast. I was parked alongside the edge
of the stable tent, which was tied off to the lorry, as the ground

was too hard under the mud for the stakes. Yesterday when I had been filling haynets with Anna, talking, we were interrupted by a loud man's voice, coming from around the side of the stables. 'Hey up. Where's the tart with a heart? Are you there, Anna?'

Anna knew whose voice it was and shouted, 'Round here, Willie.'

A dwarf man walked around the side of the tent. He was four feet high with short muscly arms and a smiling face. We jumped off the lorry and Anna leaned down and gave him a hug.

'Who's this, then, Anna? Where do you come from, love?'

We carried on doing our jobs and Willie walked around with us for a bit. He told me all about being a dwarf. He said that most dwarfs don't like children as they stand and stare and point in the street. The little people, which was how he referred to other dwarfs, grow resentful of children and try to scare them. But Willie loved children, he didn't want to scare them. That was why he worked in the circus as a clown. He said he would love to get married, to be really in love with someone and for someone to feel the same way about him. He had had plenty of girlfriends. Anna and I gave the horses their eleven o'clock water. The sun was starting to come through the clouds and the puddles in the scrapyard into the stable tent. Farouk drained his bucket and I gave him another. For a few minutes the horses were all quiet. Willie was leaning against one of the centre poles of the tent. The air was red and the red was intensifying as the sun smoothed over the tent roof. 'You see, they like me as a novelty, the girls.' He didn't sound angry and he didn't sound sad.

'My sister's a bitch too, isn't she, Willie?' Anna said.

'Oh, yes, her sister's a right bitch. They just want to take you to the pub and pat you on the head at the bar and then all the other girls say, "Oh, isn't he sweet" for a while, and then they dump you because the novelty passes.'

He stopped talking and walked over to the tent entrance. 'I suppose Polly will be here soon and Little Richie. Christmas shopping.'

He looked at me. 'You don't like these people, do you, Nell?'

I said I didn't like being shouted at all the time.

'You know what I always say about the Richards family. Their bark is worse than their bite.'

And that same evening another clown arrived with a big lorry and trailer. I didn't meet him but I saw a figure filling a kettle in the dark by the water taps, and I heard him talking with Phillip, and he was asking who was there and what was going on at the moment, and Phillip, whose terriers were sniffing about around the tent, said, 'Not a lot.'

One morning I walked back down the hill from the Burger King. From the top of that little hill the rows of caravans and lorries usually looked deserted. The Moroccans never came out into the wet. Josie stayed inside all day, making costumes. I saw her occasionally, wearing bright pink rubber gloves, hanging out the washing. Anna and I were usually the only people about; everyone else sat inside in the warm and watched television. The scrapyard was black-brown, the lorries and caravans were white and cream, and the stable tent was dark red. That day, however, I could see some of the children running about in their tiny clogs, yellow and pink. There were two people standing in the yard in bright clothes and some others hanging about talking to them. I walked down across the field and into the yard. Willie had his back turned to me. When he looked round his face was all painted up. The other clown was filling his kettle again. His face was painted in an intricate design of red and white lines and black circles. He had baggy trousers and big shoes. He had been in a café down the road, doing some publicity for the circus.

'Didja get the mozzies' number then, Jan Eric?' asked Willie.

He said he did. Jan Eric filled his kettle and picked up his prop, a giant sword. Willie called to me from his caravan door, 'Where's Anna gone?'

I turned round, and Willie's face and small figure, painted up and garish, were framed by rubbish and the mud and the old tyres, and an abandoned satellite dish, the dirty collage of the scrapyard.

Accident

The brilliant stars disappeared.
A Peep Behind the Scenes, Mrs O. F. Walton

~

I was supposed to be revising for my Oxford interview but I was fast asleep in my big brass bed in Minety, and it was ten o'clock. The date was 25 November 1991. Mum came in and asked if I wanted to go hunting with her. I was irritated. I hate to remember this, the adolescent spurning of suggestions. The night before, she had asked me if I wanted to go to church, to evensong. She had been standing at the door that led to the entrance to the back stairs, smiling, looking kind, loving me, and me hating her because I was eighteen and had decided that the world was all against me. I said I didn't want to go to church. I was proud of my autonomy, a suggestion of atheism, decided alone. No, I didn't want to go hunting either. Philistines, I thought angrily to myself, and me with my exams to do and academia ahead, the pressure, the clever questions and good answers expected, the balances to be weighed up and organised, quotes to summon, ideas to develop, understand, undermine, qualify, quantify, they didn't understand this, she didn't understand this. Hunting – as if I had the time, as if I had the inclination.

I got out of bed to plait her horse for her. It was a thoroughbred, a neat, smart little mare, and I'm good at plaiting manes. I enjoy it. You divide the mane into sections and plait each one, then roll it into a little ball. Then the horse's neck looks well curved and sleek. We put the horse into the trailer and I said goodbye. She looked smart, very sweet, she said, 'Goodbye, I love you.'

'I love you too, I love you once more.'

She drove away down the lane to the road, and I went inside and upstairs and started the revision.

Two hours later, when I was downstairs in the kitchen eating toast and jam beside the Aga, the telephone rang. A cosy Minety kitchen. All that went away with that call. Mrs Crocker said that Mum had had an accident. It still stops me in my tracks now and will until the day I die. She said that they had been riding across the disused part of Kemble airfield by the wood. 'Your mum fell, on the concrete. The horse slipped.' She was in Cirencester hospital.

I was annoyed and a bit worried – she might have broken her leg, or her arm. I wanted to go and see her, and a part of me was starting to enjoy the drama. 'Is she all right, though? Not serious, I mean?'

And the voice said, 'I'll take you to see her. I'll come and pick you up.'

I went to the hospital and there was a real-life *Casualty* scene going on outside, flashing lights and white coats. I walked past and into the hospital and the nurse put me in a separate waiting room. I didn't know why they were all so formal and worried-looking. I was used to accidents. I had broken both arms falling off ponies. All this was an overreaction, idiotic.

A doctor came in and he tried to describe to me what had happened. I didn't understand what he was saying. Then a nurse came in and said that Mrs Stroud was being transferred to Bristol hospital, did her daughter want to see her before she left, and I said that I did, of course, and where was she? And I was looking forward to seeing her sitting in the bed so that I could say, 'Are you all right?' and we could make a few plans, quickly, before she went. The nurse led me outside and there was more of a commotion than before, more nurses and an ambulance.

It was like a sledge-hammer between the shoulder-blades. She was lying on a bed and her face was covered in blood. There were huge purple rings under her eyes, which were shut. She looked as if she was dead. Let her die.

I couldn't breathe and started to fall over, I was falling, falling right away from it all, 'It's her daughter, take her away, take her away.' And I thought, Let her die, let her die, in reply, but they wouldn't hear that then, in the past. The sound doesn't carry.

She went down the motorway to Bristol at a hundred miles an hour, with a police escort – you see them go past sometimes, on the motorway, wonder what has happened for a bit. Now you know. A police escort and all the lights. I told my dad this. 'Were there outriders?' he said. He was disbelieving of what was happening to him, to us, to Mum. 'Will she be all right?' he said to me. It was the first time that I saw beyond him as my dad. How very un-all-right we couldn't imagine. Death would have been all right.

The house filled up quickly with people. After Cirencester we picked up Clover from school, ran into her classroom in tears, with a teacher, which she had always known would happen one day. Called from the classroom because your mother is dead. We drove home. Nothing we could do just yet, said Mrs Crocker sensibly. Rick, my dad, had come back from London, and people had returned from hunting to help. They made tea and Clover and I smoked and smoked and shook and smoked.

A close friend of Mum's, Dawn, drove us to the hospital. It was 25 November, it was freezing cold and there was a thick fog. It was a forty-minute drive down the M4 to Bristol, Frenchay hospital. As we drove into the car park there was one of the big signposts that are the landscape of hospitals: In-patients, Out-patients, Maternity, Accident and Emergency, Rehabilitation. Rick read that and he winced. We barely knew what it meant but we knew we were on to something big when that kind of foreign phrase was suddenly slap-bang in the centre of our vision. Rehabilitation. We would know what it meant, or what it didn't mean, soon enough. We waited in the ICU waiting room. We were soon to become fluent in hospital jargon, Intensive Care Unit, Rehabilitation. The hospitalscape of tall towers and constant smoke, deep gullies between buildings and fag-end-strewn yards, televisions in empty rooms, and the new words to scare you.

The walls were green for calm and we read magazines, waited and waited and waited. We had tea and we talked together. Dawn kept our spirits up; she talked to Clover, and we fell silent too from time to time. Occasionally Clover and I went outside to the corridor. It stretched to vanishing-point in either direction, away and away, and the floor was shiny and there were white bundles at various intervals all the way up it, on the ground. Nurses clicked past with trolleys. Some of the people on the trolleys were asleep and some were awake.

After some hours, the surgeon came into the room and he told my dad that it was very serious. He gave us the prognosis. 'We have a fifty-two-year-old woman who has received a catastrophic blow to the head. The brain has haemorrhaged and we may have to remove sections of the skull to relieve the pressure as the bruising comes through and the brain swells. She has a one-in-three chance of surviving the night. If she does recover then we can say for sure that she will be a vegetable for the rest of her life.'

I thought of when Mum dropped Clover and me off at school on wintry mornings. Clover would put her hand over Mum's mouth and say, 'Fill my hand up with kisses, fill my hand up with kisses,' and Mum would kiss into her hand again and again, then Clover would shut her hand and say she had kisses for all of the day. Don't let the sun go down on your anger, girls.

'She has lost an eye in the fall. Do you want to see her now? Are you sure that you want your children to see her at this stage?' And my dad said that he was sure.

I can remember being five or six and sitting on Mum's bed. I can still see the dressing-table, the sash window, the sky outside. 'Do you love me more than all the money in the world?' I asked her. She was standing somewhere to my left, taller than me, the strength of a lion beside me. She said that she loved me more than all the money in the world, of course she did. I didn't quite believe her and I didn't know how further to assess this love that I am only now starting to understand. 'Would you rather have me than a thousand monkeys?' I was obsessed with monkeys.

She laughed and hugged me. 'Of course I'd rather have you than a thousand monkeys, of course I would, my darling.'

Clover and I walked behind Rick into the intensive-care room. The floor was more shiny than before, we went through two sets of double doors and it was quiet. The floor seemed to be sloping this way and that, I couldn't make it out, couldn't navigate it properly. I wasn't even quite sure if I was moving or the floor was. I didn't know where Mum was. No, she was quite lost. We arrived at a bed and looked at the person lying on it. Between us, and in silence, we decided it must have been her. Her head was twice the normal size: all the slack skin that normally sits on a face was taken up and painfully stretched in swelling. She had a bandage round her head. Christ knows what they had done to her, in the operation, what terrible snipping and pulling. Leave her to die in peace. She has the heart of a lion and the strength of a bull, and you don't know what you are dealing with. Her eyes were two purple balloons but her mouth was still her own. The ventilator in her neck breathed slowly in and out for her, and her hands were still her own, still the strength in her arms. In her face she was more herself then, somehow, than ever she would be again. Clover and I sat on either side of her and we held a hand each and what we did was cry and cry and cry and cry. Her hands were her own.

She never came back to us, although she did not die.

It is impossible to know what she went through during that time, the battles she fought, the places she went to. She was way out and beyond normal consciousness. Did she feel the wet tears on her hands and did she hear the voices talking to her? If she did, I don't want to consider too hard the anxiety she must have felt for us. Much later, when she was on her feet, she would write strange, scrawled, spidery messages to us. The first word she wrote was 'Basingstoke'. In a rehabilitation centre in

Chippenham, she wrote 'jewels for divers', and that was a time when my godmother, Candida, was there. She wrote me a message once, on a card or piece of paper, 'Keep eating', it said, and this made more sense than Basingstoke – she was always a bit worried about her daughters being anorexic.

She has never learned to talk again, she is confused, her personality altered. She is disfigured by the accident. Disfigured. She doesn't know who we are; nothing is clear about her and her world on the inside. That is beyond reckoning. I don't know. I really don't know. I did try very hard, Christmas by the inert body in bed – she was in a coma for two months – and the eye that worked rolled in the socket, watching us, a terrible and reproachful, curious, pained eye. Helping her to sit up, learning all about speech therapy, helping her to the loo, playing games like Scrabble in rehab, always in rehab, in Bristol and Milton Keynes and Oxford. She was physically very strong, she learned to march off, fight, escape. She would try to hitch-hike, try to take back control of her life, which was changing faster than she could regain consciousness. She lived at home, every day, and Clover and I were falling apart at the seams, it was all going wrong. When Mum is better, when Mum is better. But she never did get better.

Before the accident Clover and I had gone with Mum to a memorial service. Mum had had a very close friend called Elizabeth. Her children were the same age as Clover and me. Elizabeth had contracted cancer and she had deteriorated quickly. She wrote to Mum and asked her to look out for Hannah, her daughter, when she died. I can remember all this very clearly; with hindsight the event was heavy with symbols that foreshadowed my mum's accident. We cried in the service; Elizabeth's sister spoke. She was shockingly defiant of the death:

'This should not have happened,' she had said, 'she should not have died.'

Afterwards everyone walked up the hill to her house: it was a cottage a long way from the road and it had no water or electricity. It was a strange place and very beautiful. Elizabeth's husband had built a huge table and chairs at the back with pieces of timber and there was a forest of bamboo that we used to play in. Mum said as we walked up the hill, leaning into the slope then looking back and seeing the other people as well, filling the slope in little clusters, and all enjoying the exertion of the walk, that it was a pilgrimage for Elizabeth. Then we saw Hannah, Elizabeth's daughter, standing at the top of the slope, looking down to us. She never cried, as far as we saw, she was solemn and withdrawn and she didn't show pain. At the time Clover and I were respectfully curious of her. 'Hannah's waiting girls,' Mum said. 'Quick, rush up to meet her.' We were not very old but we understood this pain. We ran up to meet her. I can't remember if we hugged or if we were more cautiously affectionate, but later I saw it all, brittle with significance. We ran to meet her, she was standing waiting for us, a still figure of grief. And we joined, we didn't know the extent to which we joined her. We three stood at the top of the hill and we turned and saw Mum walking the rest of the way, and in my mind's eye Mum vanishes, and it is just the three of us and the thing that is between us that we were too young to understand.

All this was to come, though, this reckoning. We sat with Mum for a while, a long while, and I can't remember. I can't remember the drive home, or the real feel of it. I don't want to. I can remember Clover's blind pain, panic. She's the youngest child, and the closest to Mum, the very closest. We all thought we had it worse, but I think maybe Clover suffered more than anyone. She was so young, her pain so horrible, black, she was as unreachable as Mum. We arrived back at the house and it was the middle of the night. Nightmares to come and difficult nights. We walked into the study. Our eldest sister was standing beside my dad's desk and she caught hold of us and held us. The world was, at that time, beyond reckoning.

The Word That Doesn't Mean Anything

And so they chattered on in the roar of several hundred people doing the same until with a crash the orchestra struck up and the show began.

The Belle in the Top Hat, JAN LAING

The twenty-fifth of November, and we were still in the scrapyard outside Glasgow. Life resonates with the mystery of tragedy and bad luck. (We never thought it would happen to us.) The twenty-fifth of November holds the resonance in a fixed, humming point. The afternoon was brilliantly sunny and the Richards family had gone to London. The clowns were out in Glasgow and Anna was asleep. I went into the field at the back of the scrapyard. Ivan had taken Mantel out there. He was giving him some grass and playing with him. Mantel's coat shone dark gold and Ivan's face was in shadow under his baseball cap. He didn't notice me as I climbed over the fence. He jumped up on to Mantel's back. Of course, he can do that easily! He's a trick rider – he runs across the rings and springs on to Mantel's back and stands up and does somersaults. Watch him climbing up the side of a lorry: he does it in one flick of his body.

He turned the horse in a circle. He saw me standing beside the fence and rode over. As I watched Ivan I imagined having my own horse in the circus. I could ride and ride wherever we went. The sun was lowering, shining through some beech trees at the far end of the field. 'Can I have a ride, Ivan?'

'I can't let you. Mr Richie would kill me, if I did. I can't. Suppose you fell off?'

'I will never fall off. Come on. It's a strange day for me today. A bad thing happened to me a long time ago today.'

It was the afternoon. Mum's accident had been exactly four years ago. Then, we were starting dimly to perceive the terrible thing that had just happened. We were turning a long corner. We were still turning. A very bad thing like that happens and the fact of the matter is that you don't really feel the consequences until years later. I mean, the day after the accident life was more or less identical to what it had been before it happened. More tears, more tea in the kitchen, friends visiting for a different purpose, someone else cooks.

'OK, Nell.'

I climbed up on to the horse, behind Ivan. The sun was shin-ing in our eyes now. I put the side of my head on his shoulder. We rode down across the field away from the yard. The grass had water on it and the sun had a last hint of autumn warmth. The horse had a short, steady gait. There was a canal at the end of the field and beyond the canal, among layers of ivy behind some iron fencing, there was a stone church. The field sloped down to the canal. I said to Ivan that I wanted to walk along the canal a bit. He said he would drop me off beside the fence. He rode off back up the field and I waited down by the water. There were some people walking, some children in pink jumpsuits and an old man on a bicycle. The church was locked; but it didn't matter. It was quiet down there and the sun was slowly sinking to evening.

I walked along the canal for a while then back again. At the other end of the field where Ivan had been riding a high bank sloped down to the brown water. As I was walking back I saw Ivan standing at the top of the bank. He walked down the bank towards me and I started climbing up. We met half-way, under the trees. The lorries and the stable tent were out of view. We mucked about around the trees. Ivan swung on a branch and we chucked stones down the bank, into the canal. There was a wooden table and chairs, a picnic table, for the summer days. The light was indigo as the sun had gone down. We sat there for a while. Ivan was talking about the circus. He has never known any other life. He has no accent, except for a kind of precision in the way he pronounced things, as if he were American and talking with a trained English accent.

'When I was little, the kids used to come and watch when we arrived in a town with the tent. If you bunged them a few quid they would help with the seats. In those days people came to the circus, you know, there were queues of people at the front of the ground. People really liked it, took an interest in it, dressed up for it. Now all they do is give you hassle. They don't come to the circus any more, they just hassle you all the time.' He stopped talking and he looked at his hands. 'The councils ban animals from their land and the animal-rights protestors come round and smash up the lorries. What do they know about the circus?'

I stretched out my feet on the seat of the bench table and crossed my ankles. There were no walkers beside the canal now and the surface of the water was lost at the bottom of the slope in the dark. I looked at his face. The light lost intensity by a degree. His face seemed to turn blue and pinched in the cold.

'One of these days circus will be one of those words that doesn't mean anything any more,' he said.

One of these days circus will be a word that doesn't mean anything any more. I can still see Ivan's cold face in my mind's eye, his white skin and his eyes. It was too dark to sit out on that bench any longer and so we walked back across the field to the caravans.

Scarper

Ei! Ei! What a circus! My Circus McGurkus!
My workers love work. They say, 'Work us! Please work
 us!
We'll work and we'll work up so many surprises
You'd never see half if you had forty eyeses!'
                                    If I Ran The Circus, DR SEUSS

Some time in the first week of December the circus moved into the car park of the Scottish Exhibition Centre, beside the Clydeside Expressway. The afternoon in the field beside the canal was the last fine day I can remember of that year. The show would be in the building, beside the indoor fairground. As we built up the stable tent, the fairground lorries were arriving, drawing up alongside the car park and slowly turning through the high chain-link fencing. Our hands were cold and our breath freezing. The temperature did not move from minus fifteen. It froze all day and all night, and the plastic folds of the stable tent were as stiff as card and sticky with ice. There were five boys to help us put up the stable and they were all from the fairground. They were Scottish and quite unfriendly; they had closed, piss-taking faces and black hair. Ivan had told me that the circus people called the fairground people travellers, whereas they, the circus people, were showmen. He said that the travellers were very flash and had a lot of money. They drove new jeeps and wore Timberlands. They only went out *en masse*, then everyone bought a round simultaneously. Twenty people each bought twenty drinks. The tables were full of glasses.

Everyone said it was colder than Moscow, that year in Glasgow. I took to sleeping in the lining of a padded tank suit. I left the bars of my electric fire on all day, but the thin walls of the caravan and the curtainless windows leaked cold air. I spent one morning in town, buying eyeliner and stage foundation for the elephant riding. The dance shop was warm and mirrored on all sides. The girl with the lipsticks and rows of mascara asked me what it was for, and I said for the circus. She looked delighted. 'Oh, the circus! Some people have already been in here this week from the circus.' I felt stupidly proud to say that – from the circus. I had had a shower in the exhibition centre and was wearing my town clothes so I looked reasonably smart. I had painted my fingernails and brushed my hair. She wasn't to know that I spent most of the time shovelling horse shit and filling haynets.

Mr Richie started to practise the horses again. The mornings were earlier. We had to be in the stables by seven o'clock. The ring had coconut matting, rather than sawdust. One morning when he called them in, Anna and I had washed all their white socks and groomed them properly. Polly had come into the stable just as we finished. While we were standing at the ring doors, watching them practising, the horses circling in front of us, their clean feet neat on the soft mat, Mr Richie in the middle, the horses' wary white eyes turned to him, she had whispered to me, 'It's a good job we cleaned them all this morning, isn't it?' – only she had done nothing that morning. I hated her for that. In Glasgow she spent less time in the stables than ever, and the work, because of the cold (the taps freeze, the plastic of the tent becomes stiff and difficult to lace, the cold burns through your hands whenever you touch anything), was harder than ever. We used to have to bring the horses round through a narrow door into the building. The floor was polished concrete.

One time when I was adjusting a martingale the horse reared then fell down on top of me. Mr Richie came round the corner of the seating stand. I was trapped beneath the horse. The horse struggled, stood up and, as it did so, its bridle came off. It was a difficult horse, and I knew that if it realised its bridle was off it would take fright and perhaps gallop off through the building into the fairground, where there were families and children, and the fairground machines. I caught hold of it round the neck but the bridle was trailing. Mr Richie carried on walking round the seats towards the entrance to the ring. I shouted, 'Mr Richie, *please* come and help me a moment, otherwise Suma is going to get loose.' My voice bounced off the building walls and back to me. He stopped, turned round and walked over to where I was with the horse. He picked up the bridle and gave it to me. He didn't say anything. Then he walked away. I hated the way he walked, toes out, pelvis forward. I dreaded that silhouette and the noise of the keys. He only drank Irn Bru. Someone told me that when they worked abroad he took a van full of it with him.

He never smiled and now there were no smiling Hungarians to antidote the shouting. Some harness broke in practice and I took it round to Mr Richie to have it mended – he did all the repairs himself. I had become pathetically anxious to do the right thing, to avoid being shouted at. I gave him the harness and he said he would mend it that afternoon. At the start of practice the next morning I realised that I had not been round to his workshop to pick up the mended harness. 'WHERE ARE THE MARTINGALES, NELL?' I said I had no idea, the last time I had seen them was yesterday, when I gave them in to be mended. 'AND I GAVE THEM BACK, DIDN'T I?' I said that I honestly did not have them, and I didn't know where they were.

Anna ran out of the ring and reappeared a few seconds later with the missing harness. She said that it had been on the other side of the seats, on the floor. I guessed what had happened: he had given it to Anna, who had put it on the ground to pick up later and forgotten about it. She didn't smile and she looked at the floor. She knew that I was about to get shouted at and that, to some extent, she was to blame. But she didn't want to stand between me and Mr Richie and get shouted at herself, and I don't blame her. Mr Richie started to shout at me. 'THERE, YOU SEE? DON'T TRY TO STEAL MY HARNESS.'

The water lying on the ground outside the caravans on the tarmac was cracked and broken and white. At Minety there had been one winter when it froze very hard like this. The big freeze. Mum and I carried buckets of water from the house to the stables, and the horses had extra rugs. The moat froze solid and we skated every day. Rick and Mum and I were standing in the garden looking at the frozen ground and the white fringed leaves of the still shrubs. Rick said the freeze was like a drought, in a way: in both instances the land dehydrated.

'I didn't try to steal your harness.'

'Don't fucking contradict me. You're mad, aren't you, eh? NOT ALL THERE.'

I didn't say anything.

The car park was filled with artists' caravans. There were some Russians, and a couple who did an ice-skating act, and a gay couple who did a trapeze act in which one wore a monkey-suit.

There was a famously skilled juggler, who Polly said was her cousin. He had a red and silver motorbike with a pony-skin seat, and he stood on a little platform at the back and juggled. Ivan was to ride the motorbike and he wore black trousers and a black shirt with silver buttons.

On the eve of the opening night there was a dress rehearsal. The winter show was ambitious, with a band and a new heavy red curtain. Charmagne came back from London and helped Josie to finish the elephant-girl costumes. I went round to Josie and Phillip's wagon that evening to try mine on. Phillip had been working in the circus all day, helping to put up the bandstand. The costume was a tartan tutu and a tartan cropped top, with a white lace frill, and a tartan beret. I stood on the loo seat and looked in the mirror and drank a glass of cider. The china horse was in the corner and it was warm. Charmagne and Josie said the ungrateful bastards wouldn't say thank-you, but the costumes look sweet, don't they? There were fibreoptic sequins glinting in the lace frills. Charmagne gave me two pairs of tights, some thin flesh-coloured fishnets and a pair of shiny tights to wear underneath. I didn't have any sparkly jewellery so she lent me a pair of clip-on diamanté earrings.

The dress rehearsal went on all night. A reasonable man directed the show, and when the shouting started, he calmed Mr Richie. A Russian troupe had been rigging their bars and I don't know what they had done to annoy him, but he started to shout. The reasonable man, Ian, actually told him not to shout, very quietly, very tactfully. I had never heard that before. The hall was brightly lit and the circus was within a curtained-off area in the hall. We could watch the show from the gangways in the seats. That night the juggler's red and silver motorbike jumped out of gear and crashed into the bandstand. Some of the band members fell on the ground and one of them broke an arm. Ivan said that Mr Richie knew all the scrapyard men around here, and the broken bandstand was standing again by the opening show at six o'clock the next evening.

Our practice on the elephants took place before the bandstand broke. Charmagne and Jena and I rode into the ring on the elephants. They circled the ring, pirouetting at five points. They lined up in the centre of the ring and lay down slowly. As the elephants sank to the floor, we edged up them until we were sitting on their shoulders. Mr Richie said to point our toes and take a call there, then jump off nimbly, skip to the edge of the ring and clap, in time to the music, so that the audience clapped too, while the elephants carried on with their tricks. Then we were to get back up on to the elephants, climbing from the elephant's raised front leg and swinging from their ears; they would stand on their back legs and finally do a sort of slow march out of the ring while we leaned back and smiled and waved – 'Smile all the time, Nell, smile, smile, smile.' On the practice night I asked Charmagne how you walked to the edge of the ring. She moved with absolute precision before an audience. She had a complete understanding of how her body looked and the shapes she was making with her hands and her legs and her arms. She didn't know what I was asking her. 'Oh, I don't know, Nell, you just sort of jol over, don't you?' and she looked at Jena and laughed.

The reasonable man who was directing said, 'Hang on a minute, it's a sensible question, Charmagne,' and he showed me how to hold my arms. Charmagne could do everything as a reflex. For example, when we had to climb up on to the elephant, she just placed one small foot on the elephant's knee, caught its ear with one hand and swung up on its back, in one movement, landing like a puppet behind the elephant's ear. I slipped and fell and struggled, ripped my tights and slid backwards. I needed practice, and it did become easier. After we had finished practising, on that night of the dress rehearsal, Phillip and Ivan were standing in the ring doors and they were laughing, with Polly. 'Why are you laughing?'

'We could see your knickers, Nell!'

We had to wear red satin knickers over the outside of the fishnets, as the tartan tutus stuck out at right angles. I was wearing a pair of white knickers under the fishnets and the edge of these were visible. Polly told me to buy a G-string, or just pull my knickers right up so that they were hidden.

Show-time in Glasgow was exciting. Little Richie styled some of his clowning on Charlie Chaplin. The juggling music was loud, fast drumbeats, and the people loved it. The juggler, who was called Lotsi, played the end of the act well, the clubs fell into his hands with an escalating momentum, like a heartbeat, growing faster, lower, and the people loved it, were there with him in the ring, following the tempo, clapping, and at the end, cheering. Ivan, Lotsi and Polly's boyfriend would hang around behind the curtains, in black trousers and shirts, practising and warming up, in dark silhouette. Anna and I walked the horses around on the concrete beside the circus, within the building. Behind the curtains, which dropped from the very top of the huge building, were the seats and we could hear the music, and the semi-darkness was flashed through with escaped lights from the show. It was so cold outside, in the frost; the building seemed warm and luxurious.

One night Jan Eric had a party in his caravan. The artists did not have to get up until a few hours before the show so they spent most nights in the bars in town or in each other's caravans. I remember feeling exhausted, and nearly going to bed early, but I hadn't been out for a long time. Sometimes the routine life of the circus – every day is exactly the same as the previous day, the routine only interrupted by moving, which becomes a routine in itself, but we were in Glasgow for five weeks – becomes boring. Most jobs, aside from the circus, are repetitive: the problem with the circus is that there is no respite from the work, no weekends away, no variety whatsoever. Much of the time, circus work feels like a treadmill.

I sat on the soft seats in Jan Eric's caravan and talked to a girl called Colette. She and her boyfriend were jossers too, and they had a roller-skating act. I had seen it briefly, through the seats. He twirled around on a little round platform and she worked off him, swinging from his arms. Jan Eric's caravan was full of people. I said that I wanted to be an artist, eventually. She asked me if I had thought it through properly. 'It's very hard, you know, appearing new every day, sometimes when you don't feel like it, you know, tired, a bad-hair day.' She had dark hair and blue eyeliner.

Her boyfriend said that if he won the lottery he would have his own circus. Jan Eric and Lotsi said he was mad, and looked at each other and shook their heads – 'There is no business out there.' They talked about the last day on a show, when people played tricks. Lotsi was short with brown hair and a neat, Italian face. He was stern and professional. He said that he had always been taught that you never, ever, ever messed with someone else's props. You didn't touch them. It was too dangerous to mess about. Colette asked me what sort of act I would like to do. I said I didn't know yet, but I might like to do something with horses.

The door banged open and some more people came in. The cold air rushed through and replaced the warm. I did not recognise the new faces. Colette asked if I wanted to be in the circus all of my life, and I said I didn't know. There was an old Scottish man, who introduced himself as Jock, with a young Scottish clown called Tweedy. Charmagne was standing beside the sink mixing up some cocktails. Tweedy was drinking them. Jock said to me that he had known all these people since they were children – Jan Eric and Charmagne and the juggler, and Ivan, who came round to the party for a bit, and Phillip, and Josie, who looked unusually pale and thin and didn't stay very long. He had watched them grow up.

I talked to the gay couple, who had the trapeze act. They were called Lenny and Terry: one had ginger hair and a moustache, the other was tiny with a permanent smile, sparkly eyes and slightly buck teeth. They were very friendly. They said I looked tired. I said it was very hard work in the stables, especially with the cold and having to ride the elephant as well, although I loved riding the elephant. I didn't mind the hard work, I said, but I hated all the shouting. It got you right down after a while. They both nodded. They had worked as grooms before, for another English circus boss, it had been the same thing, they treated you like shit. Colette's boyfriend asked them why they styled the act like that, with one of them in a monkey suit. They said that none of the circuses would let them play it as two men. He said that sometimes they could play on that, camp it up, leather jackets and everything, but English circus was too traditional for that. None of the directors would risk it.

There were some girls at the door for Jan Eric. 'Come on, let's have another drink, Colette,' Charmagne said. 'All I've got to do tomorrow is ride the bleeding elephant.' I would be up at seven

in the stables. I knew how much a hangover slowed up the day.
I said I was going to bed. Outside, the run-off from the caravans
had frozen solid across the ground and the tarmac was shining.

Just before Christmas it started to snow. You could see it in
the neon lights at night, and during the day it drifted and piled
up around the stables. Alfie's caravan had a drift along the back
wall; at the front, around the door, it melted and grew slushy, as
he had his gas fire on all day and all night. Phillip and Ivan
installed a gas heater in the stables, and the roof of the tent
dripped and glistened with melting ice and condensation.

Auntie Sheila asked me why I was walking so slowly. I said I
was exhausted. The next day another groom arrived. He was
called Ted and he was Irish. Anna, Ted and I would sit in the
back of the horse lorry, where we kept the hay, filling haynets. He
sang some Irish songs and he said that the circus in Ireland was
completely different from this, no shouting. 'Let's run away to
Ireland,' he said. He told me that, over there, he had his own act,
with some little dogs. I didn't particularly like Ted. One day he
said he had to go to town for some Christmas shopping. 'Ted's
going to town for the morning, Auntie Sheila,' I said, and she
stood at the top of the steps to her caravan and said he had
scarper written all over him. He took his full bag with him and
he never came back.

I stopped going to the cinema with Ivan. I saw him in his
Land Rover driving off the ground with a girl who was the
daughter of the man who managed the Scottish Exhibition
Centre, and another girl with blonde hair who did a Western act.
I barely spoke to him any more. One time he was sitting on the
ring fence with this Western girl. They had known each other
since they were children. Practice had just finished. He was
telling her about a time when he was sixteen when he had

slipped and knocked himself out on the draw-bar of a trailer. They were discussing all the accidents and injuries they had had over the years, and their voices were low and quiet, full of sadness, resignation and pride.

Just before Christmas Clover came up to Glasgow and stayed in the circus for a night. Rick sent me a hamper from Fortnum and Mason. Christmas was beginning to feel like something that other people did. I heard the Christmas programmes on the radio, and the circus and the fun-fair was a Christmas outing for Scottish families. There were big plastic garlands of holly and ivy in the exhibition centre. Clover and I opened a packet of chocolate biscuits from the hamper. In the afternoon we sat in the caravan for an hour. It was snowing outside and we could hear the lorries going past on the other side of the chain-link fencing, on the Clydeside Expressway. They were very near and they shook the caravan. The biscuits had thick milk chocolate. The hamper was stuffed with fake straw and there was a bottle of champagne, and caviare, and jam laced with rum, and sugared almonds, and tinned duck in sherry. I said I was becoming very unhappy in the circus. I explained to her that the shouting seemed worse, and the work twice as hard. This hour off in the afternoon was an exception. Mainly I just worked all the time. I was being treated like a slave, and the harder you work the more they bully you, I said. 'Really, the only reason I don't leave is because I love riding the elephant. I love it.' She said I might as well just try to enjoy it. She was laughing. Clover had just started at Oxford that year. She is sympathetic but never sentimental. She said that if it was so bad I should leave.

That night she came to see the show with some friends from university. Polly had been very excited. 'All your friends are here tonight, Nell,' she said, in the interval. Then, after the show, she told me that they had all stood up and clapped during the elephant act. When the show was over and the horses had been done for the night, I stood in the cold car park and talked to them. 'You looked so sweet,' Clover had said, 'skipping about in the ring,' and she gave me a hug. 'Are you coming to Jackie's party tomorrow?' I would try to. I had become very proud of the elephant riding. I mean, grooms and showgirls all over the world ride elephants, but still, I wanted to get it right. I did not want to slip when I climbed up on to the elephant's neck and I wanted to be like Charmagne in the ring, neat and precise and professional. They went off back to Jackie's. I felt quite alone then, in the circus. The fair was open for another hour so I walked round it with Jan Eric. The entire fairground was inside apart from one big wheel. All the rides were painted with film stars, like Arnold Schwarzenegger, and J.R. of *Dallas*, the old icons of this age.

'I would marry Arnold Schwarzenegger,' Clover had giggled. 'He's just so sweet.' After that I went on the big wheel alone. It was cold and clear at the top. It was a relief to see further. Across the city landscape the buildings burned and twinkled with Christmas.

Jena, Charmagne and I changed for the elephant act in a little dressing room beside the circus, within the building. The exhibition centre had been used for a trade fair recently and the dressing room was left over from this. It was a white plastic room made of plastic panels. It was warm and bright, and there was a rail for the clothes and a mirror. I would try to get in there as early as possible – it was an escape from the dark, dripping stables. Charmagne would swagger in at the last minute. Jena was not from the circus, although she had worked in it for a long time. She said she had practised the rope for a bit but it had hurt her legs too much. She is the sort of girl who is frightened of pain. She had ridden the elephant for two years and she still held on with one hand. We chatted, arranged our hats and ate chocolate. Charmagne was the last into the dressing room, but always the first dressed: in seconds her clothes were neatly folded, her hair perfectly placed and her jewellery on. We wore clogs over the suede ballet pumps, and when we were ready, we walked around the back of the circus, past the entrance to the ring, where the ring-boys hung out in the dark and whistled to Charmagne, who jauntily returned their banter, familiar, distant at the same time, knowing them well, though she didn't know them at all, then round to the doors where the elephants were brought in.

The elephant riding was the only reason why I was in Scotland. They went into the ring in single file, and we had to duck under the curtains. The band played 'Scotland the Brave', and for four of the five minutes of the act you were on your own, in the light, with the band behind you, and it was impossible to be depressed. Nothing mattered. Nothing could let you down. Nothing bad could happen. The band was playing for you and the audience clapped at your suggestion. Full exhilaration could be expressed through the body and full pride in existence, just the very fact of being there, alive and mobile, could be expressed. Phillip said I looked completely different in the ring, he didn't recognise me at all. I learned quite quickly, started to ride with one arm in the air and one hand on my hip, like Charmagne. I wanted to do it brilliantly. I wanted to fill the ring with exuberance and precision. I wanted to be celebrated. I wanted to celebrate. The reasonable director asked me if I had ever worked with the public before, I said that I hadn't, and he said I was doing very well. I thought I had found what I most wanted to do in the world. I wished that all I ever did was ride the elephant, round and round, for ever. I had never skipped and shimmied and posed like this before in public.

As we came out of the ring, folded back through the curtains (Charmagne would make her last outline, throw a hand into the air, uncurl the finger, seconds before she vanished through the curtain), I would see my legs running with blood from where I had grazed my shins climbing on to the elephant's neck. My knuckles would be bleeding too, from being ground into her neck under the harness. Charmagne was blasé, bored, slightly angry, where I was stage-struck and uncool. 'Bleeding cows,' she would say, 'dropped me right down then, didn't she, the bitch?' I knew what she was doing with these complaints and curses: she was setting me outside her closed ring of circus blood: only jossers bleed when they ride the elephant. But I didn't care. I was high on the high of working in the ring, and for a while that high negated the increasingly difficult pressures of working in the stables.

Jackie's flat was as it always is at parties. She had put paper-chains up around all the rooms. Glaswegian boys with crew-cuts played records on the decks in the corner of one of the big rooms. Clover was dancing in there with Jackie. I couldn't stay very long as I had an early morning, and the voices were shouting, they did not leave me night or day, in my mind as a warning. I can't remember talking to anyone apart from Clover about her first few terms at college. I'm sure that friends were there, from school, from the past, but I can't remember who. I felt unable to speak to anyone. I felt very strange and when I looked in the mirror in the bathroom I didn't recognise myself. My face was puffy and my hair was very bright blonde. I was still wearing show makeup. My hands were chipped and covered in little black lines.

I caught a taxi back to the circus from the cold streets of Glasgow, where the glow from full pubs came through the stained glass and the high buildings guarded the full streets.

On Christmas Eve Anna and I decorated the Shetlands' reins with tinsel. They gave rides in the ring before the show. The fairground boys helped us. I walked with a pony and one of the boys, Gareth, held the children. He said that he and his dad had had a juvenile ride, a ride for children. They had made it themselves, some spinning tea-cups. When a child sat on the pony he would tell them to press the front of the saddle to make the pony move. He would chant a bit, like the chants you hear on the fairground. 'Come on, then, kids, here we go, hold tight, come on, then, off we go, do you want to go faster?' and so on.

Polly appeared around the corner of the stables. She had just been Christmas shopping. We were leading the ponies out of the stables to the building. The ramp on the horsebox was down because it was laden with snow and the springs had broken. We were supposed to lift it when we had finished doing the haynets. She started to shout. 'Why is the ramp down, girls? You're getting very, very lazy, and I don't like that at all.' She flicked her hair and pressed her lips together.

Something went inside me. My back was hurting and my hands were blistered. I gave the pony to Anna. I said I was leaving, I couldn't take any more of this shouting.

'Well, FUCK OFF, then,' Polly shouted. I was starting to cry. The black eyeliner stung my eyes. I was too tired and too got-down by the shouting. I should never have cried. I went round to Auntie Sheila's trailer, ran up the steps and knocked on the door. They don't ask you what you want, they just stare at you or perhaps jerk their chin up as a question. I said I was leaving. I was working hard and all Polly ever did was shout and shout. I said I honestly couldn't work any harder than I was.

Auntie Sheila frowned. 'But you never do any work, love, you just walk around all day.'

I couldn't stop crying and the eyeliner poured down my face. I went back into the circus and did the pony rides. Gareth said I should go and wash my face. 'They're terrible aren't they?' he said. 'We're all getting stressed out,' he said. I stayed for the two shows that evening. I rode the elephant for the last time. In the dressing room, Jena and Charmagne were sympathetic. They said they wouldn't take that sort of thing from anyone. During the first show I had taken one of the Arab horses into the back doors, just behind the curtains, a few seconds too early. Mr Richie had turned on me, said I was mad, just not all there. The ring-boys shook their heads. After Mr Richie had gone back into the ring they said that they had never been shouted at so much in all their lives.

I did not decide to leave. I just left. I did not want to leave the circus and the elephants. But I had no choice. I found myself piling everything I owned into the back of the van and thinking only of how I could make it to the motorway. It was eleven o'clock at night. The horses were done. Everyone was inside. The snow was lying about three feet deep with deeper drifts on all sides. I couldn't take the caravan. I went to say goodbye to Charmagne. I knocked on Josie's door. I thought that Charmagne would be in there, but she had gone out.

'Goodbye, Josie.' She looked so pale she was almost transparent.

'Goodbye, Nell. You're doing the right thing. Don't take any more of this shit off anyone. Don't let them treat you like that. Take care on the roads. Tonight is no night for driving.'

I said I would leave Phillip my gas bottle, which I cut off with a knife just behind the regulator. I had no money at all, and they lent me twenty pounds for diesel. Nobody came out. I'm sure they knew what was happening, the Richards family, but this is what happens when you leave a circus like that. The doors shut. The curtains are drawn. You are on your own. I asked Ivan if he would help me couple up. He said he couldn't be seen to help me leave, so I left the caravan. My van's ignition key snapped, and the broken half was lost in the snow. I called the AA and waited for an hour. The snow was still falling, and Alfie, who saw me waiting in the car park, said I was mad to try to leave tonight, it was too dangerous. But I had to leave then.

The AA man thought I was trying to run away from a boyfriend. He took an hour getting the van started. He said, 'Are you sure you want to go tonight, love?' and I said I had to get out of there. I was going to Newcastle to see my aunt, I had to get out that night. He broke the lock on the steering wheel and showed me how to start the engine with a screwdriver. The snow had not stopped for an instant. There were some papers to sign, and I asked him if we could meet at the petrol service station down the road: I wanted to leave the car park as soon as possible. I had started to panic.

I left all my clothes in the wardrobe in the caravan. I never got them back. Mum had given me a lovely brown teddy-bear fur coat when I passed my A levels, and I lost that. But at that time there was one objective: to get out of that car park and drive and drive until there were hundreds of miles between me and the Richards family.

The AA man shook his head. 'Well, this is going to be a story,' he said, 'middle of the night on Christmas Eve, whatever next?'

I followed him to the petrol station and signed the forms. He asked me what the story was, what on earth I was doing.

'I couldn't explain in the car park,' I said, 'too overheard, you know? I just am running away from the circus because I have had it with being shouted at all the time.'

The streets were full of drunk people on their way out of the pubs. The AA man said I would have to be careful on the roads tonight. He said he was going to put a tick in the dodgy box – he thought I was stealing the van. 'To be honest with you, love, in that car park back there I thought your boyfriend would walk around the corner any minute with a sledge-hammer.' He led me to the motorway, and I followed him until he pulled off back into the city. As he drove up the slip road he waved out of his window and blew his horn.

I drove the whole night. The roads were covered in snow and the signs were thickly veiled. The windscreen wipers seized up. I had to keep getting out to wipe the windscreen clean. The van slid when I braked. I called my aunt on my mobile. 'I'm coming to stay for Christmas.' She map-read me over the telephone for some of the way and said to call when I was nearer. In retrospect it's an amusing story; at the time I was freezing cold and terrified that I would skid off the road into a snowdrift and never be found. The only other people on the road were lorry-drivers; the bright lights bore down on the van and sent it shuddering across the road.

At seven o'clock in the morning, about three miles from my aunt's farm, I ran into a snowdrift. I couldn't go any further. I telephoned her. She said she thought she knew where I was, and drove out to find me. There was a whining wind coming across the hills, carrying on it more snow. Nothing figured any more and I had only a dim idea of what was happening. Teesa, my aunt, picked me up in a Sabura pick-up. There were dead pheas-ants in the back. We drove up the drive, right up into the hills. She had all the fires burning in the house to stop it freezing up. There was a bed upstairs in the spare bedroom, warm from an electric blanket, and on it was a full stocking, crunchy with new soap wrapped in newspaper. On Christmas Day we rode on the fell. Teesa's husband, my uncle Derwent, stayed in bed. He had food poisoning from a goose they had eaten that evening. I gave him the hamper but the thought of the duck pâté in sherry made him feel more ill. So we didn't have a complicated lunch and Christmas television: Teesa and I just rode the horses on the fell and watched the bright, snow-spangled horizons, which were dark blue on one side, and in front, ahead of us, above the valley, bright burning gold, beaten gold, where the sun was starting to set.

After Richie Richards

And when once in a while some leisurely passer-by stopped, made merry over the old figure on the board, and spoke of swindling, that was in its way the stupidest lie ever invented by indifference and inborn malice, since it was not the hunger artist who was cheating, he was working honestly, but the world was cheating him of his reward.

'A Hunger Artist', from *Franz Kafka Collected Stories*,
GABRIEL JOSIPOVICI (ED.)

~

I stayed with my aunt Teesa for about a fortnight. I never went back to Richie Richards' Mega Circus and I never wanted to go back. I would not work there again for all the money in the world. I knew that if I went back I could ride the elephant for ever, if I wanted, and perhaps work in the office, out of the grind of the stables, but the price was a lifetime of shouting and gossip. Nothing was worth that. Nothing.

A month or so after leaving that circus I called Charmagne on her mobile. She said that she was with her mum for a month and that then she was going out with another circus for the season, in England. She said that she did not know which circus it was yet, which meant that she didn't want to tell me. If you ask a circus person a question and they say they don't know, it means you have asked the wrong question. It means, 'Don't ask.' I said I wanted to join a show, but that I didn't want to work in the stables any more. I wanted to learn an act. There was a pause at the end of the telephone. Charmagne has a thin, cheerful voice. 'Well, you're better off joining a small show and getting someone to teach you. There aren't any circus schools in England that I would recommend.'

I saw in my head another Richie Richards, another show where there was no time to eat, let alone practise, another season of climbing about on a skip full of manure in the pouring rain, watching the traffic passing on the road.

'Listen, Nell, I can give you the number of a woman called Bernadette who lives in Bath. She teaches people tight-rope walking and that sort of thing. She might give you some advice.'

Some time in the spring of 1996 I went to meet Bernadette. I had been working in a solicitor's office, filing infinite paperwork in a gloomy basement, and spring-cleaning people's houses, baby-sitting, doing any job that came up. I had sold the van. I felt distant and alienated from the circus, and fraudulent to myself. I thought that I worked in the circus, and yet had no career in it. I had only a handful of bad memories. I was casting about for advice, clues, suggestions.

The house was large, Georgian, at the end of a terrace. Wide steps led up to a heavy front door, and there were intricate designs on the thin blue lace curtains in the downstairs windows. An old man opened the door and I introduced myself. 'Bernadette is my daughter,' he said, smiled, stepped back and indicated that I should walk into the hall. He had a thick foreign accent, a low voice, and he moved precisely.

The hall was high and there were coloured stone tiles on the floor. The walls were full of the circus, old posters, programmes and pictures in frames. The style of the posters was completely different from the TV-cartoon Richie Richards posters, and the circus posters that I had noticed in shop windows and on telegraph poles. They were rich and carefully designed. There were ornate baroque posters, the acts exploding on the paper in a multitude of typefaces and exclamation marks, outsize elephants and mythical depictions of horses, wordy lists of acts – 'Herr Ulric, in His Great Barrel Performance Mid-air', 'La Place Bros' graceful Performance on the Revolving Globe', 'Vaulting, or Trial of Skill by the members of the company' – and stark woodcuts, a black pony and a girl in an evening dress, turning away. Among the posters and programmes were large black-and-white photographs, all taken in circuses: there were acrobat troupes, and a girl in ostrich feathers and sequins smiling beside the head of a grey horse. The background elements of the shows were different from what I had seen in England: the rings looked larger, the curtains heavier, the seats higher. There was one photograph of an acrobat troupe working in the ring. In the background you could see the high lines of seats, reaching right up in darkness and full of people. There was a photograph of a man in a tail coat, with brilliant shiny black shoes and glossy hair. His back was to the photographer and he was raising his arms in the air before fourteen dapple grey horses, standing on their hind legs, in jewelled harnesses with plumes on their heads. They were outside, with nothing beside them but the sky, and the odd wheel-arch visible through their legs. There was a man in a top hat on a grey horse, the horse standing with one leg lifted, as if trotting at a standstill, and the man was still, hands steady, looking at the camera, everything shining, and a summer day behind.

The man in the hall started to walk up the stairs. 'Come with me,' he said, and I followed him out of the hallway and up.

We walked up to a sitting room on the first floor. An old lady was sitting in an armchair in the room. 'This is my wife,' the man said, and I sensed that she spoke little English. She nodded, said hello, slowly and carefully. The man gestured to the sofa. 'Sit down,' he said. 'Bernadette is having a new prop made. She will be up in a minute.'

The room was very large and had few pieces of furniture in it but many ornaments, shire horses, little white rearing horses, elephants, clowns, a dark yellow claw on a wooden base, and more photographs. There was a colour photograph of a wire-walker and more photographs of the man on the grey horse, a ballerina standing on a black-and-white horse.

'That is my daughter, Bernadette,' the old man said, and I looked at the colour photograph. I looked back at the photograph of the man on the horse, and he smiled. 'You like the horse? That man is my father. He is dead now. He was the master of *haute école*. He was the best in the world. He was brilliant.'

He picked up the photograph from the mantelpiece and looked at it. The lady in the armchair said something I didn't understand. He smiled and nodded. The door opened. A brisk, slight, dark-haired lady walked into the room. I stood up. She walked towards me and shook my hand. She was Bernadette. She had been talking with the man who was making her new prop.

Bernadette was friendly and open, her accent clipped, precise. I said that I wanted to work in the circus, but not as a groom, I wanted to learn an act, to work in the ring. As I spoke she sized me up and watched how I moved, the length of my limbs and my posture, the length of my spine and my height. She was looking for balance within, spring in the joints, strength in the arms.

That is how circus people come to do their particular act. The elders watch the children as they play, and see where their inner talent lies. The act has to come from the physiognomy of a person: it cannot be superimposed on an unsuitable canvas. I suggested that I could learn to do the trapeze.

'I don't think so. You will always be too big. You look like a horse girl to me. You would be lovely presenting horses.'

She said something to her mother, who nodded. 'I teach people to do the wire. But I don't teach many people. Most new-comers to the business now don't want to learn this to a high standard. They don't want to learn to be the best. I'm not going to teach someone now unless they can be the best. I had to teach some dancers in Germany once to do the *corde lisse*. You know the *corde lisse*?'

I nodded. It is the act in which the girl climbs the rope then makes positions on it, finishing with a spin by the wrist or neck.

'Look, I'll show you a video of a girl. Now watch.' She put a cassette in the machine and pressed the remote control. 'Look, she had no strength in her arms.'

The girl had long sinewy limbs.

'It was a promotion for the circus. We had two days. Her lack of strength was the problem. We had to work out a routine that didn't rely on strength. Look, watch how she presents herself to the audience – in the circus we call this the compliment. I taught her all this.'

She said something to her father who rewound the tape. The girl strutted awkwardly and fast out of the ring. She came back in again, slow and elegant, and she pulled off a silvery cloak. 'You see that? That is what I am talking about, the way she dropped the cloak, to one side, following the line. That is the type of thing that you have to think about, all these things. My father came to England from Czechoslovakia in the thirties. He left the circus. I wanted to learn an act so he taught me the wire in the garden here.'

She showed me a video of herself working. I couldn't recognize the circus from the circus I had seen in England with its TV iconography, its digital theme tunes and reworked melodies from West End musicals. There is no genuine circus culture left in England: it is an art that is largely disregarded. Since the circus fell on hard times it has pandered to a naïve understanding of popular taste, and in doing so has further downgraded and eradicated itself. What I was encountering in that house was something different. It was true circus culture, not mediocre acts dressed up with black lights and Day-glo and strobes but an unequivocal, obsessive focus on perfection. A real circus person will not rate a hardworking second-class artist, or cheap costumes, or incorrect detail. Circus is a discipline. Like any other art it has rules and boundaries that can be challenged only with understanding and skill. The sole objective is to be the best.

The wire was rigged low and it was springy. There she was, dancing on the wire, dressed as a Cossack and as a ballerina. The costumes kept changing. It was exquisite, academic almost. It was technically perfect. The act finished and there were other acts to follow. Bernadette switched off the television. She asked me if I wanted a cup of tea. Her mother smiled at me and nodded. The house seemed large and empty.

Santus Horizon

'Your world and the circus will never meet.'
EVA SANTUS, 1996

~

The visit to Bernadette had been a window to what was for me a new concept of circus and now I had another telephone number, in the chain of telephone numbers that were slowly bringing me closer to Santus Circus. Bernadette had shown me the low rigged wire in the shed in the garden where she practised. A middle-aged man was in there welding a piece of equipment. Bernadette introduced us and told Peter that I was looking for a circus to join. He lifted the visor back from his face and rubbed his eyes. He said he was going to visit his cousin Sara, who was working with Santus Circus. They were French but they worked in England. He said he would probably be going at the weekend. I could go with him if I liked.

The following weekend I went with Peter to visit Santus Circus. They were on a ground near Dover. The weather was hot and the roads were full of caravans heading for the coast. Peter drove his Granada at top speed down the motorway, the Rolling Stones 'Route 66' at full volume. We stopped at a service station for a cup of coffee. Peter played a computer game, 'Street Fighter'. Amazonian women executed perfect, synched karate kicks, and the mutating sci-fi scenery glimmered behind them, like dark castles and empty deserts. People came and went behind us, and the air scattered and shot with bleeps. Peter was obsessed with computer games.

In the car we talked about the circus. He was from a circus family, but had left for the moment. He worked mainly as a welder. He kept insisting to me that I needed to work with professionals. He used this word liberally. He said that there were too many jossers in the business, amateurs. I needed to be around professionals. His cousin was a professional. The jossers were ruining the business, he said.

We arrived at a field beside a pub that had a plastic tree with yellow eyes in the garden and an old boat against the fence for children to play in. Trailers, part of a scrapyard, were loosely hinged to a dark horizon, and in the foreground was the circus. An elephant was standing in the sun beside a hedge, pulling branches from the trees. It stopped and watched us as we passed. We drove round the outside of the caravans. A car was parked behind one of the lorries and a couple was just getting out of it, a woman with a cigarette in her mouth and a hard, annoyed face. I had never seen such a hard face. They didn't look at us as we drove past but pulled open the doors of the car.

Four little spotted ponies were tethered behind the caravan beside which we parked. A girl came out of the split door of the caravan, which had pink curtains. She spoke Polish, her skin was thick-looking and she had big heavy eyes that stared. She gestured for us to step into the caravan. An older, quieter woman was sitting at the little table, which had a little doll clown on it. She smiled and said nothing. Sometimes she picked up the clown and looked at it. She looked at us and smiled.

'All right, Sara,' Peter said. 'It's Pete and I've brought this Nell to see you.'

He was not addressing the woman sitting at the table. A voice came from the other end of the room, from the bathroom. 'Hang on a minute, Pete, I'm doing my hair.'

In a few seconds the door opened and a girl walked out. I had seen those looks already. They were Charmagne's and Josie's and Jena's, and they were the looks of the aerialist, Sky, in America. Bernadette had had a shadow of the same looks. Big eyes actually stained around the inner rim from a lifetime of eyeliner, set in a little face. She shook my hand in an endearing kind of way. There was a discussion about the trapeze. I wanted to learn the trapeze but that was not the point any more, and I had lost the point a way back. Outside rain was starting to fall and through the web of the curtains I could see some children leading the ponies to a tent. My back was to the window that looked out to the inside of the ring of trailers around the big top. All the world was inside this ring and the ring inside this yet. Within those encircling you just might find who you really are. I was looking over my shoulder where there had been a camel, which had gone now as well.

Peter and Sara were talking about a new prop that he was making for her, a type of trapeze, a four-sided frame that sits static in the roof of the tent. The idea seemed to be that Sara's boyfriend would work on it too.

'I want the ends of it in that plastic stuff, but wide, you know what I'm saying, Pete, so that I can make my positions on the end without worrying how wide it is.' She made a quick pose to illustrate the point and for a moment I saw it all: the crowds looking up, and these people for whom this difficult world is an entire existence for ever.

The door banged open and a huge blond boy with a massive lopsided face stepped in. The woman who didn't speak English smiled more. This was her son, and he was Sara's boyfriend. They discussed things I didn't know about. My overwhelming impression was of that particular circus. I forgot about the trapeze: it seemed to have been a device only for bringing me closer to the circus – closer to a show that would define the word circus.

A week later I went back to the coast, with Peter, to see Santus Circus again. They were in Margate. The main road comes in over the horizon and, held in the arc of the road and below its surface, was the circus, the tent, the lorries and the caravans parked behind. In Dover, business had been bad. Now, though, in Margate, there were rows of cars parked at the front of the circus, though I did not understand the importance of this as I do now – the sight of three cars or thirty, and the difference that makes to morale. We were late for the show and could hear music and a man's voice in a microphone as we parked the car and ran over to the tent. We went through the wallings and inside. The air was blue, and I saw why: two blue lightbulbs were screwed to the underneath of the lighting stand. I loved that light, swimming half-blue lunar light, making its own mystery. The roof of the tent was covered in stars and the curtains were gold and red, covered in stars too. The ring boxes were gold and red, painted with scrolled lettering. Santus Circus. Santus Circus. Santus Circus. The quarter poles, which are the poles supporting the middle section of the tent, around the outside of the ring, had a spiralling cream ribbon around them. Every detail I saw I liked. It was a circus that was not trying to be anything else. It was the most genuine circus I had seen in England. It was not an imitation of a circus, or an executed idea about a circus. It was just a circus, doing itself for real.

Peter and I sat down on the benches behind the ringside seats. A thin lady with glasses and loose clothes appeared out of the darkness and sat on the seat beside us. She talked with Peter. 'You know Sara's boyfriend has been deported?' she said quietly. Then she went away again into the darkness at the back of the tent. Peter said that that was Eva, Ernest's wife. Ernest Santus, he said, was the director of the circus. It was his circus. Eva didn't live on the show all the time, he told me. She painted pictures. She was at college in Canterbury. They used to be circus artists them-selves, they worked on a lot of different shows, he explained. That was why they were more sympathetic to the artists than a lot of other circus bosses. They knew what it was like to be an artist on a show. I didn't understand Eva at all; she did not look like a circus wife or a circus boss. She seemed less outgoing, less bitchy, though quite severe. That was how she struck me then. She didn't say anything to me. Sara's prop was swinging in the roof of the tent. Peter said that we had missed her act. Look, her prop is swinging. It was a steel hoop with a disco ball above it, swinging and glinting.

For a moment the starred curtains were closed and blank. Then, suddenly, there was a girl in the ring in a denim boiler suit and a baseball cap. She had been walking across the ground the last time we were here. She is Romanian. Magdalena.

She came into the ring and started to dance. She was regarding the audience from underneath the cap and she was pouting. She was a million miles away in the ring and we were not watching but witnessing. She undid her boiler suit in one pull, tipped forward at the waist, ripped it right off and dropped it on the ground. Her body was in an electric blue sparkly costume and she spun hoops on her arms and around her waist. She was brilliant, perfectly delicate and precise. The people clapped in time to the music. She was rotating within the spinning hoops, her body swaying and jarring between the lightning blurred lines of the hoops. A clown followed, Tito, and he had an indigo suit and a painted face with red lips. He was like a puppet. There was a camel and a bull, and an elephant with a girl riding on its back. The show was languid, rhythmic.

I felt captured by it and drawn towards it. It seemed close up, intimate and, at the same time, a long way in the distance, as if seen through a pair of binoculars.

In the interval two men, one who presented the animals and another with grey hair, brought the elephant back from the flat gloom behind the curtains and into the ring for photographs. They were both wearing black tie. They laughed and smiled a lot. Sara was selling sparkly wands but she couldn't talk to us for long as the men in the ring had their eyes on her, she explained, to see that she was selling. The man with grey hair smiled at Peter, and he smiled at me too. The quarter poles interrupted our view of the ring and the faces seemed to play behind them. Peter said that they were Ernest and Roget Santus. It was their circus. 'Get used to this, Nell,' he said, 'because I think that you are going to be here soon.' I neither disagreed with him, nor agreed, I just didn't know, I couldn't think straight. I loved it, the tent and the show. But Richie Richards was a circus too, and how different from this, to work and live in, I couldn't decide.

As it was the weekend, the show finished early, and Peter and I went round to see Sara. We were waiting for Ernest, as we were going to go out for a drink with him. She was sitting at her table, behind the lace curtains of the caravan, drinking wine. She looked dejected. 'The bastards have ruined my season,' she said. 'They rang up Customs.'

'Who?'

'Them, the others,' and she waved her hand. 'They came during the show, the Customs men, and they asked for Tizo. How could they know that was his name when it is his nickname? Only people on the show call him Tizo. He was in his dinner-suit and he ran across the ground and into the caravan and out of the window at the back, and into the bath tub that is round the back of the trailer. You know what I mean? But they caught him and they took him away, before he made it. We were just starting to practise together. We could have been working by the end of the season.' The evening was so hot that the door stayed open, and the glass on Sara's door reflected the colours of the tent, which were still visible in the bright hot evening. She pulled at her hair. 'My season is over now. I loved him. I can't believe that he isn't here. I mean, they took him then, back to Poland. The bastards have ruined my season. Why did they do that? They must have been jealous or something, because we were practising. But why did they do that? Maybe it wasn't them. I don't know for sure.'

I didn't know what to say, so said nothing. I was unsure as to what had happened and, from the sound of it, I didn't want to get involved.

Magdalena knocked on the side of the caravan, and asked Sara if she wanted to go out, for a drink, to the sea-front. Sara said that she did, and she asked us to come too. Peter said that we were going out with Ernest, to see about work.

It was getting late. Peter and I walked across the ground, round the back of the tent, to Ernest's caravan. We knocked on the door and Ernest came out. 'OK, I'm coming now,' he said. Outside his caravan were dog kennels and wicker chairs. The grass was long and everything seemed to be disappearing into it. Ernest locked the door with a chain and padlock. 'OK,' he said, 'we go and have supper.'

There is a pub in Margate called the Flag and Whistle. We went there for a drink and there were skinheads playing pool. 'It's rough,' said Peter. 'They fight in here.'

'OK, we fight!' laughed Ernest.

I took to him immediately. There was no Richie Richards snobbishness in his manner. The sun was low and bright over the sands outside, going down over the gaunt houses. We talked about the circus, deals lost, burned buildings, stolen artists. The sun dropped into the water. The skinheads were cheering each other on. We finished the drinks and went to a Chinese restaurant round the corner.

The day was over but the streets were hot, and the doors to the restaurant were wide open. On each table there was an empty vodka bottle with paper roses. 'It is bad for Sara, her boyfriend arrested, I know this,' said Ernest. 'I don't know what to do, she was crying and everything.' We ate Chinese food. A holiday family came and went while we were there. I was intrigued by this circus and this French family. Peter went out for a minute or two. 'OK,' said Ernest. 'You can have a job in my circus. You can do the paperwork. You can type?' I said I could, though slowly. 'You can help in the office.' The doors were still wide open and it was very hot. 'OK, we can give you a caravan to live in. You can start next week.' Peter returned, and the lights were dimmed in the restaurant. Shadows dropped down across the faces of people at other tables like shutters.

*

The next weekend I went back to the circus on my own. They were in Whitstable. Long ago there had been something in a dream about an old airfield, an old airstrip, and events on that airstrip that meant I would be living in Kent. I dreamed that a long time ago, before the accident.

My mind's eye carries pictures of my childhood like perpetual dreams. Clover and I are sitting in the garden at Minety on our ponies. The lawn in front of the house was called the croquet lawn but, because Clover and I had ridden all over it, it was rough and impossible for croquet. It has a pond that runs around two sides of it. It is the remains of an old moat, and that is what we used to call it, the moat. In the summer we caught tadpoles in it and in the winter we skated on it. There we are, Clover and I, sitting on our ponies, bareback, in summer, way back then through a passage that has collapsed; we can't get back through it and those two figures on the quiet ponies can't get out either. They are watching the Red Arrows practising in the sky, the ponies are half asleep in the sun and up there, right up there in the dizzy blue sky, the aeroplane dips and wheels, and red smoke is pouring from it and staining the sky blue.

After the accident, Rick and I went back to Kemble airfield, to the very place where my mum had fallen. This is what it is like: an old tarmac strip with a wood on one side across the field and a view out over the vale, in front, southwards. Rick thought he knew where the place was, just after a post-and-rails fence. He put the palms of his hands on the gritty tarmac and slowly pressed his face to the ground, eyes shut. The pain dismays me over and over again, undoes me, leaves me deserted, at times, despairing. I fight, I want to climb back, back through the collapsed passage and out again the other side.

I walked on to the circus ground. I had just bought an old diesel Sierra and it was full of my possessions. I saw Ernest standing beside the tent trailer with two of the boys. He came over and said hello. He turned away from the boys and looked at the ground. Then he said that the ring-master was leaving that weekend. 'Do you want to be the ring-mistress?' The sun went behind a cloud and two swans flew over, close above our heads, the wind rushing in their feathers and their wings beating silent time. I said that I would love to be the ring-mistress, though I had never done anything like that before.

Exotic Parade

～

There exists in England a stalwart supporter of the circus called the Circus Friends Association. The members meet to visit circus shows, organise trips to Europe to see other shows, and they produce a journal called *King Pole*. Old-fashioned and fanatical, the Circus Friends Association views the circus as a trainspotter views trains. I found this write-up of Santus Circus in a 1996 issue of *King Pole*. The term 'exotic group' is an anachronism from the days when the non-domestic animals of the circus, arriving in villages, curiously patterned, smelling alien, issuing unfamiliar sounds, would have seemed genuinely exotic.

SANTUS CIRCUS. Barkingside, 7–12 May
Good poster coverage of the area led to the green and yellow four-pole tent wall positioned on the main road. A

small audience for the Friday evening performance was welcomed by Ernest Santus and clown Jetto, and again, inside the tent, by the artists. Ring-master John-Paul, in 'pink', clearly announced the acts and reacted well with the audience in introducing:

1. Claire and Elaina, an impressive start with simultaneous *corde lisse* routines attractively presented on each side of the ring.
2. Farmyard frolics. Anne Marie Santus with goats, pony and chicken culminating in two high by goat and chicken on the pony.
3. Introducing Tito (with Emu) and Jetto in the first of their clown entrees.
4. Trio Russo. The first appearance of this family from Romania with a well-dressed, clever juggling routine using hoops and clubs. The act culminates with the audience counting the plates thrown by the ladies at increasing speeds across the ring to be caught by the man.
5. Sandrina. More aerial glamour from Sandra Sandow on aerial ring.
6. Tito and Jetto, now getting more response from the audience as they cover the ring, change for:
7. Rhanee the elephant, shown by Roget, with a walk over Elaina.

Following the interval:

8. Magdalena. A very lively hoop routine with good presentation emphasising both skill and glamour.
9. A short routine in all sense with the ponies with Roget Santus.
10. Tito and Jetto again, this time with buckets.

11. The Nevadas. Jason and Claire presented a strong Western act with ropes, whips and knives. This improving number must now be one of the best of its type, ending with Claire on the Wheel of Death.
12. Tito and Jetto involving John-Paul and the audience in 'can't play here'.
13. Roget Santus shows the exotic group of camels, Ankole and llama.
14. Trapeze Washington very competently presented by the attractive Elaina from Romania.
15. Tito and Jetto with their last appearance, balancing a tray of eggs.
16. Duo Russo give a strong ending to the show with Magdalena mounting to the roof of the tent on a perch supported on the feet of the bearer. The high spot has Magdalena and the bearer each balancing with only one foot.
17. Finale, with all the artists returning to well-earned applause.

The Circus Friends Association works hard for the circus community and their unremitting enthusiasm seems to bind it together. *King Pole* journalists and photographers report on new shows and new acts as well as circus-family news. So circus people know what other circus people are doing, in England, Europe and America.

The journalists are clearly aware that shows in England, compared to those in Europe and America, are of a low quality; and they report promptly on any positive developments within English circus. But this is not enough to push up the standard of English circus. In the media much discursive material is produced that relates to the other arts – theatre, opera, ballet, modern dance – but the circus is almost completely ignored. The Circus Friends Association never lacks enthusiasm and perhaps it is too unquestioning, their observations too prosaic.

For instance, in the article quoted above, they said of Elaina's act: 'Trapeze Washington very competently presented by the attractive Elaina from Romania.' In fact, it was a demonstration of sheer nerve and skill. The 'attractive Elaina' stood on her head on a bar that was spinning and swinging at the same time. It was an overtly sexy routine: she would climb a thin rope in stiletto heels, then sit on the trapeze and fling open her legs to initiate the spin of the bar. It was too dangerous an act to be bawdy, but too dangerously sexy to justify the blushing adjectives 'competent' and 'attractive'. For anything to progress it needs to be criticised and commented upon; it needs more than the observations of a small group of fanatical devotees. Elaina's act was brilliant; and the indifference to circus art evident in the media throughout England should be seen as a crisis.

Circus

Tomorrow morning the circus will also leave the city, for the gipsy must ever wander on. The rain falls where he rests, the fragrant blossoms and the ozone of the sea woo him, he knows the charm of tender nights when the moon is full, and nights when the storm wind whistles. He knows river valleys and mountain chains, the song of the cuckoo and the cricket's chirp. Whether the grain be swaying in the breeze or the autumn mist pressing the leaves to the ground, the circus travels on through the world, with man and beast, the big tent rises aloft with its steely song, and there is nothing above the bliss of its roaming save the eternal tented roof of the stars.

Circus-men, Beasts and Joys of the Road, PAUL EIPPER

At Santus Circus, as with any other travelling show, time was the most valuable commodity available. Time was borrowed, lent, stolen, argued over. No single person in the circus had one job to do. I worked in the booking-office in the mornings; for an hour and a half in the afternoon I helped with publicity; and I worked as the ring-mistress throughout the show. The girl artists worked in the interval doing the selling, in the office in the morning, and in the circus shop before and after the show. The boys did pony rides, helped with the lighting and music, and carrying the heavy props. The boy who worked in the stables had one task, looking after the animals, but this took him all day and most of the night. Grooms in the circus are allowed the least time of all – but I knew this already.

Ernest seemed to do everything – the lights, the music, the tickets, the driving; he would unroll the canvas, knock in the stakes, winch up the king poles, put the seats in, and everything in reverse at the end of the week, then drive the lorries, set all the caravans on the new ground, drive more lorries, knock in yet more stakes. He never sat in his caravan and gave orders, he never shouted and he never lost his temper. He was endlessly, tirelessly good-humoured. At the end of a forty-eight-hour day he would go to the pub with the whole show, buy everyone drinks and tell jokes.

Every single day in the circus is back-timed. This makes for a highly successful life. No day in the circus drifts haphazardly towards evening. Every action and task is set to a certain time so that everything is ready for show-time. Each person sets their own routine to ensure that they are never late for a show and that they are always presenting themselves as perfectly as they can. It is unheard-of, a sin, to be late for a show. This applies also to the grooms: but there is one major difference for them in that they don't have to turn themselves out for the ring. They brush their hair, and perhaps put on a circus-issued uniform for the brief moments when they are on the other side of the curtains to lead animals in and out of the ring, but they don't have to attend to the complicated business of hair and makeup, jewellery, fishnets and costumes.

The ring-master, or ring-mistress, wears a top hat and tails. The ring-master wears black trousers and shoes, perhaps white gloves. The ring-mistress wears a leotard, cut like a modern swimming costume, fishnet tights and knee-high boots, sparkly jewellery and makeup. Of course, the role is open to individual interpretation a bit, but the overall look is something like a cross between an old-fashioned show-girl and an assistant on a television game-show. I used to put my makeup on while I was sitting in the box-office. I had a little hand-held mirror. I wore black lines on my eyelids and red lipstick, and a lot of powder to stop the makeup running. I was not very practised at this type of makeup, and to start with I made panda eyes and clown cheeks, applying blusher in round circles underneath my cheekbones. After a while, and following Eva's advice (she was a master at discreet, striking, *classy* makeup) I looked more professional, less like an amateur's raid on a makeup box. I would run back across the ground about ten minutes before the show started, and change into my costume. If I rushed, my tights would catch and rip on my jewellery. Five minutes before the show I would go into the back of the tent, set the tapes for the show and make the five-minute announcement over the microphone, requesting that the audience did not take photographs or smoke in the tent.

The ring-mistress has to carry the audience through the show, announce the acts, fill in any gaps, banter with the clown. It is a tiring role because you are on your feet throughout the two-hour show, and there were two shows a day. I was a very imperfect ring-mistress. I was never fluent in the off-the-cuff banter. For two months I wore boots that were too tight and had to sit down on a chair in the back doors during the acts as my feet were so excruciatingly painful. When I first started working I fiddled with the lead of the microphone and spoke too softly, walked backwards as I spoke, as if trying to escape from the audience. The old ring-master gave me a piece of advice. He explained that when you are alone in the ring you are all that the people are looking at. The more still you stand, the more focus is held.

Thus I started to learn the intense self-control that is needed for working in the ring. Every unintended movement is a mistake, reveals your lack of expertise. A true circus artist will not make a single unconsidered movement in the ring. A brilliant artist will move in such a way that the people are transported out of themselves as they watch him or her. Charlie Chaplin, for example, was a brilliant artist. Every gesture and gait related to the inner mood of the character, to illustrate and create the role. Circus artistry cannot be learned quickly. I was never an artist, though I was learning about the peculiar environment of the ring. And sometimes I got it very wrong. I used to wear a pair of old grey clogs between the caravan and the tent, then change into my boots at the last minute. Once I went into the ring, trying my hardest to look suave and controlled; about half-way across I realised I was still wearing my clogs. Rather than continuing with the first announcement and changing during the opening act, I turned round and ran out. All I could hear were the rope-act girls falling about with laughter, and all I saw was Ernest's dismayed face as he realised what had happened.

I had already seen, on the other shows that I had worked on, that the better equipped you are, the more time is available. If you have more time you are less tired, and if you are less tired you are more precise in the ring. The more time you have, the less tired your face looks. My old caravan, which I had left in Glasgow, had no shower, so I lost time driving around looking for sports centres. The day after arriving at Santus Circus I bought an old Tabbert caravan from a taxi driver. It was parked on the concrete outside his house, and he sold it to me for under two thousand pounds. Circus people in England tend to live in either American trailers, which are roomy and luxurious, or German trailers, either Weippert or Tabbert. Both these makes are heavy-duty, well-insulated trailers that are designed to be lived in full time. The lighter English touring caravan is too insubstantial for full-time use. My Tabbert was seventeen feet long and had hot and cold running water. It had a shower and a big free-standing table surrounded by a wide, spongy sofa bench. There were little lights hidden behind pelmets and it had an efficient gas fire. Maintenance consisted of changing the gas bottle every week, filling the water tank every day, and rigorous cleaning and tidying. Once a week I would empty the chemical loo into a sewer. It was my first proper caravan and I lived in it for two years. It is hard to emphasise the importance of luxury when you are living in the circus. Almost all the time I was tired, so it was of vital importance to be able to sit down in peace to have a cup of coffee in the interval and read the paper. Circus people lead good lives, but they lead very hard lives. The life is demanding because work, art and family are all welded into one, because you are constantly moving, and the routine demanded by the shows cannot be escaped. So relaxation, warmth, free time are treasured, because they are infrequent and so laboriously acquired.

Heroes

Circus women have a peculiar charm of their own.
Circus Nights and Circus Days, A. H. KOBER

~

I had been with the show for about a week when I went round to Sara's caravan one evening after the show. Magdalena was in there. They were both going to a disco that evening because it was Sara's birthday. Magdalena was dressed all in white and she was turning around in front of the mirror, looking at herself over her shoulder. Sara was in the bathroom doing her hair. There was a diamanté-framed clock on the wall and a pile of costumes on the seat that ran along the side of one half of the caravan. Sara came out of the bathroom, slid plastic hangers into the costumes and hung them in the wardrobe. Magdalena sat down at the table and drank a glass of Coke. They said that they were leaving in half an hour, and asked me to come too. Sara's cousin was picking them up. I said that I would have to get a sub from Ernest, as I had run out of money for the week.

The stables were still lit and the lights were on at the top of the tent. The caravan sat in its dark shadow. I felt nervous. Memories of knocking on the Richards' caravan door filled me with dread. Sasha, their son, opened it. He had been sitting just inside the doorway playing a computer game. I heard Ernest's voice behind. 'Who is it, Sasha?'

'Nell.'

'Come in, Nell. You want a quick whisky?'

I stepped into the caravan and explained that I was going out with Sara and Magdalena, as it was Sara's birthday. The caravan was dark inside and full of Eva's paintings. Right in front, above the window, was a painting of Sasha as a child, and beside that a tight close-up of a clown's face, eyes shut looking deep in thought through the concealing makeup. The pictures seemed to be hanging in the air. There was a little table with a dark-coloured oilcloth and on the shelf behind the sofa there were pictures of clowns and photographs of the family. The curtains were red velvet with tiny red velvet tassels. Some of the tassels were missing. The carpet was red and the sofa was covered with dark pink throws. Ernest said he must get the dog in. He said it was the only dog allowed in the caravan because it was such a good dog, the best dog he had ever had. Its name was Sorrow. He poured two glasses of whisky.

'*Santé*. You OK?'

There was a knock on the door. Sasha opened it. A tall man came in. Ernest introduced him as Robert. He was driving a load of antiques to Czechoslovakia. He had to catch the boat at Dover soon. He stayed for a quick drink. Sasha was still playing the computer game. He didn't look round. Ernest and Robert discussed circus business. Robert said you had to have the right marketing, you just had to have it. You couldn't make a show work without it. After a while he left to catch his boat. Ernest explained that Robert used to be married to Yolande.

'Yolande?'

'My sister. She is in France at the moment.'

Ernest said they used to own a farm in Essex. They had stables and a big barn with a trapeze. When they were away during the season the local boxing club used it for practice. Then the taxman came and took it away. That was terrible. Under the table Sorrow turned in his sleep and I emptied the glass of whisky. All that could be heard from outside was the noise of the generator and a dog barking. He had wanted to give up the circus, then. 'I was too tired, too tired. But everyone told me to keep going, not to give up. The business is so bad, though. It is a very hard life. You know, when I was little the shows were packed, maybe three or four shows in every town. Everyone went to the circus. My grandparents stood on a platform in front of the shows, you know, in the market-squares in France, maybe played an instrument, something like this, showed the snakes, and all the people came! You know, it is not like this any more, no, especially not in England. There are many problems for the circus.' He shut his eyes. 'Robert is right.' He opened his eyes. '*Si*, you want to have good business you have to have good marketing.'

A little while later I heard a car on the other side of the caravan. 'I am going now as Sara's cousin is here,' I said. Ernest gave me ten pounds from next week's wages. 'Have a good time. See you tomorrow.'

The next morning I sat in the box-office reading the Sunday papers. Although it had rained a bit during the night, the weather was light and warm. Eva drove on to the ground in her car, the back seat covered in plant pots, paintings and clothes.

She came into the box-office to talk. I was just starting to know her. She was tiny and dainty with long hair and glasses, and her finesse, her light walk and delicate hands, did not seem to correspond with her powerful mind and survival in a deeply eccentric, difficult, fractured life. 'I am not a typical anything,' she said, and she isn't. Her father was a magician. She held her hand in a fist then opened it and a pink scarf bounced to life on her palm. She said that he would hide it between his fingers. She curled her fist then released her scarf, over and over again so that the material vanished and reappeared.

She went to boarding school in Ireland and then moved to London in the sixties. 'I was a swinger then,' she said. She had a baby when she was seventeen and started a business doing up Jeeps for pop stars. She met Ernest: 'I was *mad* about him, crazy for him. It wasn't the circus I fell in love with, it was Ernest.' She said that she had to go and cook lunch any minute. I sold a ticket to a man with a Scottish accent wearing a round skullcap. Eva asked him something and he laughed then said that he was not an obeyer of man's laws. He was difficult to figure out. Most of the faces that came to the window were easy to figure out. He said thank you, then got into his car, which was parked in front of the box-office. I asked Eva if he was bullshitting, about not being an obeyer of man's laws. She pointed out that he had opened the door of the car, got in, started the engine and driven away like someone who had been trained. 'Did you watch? He was precise, slightly aggressive.' We were quiet for a while.

'Never fall in love with a circus artist,' Eva said suddenly.

In front of the box-office, across the ground, a football match was starting. The figures wore either red or blue. I thought about the previous night. I had felt very out of place among the circus people I was with. 'Listen to what happened last night, Eva,' and I told her this story.

Magdalena and Sara and I went with her cousin to the show where Sara's parents worked, and where she grew up. It was a large, traditional circus, with no jossers working on it. They were parked about five miles away from Santus Circus. We went to eat birthday cake with the family, to pick up Sara's sister, then go on to the disco. Her mum looked like a tiny aggressive bird. Her legs were muscled and she wore high heels. She opened the door of her lorry and hugged Sara, scolding and chattering in Spanish. Sara's parents had converted the lorry into a kitchen. It had been beautifully done with a large copper chute above a substantial cooker. A group of people sat round a table at the far end of the room eating Chinese takeaway. When they had finished and the table had been folded away, they sat and talked about circus matters (circus people rarely talk about anything else) and teased the young people.

There was a man in the corner whom I recognized: he was a famous clown. His son was Jan Eric, whom I had met in Glasgow. 'My children, terrible they are,' he exclaimed, 'ring me up all the time, needing money, "I have a problem with this or that." They ring me, they are terrible, fools!'

There was a loud knock at the door and a boy bounded into the room and talked loudly to the older people, winding them up, making them laugh.

'Fools, they are terrible with money!'

The boy stood in the middle of the room and everyone was looking at him. He was half Irish and half Spanish. Sara said he was moving to Las Vegas next year.

Magdalena looked down and up through her eyelashes at him, and he looked on, reassured. Magdalena, the hula-hoop girl, queen of the tiny costume and thin limb. She wore little white boots with a heel and silver studs, immaculate white trousers and a white top, her hair in a pony-tail or similar arrangement, with a curl sexily at the front. The skin on her face was so perfect it looked like ice. She won the approval of all. She was on the inside. Sara's granny brought in a birthday cake. Everyone sang and clapped and passed the cake round on small pink plates. Sara hugged her and said that this was her nan who had taught her everything. Her nan said that Sara was a lovely girl. The room was very crowded now, and Sara's dad said that we should be off. Her mum spoke to her in Spanish and she looked even more like a furious bird. We were wondering if Anita, another girl on the show, was coming with us. She had recently married a Hungarian boy and he was ill. Sara, Magdalena and I ran across the ground in the dark to their caravan. Some lightbulbs were strung above our heads on the main guys and in their light shone the backs of some sea-lions, who watched us with jelly eyes.

Anita was tiny and Brazilian with big teeth, big eyes and long dark hair. There were leopardprint cushions and it was very warm in the caravan. Her husband, Kootchie, was lying on the bed at the far end of the room, watching television. Anita said, 'Won't you come out, Kootchie? Come out, darling,' and he said he was ill. Anita leaned back on the wall and looked at him. She said to us that she might come out – she'd meet us in the car if she did.

We sat in the back of Sara's dad's car. He said he would come and pick us up later if we wanted. One of the boys got his car stuck over the rim of a rut hidden in the long grass. 'Bloody idiot,' said Sara's dad, and he towed him out, while the boys were whistling and shouting in the dark; we could see them through the car's rain-flecked windows. A figure in a dark coat appeared: it was Anita, just as we were about to pull away. She said that she was coming after all. We budged up, she slammed the car door and we were off again, towards the gate that led from the field to the road. Kootchie was in her mind, though, and she asked Sara's dad to stop the car. She said she was very sorry, then jumped out and said, 'Goodnight, see you later, have a good time,' and was gone again into the dark.

Where I was, among all those people that night, I didn't know. In the lorry Jan Eric's father wouldn't look me in the eye and I suspect that it was because I was a josser. Among the girls in the night-club I felt like a clown. I couldn't fit in with their polished self-restraint. I was wearing trainers and the bouncer in the night-club said they weren't smart enough. The juggler, Lucia, lent me his shoes – he had some others in the car. They were far too big and far from alluring, and I had to shuffle and trip to keep them on. The girls danced in a circle and slow-danced with a boy each at the end of the night. Lucia had a go at Magdalena, who was nice and soft with him. I felt like an oddity, a bit too butch, a bit too posh. On that particular evening I was on the outside looking in.

I liked Lucia, I explained to Eva. I liked his accent, he was funny and charming, and I liked the fact that he made all his sequined costumes himself; but I wasn't prepared to compete with him on those terms – I didn't know how to. And Eva knew what I was talking about and she said that it was hard to find a man these days anyway. She looked out of the window of the box-office. The red and blue figures had not even reached half-time.

'Plenty of men there,' she said brightly, 'and not a hero among them.'

Diary: Billericay, August 1996

~

It is the middle of summer and I have been with the circus for a few weeks. It was the end of a build-up day and we were at the falling-over stage of tiredness. I had just climbed up one of the side poles to hang the ring curtain, then I was back on the ground again, and around the side of the wallings came a beam of light as the sun set. Jason's face was lit by the sun, and there was Sasha too, with his eyes open talking about a video game. Sasha is tall and thin, with Ernest's melancholic eyes. He is very intelligent, good at writing, and funny. He has lived in the circus since he was a baby; still, like his mother he can stand back from it a bit, regard it with new eyes.

The corners of mystery and the wide-open symptoms of a life spent energetically in the open air. This brilliant combination of the sun and the night and the motion continually moving around us. I would cry that more is not seen and felt and recorded as the sun goes down and the colours bounce, brilliant, off everything. Nothing could further reveal the world of possibility that sits and laughs all around me. I am happy as I never have been before. The clear and ready laughter of people who excel in the world that they inhabit with every straining muscle of their bodies.

From the box-office I can see the camel's slow, gaunt walk to the shade of a tree. The other day I was in there and it was raining outside. Anne Marie came to the door with her baby, Lucian, and the pram, and she was covered in mud because she had been clearing up the elephant and filling the skip. We sat for a while with the baby while the rain came down outside. There was a musical toy hanging on the pram and Anne Marie pulled the cord and it played a tune. The baby was laughing at the toy, and Anne Marie was smiling at the baby. There was mud on her face and the rain was coming down and she was smiling and the baby was smiling too, and the little tune was playing and the whole room was there and it was not there, I was right away and I was falling under, I was falling, here and everywhere, I was not here and here and the world outside and other references and other ideas didn't matter at all: it was just this baby and the woman who loved the baby smiling at each other.

At Santus Circus, at the end of 1996, I lived in the present. I didn't lament the past or construct a future: I was simply happy in the present. I was inspired by the vigorous, uncompromising ways of the Santus family, and the authenticity of their circus. There was nothing self-conscious about the show, and as a result it held a magic, 'corners of mystery', that I have not experienced elsewhere. I felt only frustrated that I could not record more fully the bright 'open' physicality of their difficult, defiant lives.

Tent

*Lastly he sang of Her – the Woman of the Ring – flawless,
complete, untrammelled in each subtly curving limb;
earth's highest output, time's noblest expression.*
                                    The Circus Book, EDITED BY R. CROFT COOKE

It was the back end of the season and winter was on its way
without a doubt. With the winter came the winds and the fear
of losing the tent. The previous night we had taken it down in a
gale. The circus moved every Sunday night, and the show opened
on Tuesday, so we had only twenty-four hours to relocate. Pull-
down is always urgent; the work cannot be left for a moment. It
was Ernest who drove everyone, calling and cheering to the boys,
'Come on, girls,' he said, 'you can nearly smell breakfast!'

The vinyl of the tent had cracked and rolled in the wind, and
everyone had come out from the caravans, the girls and the children and the wives, to help, hanging on ropes and shouting in
the stumbling darkness. Once the poles are out of the way the
only thing that holds the tent are the guys and the stakes, and the
wind gets right underneath it and hauls it upwards. We ran
round the outside, undoing the ropes in succession, dragging the

tent round, folding it, making it heavier, piling it on to the trailer parked in the middle of the ring.

Jason and his girlfriend Claire have a Western act. He throws knives at Claire, who stands against a board. She whirls a lasso and throws cut-out metal stars at him. They wear fringed, beaded cowboy clothes, sparkly Stetsons, silver cowboy boots. Claire makes the clothes, and Jason builds the props – a stars-and-stripes stand for the ropes to hang on, a static knife board, and a big circular revolving board – 'the Texan Deathwheel'. The act is accompanied by country-and-Western dance music, and strobe lights. Its format is a modest allusion to the heyday of Victorian circus, when Buffalo Bill Cody brought real Red Indians and live buffalo to England with his massive Western Circus.

Jason is a good boy. He grins at you in the darkness, mud on his face and rain in his hair, and the only lights are the lights from the road and the rushing cars and everyone has lost their torches and you are at the outside edge of what you can take; too tired now, too long the hours, too slow the lorries, too violent the wind. Moving a circus is hard, heavy work, and there is no way round this. I liked to work with the boys, to get good at it, get stronger. Jason has slight bow-legs and his hands are not as they should be for his age. He is young but his hands are broken open and rough like wood. He was standing on the trailer. The whole of the tent comes down on to the flat-bed: once the sides have been rolled and lifted on to the lorry, the top part of the tent, the coppolla, a metal frame suspended from the king poles, is slowly winched down and the tent folds under itself with no flaps hanging over the edge of the trailer. But that night the wind was blowing and forcing the tent to hang over to one side, making it impossible to load. We pushed it back, clinging to the sides of the lorry and trying to lean on this vast, flapping, angry thing that billowed around us. There was a new boy and he tried to climb up to help, but he didn't know where the footholds were and couldn't see in the darkness where to hang on. I was at one end, trying to keep the corners in. Somebody pushed the boy up from underneath, he lurched forward and disappeared into the fold. I clung to the plastic, and down on the ground, somewhere in the darkness, I could hear Ernest calling to the boys who were turning the winch handles. The wind gusted, and just as we thought we had it, the tent jerked to one side and Jason flew off the lorry, twisting and curling as he hit the grass. I could just see him a few feet away. He lay completely still, then jumped up and walked forward, his body tipped and wincing at the weight. He stopped and put his hands on his knees, then straightened up again. Somebody shouted out to him and he yelled back that he was coming, hang on.

The next day we put the poles up, but not the tent – it was too windy, the next day was spare, we could do it then. We would just sleep tonight and hear the wind and not worry. Ernest said that he was very tired: when the wind blew he didn't sleep. If the tent went his whole life would be carried away. 'What else could I do but the circus?' he asked me once. You can see what he meant. The circus is the only medium I can think of where life and art are undivided; the essence of circus life cannot be replicated anywhere else. Once you have been in the circus you feel out of it in any other world. But I felt guilty when Ernest said that: I could walk away from a destroyed tent to other lives. I was inauthentic, a passenger with a typewriter. And I made assumptions, at the back of my head, without realising: that they must have other lives too, houses, that the circus is a distraction from this for a part of the year, a suspension of another reality. But it isn't. There is nothing else to fall back on, to go home to. This is it – the wind and the flapping tent and the lorries in the night and the camels slowly passing during tea outside the caravan.

The sun had set in a sky coloured by the storm and the faces were coloured by the sky. The tent was not up but the caravans were arranged around the ground, and the animals were grazing within this space. The field we were parked in had little hillocks and a gate on to the road. This led on to a roundabout and a motorway. You could see it from the field. It ran along the horizon. The trucks looked huge, nothing behind them, just the sky. They looked like they were driving to the ends of the earth. I felt very tired from the long night and the night before, the racing around in the dark and the falling in the mud and the work today. I became preoccupied by the lorries, the light fading, and I could not understand them. I was with Ernest, Jason and Claire beside the tent trailer, whiling away the time, watching the last light and practising handstands. I wanted to learn to press a handstand. I was heavy and my wrists felt weak.

Ernest's father, Grandpère, came over; he was about eighty and he stood on one hand with his body straight out parallel to the ground and everyone clapped.

The bull pulled his stake out of the ground and cantered about, tossing his head and glancing at us with the whites of his eyes. The boys went after him, caught him by the horns and knocked the stake back into the ground. Jason's dog barked and the boys laughed like cowboys The light was bright yellow on the horizon and all their faces were yellow too.

More wind was forecast, and darkness was ahead. It was about five o'clock. I had to sit in the box-office, waiting for people to buy tickets. It was a converted box-trailer and when I sat in there I felt surrounded by all the people who had ever worked there. Some of Eva's oil sketches were propped up on the shelf above the window, a half-finished portrait of her son, Sasha, looking over the edge of a table with his chin on his hand. 'His face is lit by a pumpkin,' she told me. He was waiting for his dad to come into the caravan so that he could show him the pumpkin, but Ernest didn't come in until very late so Sasha was sad, sitting there waiting for him. A Parisian looked out coyly from under a multicoloured watercolour hat. Somebody must have had a fascination with crime as there was a box full of murder-mystery case studies, serialized pamphlets free with the *Sunday Times.*

Anne Marie is married to Ernest's brother, Roget. Her two little children are Ruby and Lucian and their jackets and scarves hung on the wall. There was an old Monopoly board and a pile of paperbacks in the corner. The top one is entitled *The Great Mistake* and is subtitled *A Family Secret is Unmasked with Violent Consequences.* On the cover there was a drawing of a woman with glasses and gnarled hands, and the edge of the pages was turquoise and frayed. The whole book had been taped up with masking tape and on the masking tape Eva had written (it could only have been Eva): 'Only read this if you want to go mad or are masochistic.' Anne Marie read when she sat in the box-office, and I did some writing. Eva painted from her reflection in the darkening window, and Claire sewed: she has new costumes every week.

The dented steel step was set by the door and Elaina had just painted it white. She said she loved painting. Her English was broken and articulate and hard. She was Romanian and rolled her Rs. Her face was wide, cat eyes and scarred skin from chicken pox; when she smiled her lips were thin and her eyes slanted. She had arms like a monkey and a short back. She stood on her head on the trapeze and her neck was thick with muscle. One day she will be in a wheelchair from the stress the act puts on her spine. 'And then you will push me around, eh, Speary?' she said accusingly to her husband, and he replied that he married her, babe, in sickness and in health, but she laughed bitterly because she didn't believe him. Her life seemed difficult to me. They live in a lorry and she is always packing things into suitcases then unpacking them. She is very clever with her costumes: she makes feather headdresses for riding the elephant, encrusted with stones set on thick wires and stitched together, and patiently mends rips in thin tights, weaving threads of material pulled from the waistband into the holes. But she is always tired, and lazy, too, gives up in the winter, lives in her bed, watching Sky telly and eating bacon sandwiches. She doesn't know the extent of her brilliance, I'm sure of this. She put the paintbrush into a jar of water and the lid on the paint. Speary called to her and they went home for supper.

I sat in the swivel chair in the box-office. The wind was starting up again and I could still see the lorries on the horizon. There was a white cylinder container, and it looked as if it had broken down. Then I could see a man climbing the ladder at the side of it. He was dressed in silver and looked tiny, the lorry, huge. The light was going and it was dark in the office, too dark to read, and I was sure that no one would stop by. Jason was still laying the electricity cable, ratcheting around in the dark, and until he had finished there would be no light. Speary's generator started to whir from across the ground and the animals were all in for the night.

Ernest knocked on the door and looked through the glass window. I opened the door and he stepped in. The step was wet and there was white paint on his soles but he laughed and said,

'Elaina loves painting, doesn't she?' He asked me if I was all right, and said that the electricity was on now. I pulled the light cord and the bulb illuminated. 'Not much power here,' he said. The bulb glowed dark yellow and his face was in deep shadow now that all the light in the sky was gone. It was pitch black outside.

I worked much harder on the tent than the other girls. It is men's work, putting the tent up and taking it down, heavy and dangerous. The girls knew better than me: they waited in their caravans behind the curtains, the noises from outside betraying the progress of this massive operation: the shouts as the rolls of the tent are lifted on to the lorry, the squeals of the winches as the king poles come down, and the far-carrying chimes as the stakes are knocked out. A high wind, and the girls are compelled to turn out, to help until the tent was packed beyond danger of ripping.

The tent is the hardest taskmaster of all, a mobile building site and a theatre to art and work. All the cabs, the lorries and the caravans on the show are the different rooms of a big house, and the tent is the great hall, the cathedral. Birthday parties and christenings are celebrated in the tent, and people sit around the ring on the ring fence. They don't carouse in the ring: it is too respected, the ring is almost sacred.

That evening, sitting in the box-office, I was shattered, not much sleep for two days, the curve of the swinging sledge-hammer pulling my shoulders. As the little room illuminated I could see my face reflected in the window. Ernest asked me again if I was all right, 'You work so hard,' and he asked me if I wanted to go to the pub.

'I don't know,' I said.

'Are you being difficult? Do you want to go to the pub later? We won't open the box-office for long, this wind. What's the point?'

The rain had started: I could hear it on the roof.

Ernest went away and I could still see my reflection: I didn't see what I thought I was, but someone thinner, with wild hair and filthy clothes and green eyeliner left on from the show two days ago. I was tired and starting to feel quite lost.

There were no people to sell tickets to. I was too tired to read much. When Clover had stayed a few weeks ago she left behind a copy of *Hello!* We had a nice weekend: she sat in the office with me and we smoked and read magazines. I flicked through *Hello!* for a bit, then I sat, stared at my reflection and out through it into the darkness. If I hadn't been so tired I would have been bored, but the tiredness takes you away from the monotony. This was a circus night, and I remembered my first week with this circus earlier in the season. It was the week that the old ring-master, John-Paul, left.

To commemorate his departure we had supper outside, Ernest and Roget, and Anne Marie and Eva and the children. John-Paul was Irish and spoke with the ease of an Irishman. He taught me how to project my voice and he showed me how to stand in the ring. Never walk backwards as you are speaking. Don't fiddle with the microphone cable. Keep still. Don't break up the focus. I spoke far too quietly, and nobody could hear, even with the microphone. In the daytime we went into the ring and he got me to make a few of the announcements.

'Ladies and gentlemen, from the Santus Farmyard, will you please welcome . . .'

'Louder. Overdo it.'

'From the Santus Farmyard.'

'Louder.'

'FROM THE SANTUS FARMYARD.'

He was laughing and he clapped. 'Now you will be all right.'

We were by the sea and we ate crabs, lobsters and oysters, platefuls of them, a last warm night in August. There were bulbs on cables hanging from Roget's caravan, and they lit up the faces and the white tablecloth. We drank whisky. Rick, my father, was there. I felt happy, felt that I had come home. The chickens were in the wire pen across the grass and the dogs were asleep under the table. The people around the table were strangers, and yet it was as if they had been waiting here and I had only to find them. It was as if I knew them already. The sea was in the distance and I swam in it the next day, with John-Paul, drifted in the waves and looked at the sky, the sand dunes. Yes, I felt that I had come home. . .

There was another knock. It was Claire, Jason's girlfriend. She is a tall, big-boned girl, with long black hair, and she throws knives and whirls a forty-foot lasso. She is absolutely unbeatable at arm wrestling. She is good, strong, tough and funny. She looks like a Red Indian princess, I think, with her black hair and her dogs. Her caravan is beautiful: glossy, clean and spacious with a cut-glass door to the bedroom and a honey-coloured wooden floor. Jason runs it and she cleans it, and in the back of the lorry he has installed a bath, with wooden walls and a built-in radio. Costumes, tumble dryer, washing machine – it's all there. I stood up and opened the door of the office. Claire was holding two cups of coffee and, under her arm, a stack of papers. She said I must be bored with no one to talk to, it wasn't right that I had to work so hard. I said I didn't mind, that I liked it, that I *was* bored, though, thanks for the coffee, what had she got, could I see? 'That's why I brought it, for you to see, my scrapbook from when I was a kid, the pictures we were going to throw out. I kept them.' She showed me the photographs of her childhood, extraordinary documents of a strange tribe, a way of life.

Claire is not a thin little slip of a thing: close up, circus girls are larger than life and there is more to her than meets the eye. But the mythology about circus women transforms them to semi-spiritual beings. I found this in a book, written in 1784: 'A young person of sweet and dream-like appearance, rope dancer of the abstract school, full of poetry and expression, who danced on a rope with the wings of sylph and the modest graces sung by Horace.' This would have been Claire's great-grandmother, or an in-law, or similar, back down the line, spinning those mysteries in the air, but sitting in the dark night with some coffee, Claire was prosaic, frighteningly strong, with a rough edge to her voice and a threatening look in her eye – and in the photographs she was a determined child, learning the secrets of her trade, the lifted chin, the fuck-you superiority. There is Claire doing the splits outside, in a sparkly costume – and you can only just make her out in the dark – the sun is setting, the light is coming in sideways, catching the side of the lorry and throwing the camel into silhouette. There is another picture of Claire on a Palomino pony: she said she really loved that pony, it was the only pony she really loved. She is beside a red lorry, in front of her parents' big top, in a cowgirl costume. There is a monkey in a cage and a man with a lion. 'What is it like,' I asked her, 'growing up in the circus? What did the rest of the world seem like when you were a child?' She said, 'You just have an edge, don't you? You just have an edge.' It is a difficult life, carved in wind and disaster and an unearthly picturesque. How much did they see that bit, I wondered, the ongoing, extraordinary visual cliché? I could never discern whether circus people sensed the picturesque nature of their day-to-day lives. They have an untiring pride in their work, their lives. You just have an edge.

'But in any case,' Claire admitted, 'I'm only second-generation circus.' I asked her what her parents had done before, and she said that they had been in travelling theatre. She was not circus, she was travelling theatre. I am sure that in this difference lie a thousand implications and prejudices, but it is a language that is beyond me. She showed me a thin little scrap of brown paper: a painting to illustrate the structure of the tent for the theatre. It was thin and ripped, a shred of a document, and Claire said that it was lovely. She held it and looked at it, and it was sacred, too, in the dark box in the light of one bulb. We drank coffee and talked, then Claire said she was going home to make Jason dinner, that they were going to the pub later, did I want to come? I said I did.

I can clearly mark in my head the times that I have been forced to defer to this 'edge'. Ivan's 'pretty wild, isn't it?' was an overt acknowledgement of the edge. He had gone too far in that instance, though: he had been in danger of giving the game away. (They play with your preconceptions, though, laugh at josser whimsy and romance, but create it none the less, spin the mysteries, because the elephant's hay and the food in the pan depends on it.) When Charmagne swore at the elephants, bleeding cows, when I had blood on my hands and legs and she did not, that was the edge, too.

It had been the same on another occasion. I had gone with Sara to see the show her parents worked on – we had a night off and the show was nearby again. We caught the second half. We were sitting up near the spotlight, which Sara's cousin was working, and we were with some friends of hers, who smelt strongly of perfume and cigarette smoke and told Sara about their new boyfriends, who were Hungarian, the boys who did all the tricks on the bikes. There was an act with some tigers. They had soft paws batting the air. I loved the tigers and so did Sara. 'Lovely, aren't they?' she said, and I agreed. Then she pulled herself up. Like Ivan's 'pretty wild, isn't it?' she was giving the game away, so she added, and this was a showman's touch, could only have been said by someone with circus blood in their heart, 'Nice tigers.' I couldn't say anything to this: it was a phrase from an unfamiliar idiom. I fell away from it, nice tigers: I had never seen any other tigers apart from at the zoo, a punter's child.

Claire left and I sat for a bit longer. The rain was hard now, and the wind stronger. I was feeling more and more tired, feeling things slip away, feeling that I had come too far to go back, if I went I would get lost, lose the track. I shut my eyes and I could see the green-yellow light of the sunset, and Ernest's trilby blowing off, lifting and flying in the wind, a clown's hat. The office thundered and shook, and for a split second I thought that it was someone running around upstairs, footfalls from another time.

Wintering

Then the circus was over. People cheered and clapped and then went out. Half asleep, Susy-Anne and Pip went too. They tumbled into bed, and dreamt all night long of the wonderful circus. How they wished that they had belonged to it too!

Enid Blyton's Circus Book, ENID BLYTON

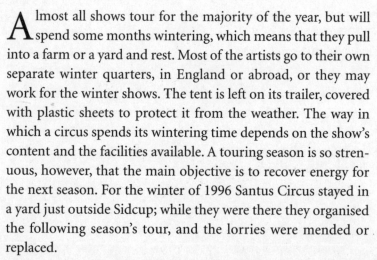

Almost all shows tour for the majority of the year, but will spend some months wintering, which means that they pull into a farm or a yard and rest. Most of the artists go to their own separate winter quarters, in England or abroad, or they may work for the winter shows. The tent is left on its trailer, covered with plastic sheets to protect it from the weather. The way in which a circus spends its wintering time depends on the show's content and the facilities available. A touring season is so strenuous, however, that the main objective is to recover energy for the next season. For the winter of 1996 Santus Circus stayed in a yard just outside Sidcup; while they were there they organised the following season's tour, and the lorries were mended or replaced.

The main road goes out of Sidcup and into Kent, a busy road with a scrapyard and gypsies trotting fast ponies through the

traffic. A track goes past a fruit and vegetable shop and some stables to the yard where the circus was parked. The road is left
behind, the sound of traffic becomes muffled, and beyond the
yard are fields, and on the horizon, a wood. The moon hangs
heavy over the wood, and while we were there the nights were
cold and clear. Anne Marie said she sometimes walked her dog
up to the wood at night and looked at the moon. The circus lorries were packed tightly into the yard, the caravans between
them. Grandpère put a lightbulb on the ground between the
caravans. It illuminated their shiny aluminium walls and dark
Perspex windows, the feet of people walking past, heavy boots
and children's wellingtons and the dogs' scratching paws. There
were alleys between the caravans and when it was wet we put
down bits of carpet and wood to walk on, but mainly the ground
was crisp and clean and frozen white. Without the relentless
shows and moving, and with the loud show music absent, life
seemed leisurely and quiet.

All the artists had gone. Magdalena had returned to Romania
with her parents, and Jason and Claire, Speary and Elaina and
Sara had all retreated to their own winter quarters. The clown,
Tito, had scarpered before the season finished. Nobody knew
where or why he went. He was quickly forgotten, as people who
scarper from the circus are. In Sidcup it was just Ernest and Eva,
Roget, Anne Marie, the children, Grandpère and me. The shops
were full of Christmas, pink Barbies in Woolworths and
Dalmatians in McDonalds. Anne Marie and I would go to the
supermarket together. She cooked for everyone in the evening,
and the caravan was warm and smelt of food, while the television bounced colourful shapes, the Dalmatians. Ruby loved
them – 'Look, puppy.'

One boy, Brian, stayed with Santus Circus for the winter. He had joined at the end of the season. He told me that after leaving the Army he had been very viólent so he had ended up in prison. He married his probation officer, then took a job selling accident insurance. He arrived at the circus in a suit. He tried to sell everyone accident insurance. Nobody bought it. The next day he came back and asked for a job. He was tall, with brown hair and big teeth and a South London accent, and he said that he had an iron bar under his bed all the time, 'Because I used to be into this and that, know what I mean, Nellie? I wouldn't mess with Nellie,' he said, when I could swing a sledge-hammer better than him. But he learned quickly, and the circus changed him. The suit went, his car broke from bumping across fields, he lost weight, his face hollowed, sharpened. He was disgruntled all the time, and very proud of the circus. He said that when he went into town to do the billing he felt better than anyone else there. He was doing what he wanted and he was free-spirited, and he had standards. When he walked out of his caravan in the morning, a very small caravan with no hot and cold water, a broken window, no heater, he looked sharp: shades, slicked-back hair, clean jeans, Timberlands. 'Morning, Nellie.' He never looked scruffy. He worked very hard and he was pushed around. That is what happens on your first ever season with a circus when you are a josser, when you are running away, when you are looking for some sort of affiliation, when you sleep with an iron bar under your bed, when you suddenly feel better than anyone else in town.

During that Sidcup winter, Brian worked in a pub up the road, and avoided the fighting there. He moved from a caravan to a lorry, and the roof of the lorry was made of fibreglass, and the cold sat on it and stared through. His gas bottle was wrapped in an old duvet. He painted the ring boxes, mended chairs, looked after the goats. He said that what he wanted to do eventually was train tigers and Dobermans. He was very good at selling and became a brilliant biller – even the RSPCA shops took his posters. What I suddenly saw through Brian was the heartlessness of showbusiness as a way of life: that hard work doesn't count for so very much – Brian wore himself out during that winter, but hard work doesn't count, only talent, just talent.

In the daytime I typed letters for Ernest. Eva made sand-wiches for lunch and we sat at the oilcloth table in the caravan and ate, drank a glass of wine, and outside, through the little windows, Land Rovers and pick-ups came and went from the farm, around the outside of the lorries. The dogs barked and their noise bounced off the sides of the lorries. Ernest stood up, pulled the curtain back a little and looked out of the window. He said that it was just Jake from the farm, and sat down again, took another bite of the sandwich. He opened a tin of olives.

'You don't mind if we do some more letters after lunch?'

'No.'

'You want another glass of wine?'

'It is Christmas.'

'Come on, let's have a drink, it is Christmas.'

Eva was looking at a copper coin on the table. She was tilting it so that it glinted in the light. 'Are you going to change your costume for next season, Nell?'

I had an idea in my mind that was not going to rest. I wanted to buy a horse and keep it with the circus. I had already men-tioned it to Ernest. 'Do you think I could keep a horse next season? I'll look after it and everything and it could open the show. At the beginning, when I make the first welcome to the circus and announce the first act, I could do it from the back of the horse. I think that the people would love it.'

Eva said she didn't see why not, and asked me if I knew where to buy a horse. I said that my aunt in Northumberland would help me to find one.

'Perhaps you could teach it *haute école*.'

The copper coin twisted and glinted and Eva said that it wasn't as easy as that, to teach the High School. There were so few people who did it any more. You needed money for that because you needed space and time. Who in the circus has space or time any more? Ernest stood up and took a bottle from the cupboard. He said that his back hurt – it was still hurting from the work in the season. 'When I was younger,' he said, 'I would catch my brothers on my shoulders when I was on the unicycle.' That was when he had damaged it. He sat down again. '*Si*, you buy a horse, you can keep it in the circus, that is not a problem.' He poured some more wine.

I had never looked after my own horse before and in my head I ran through, as I had many times before, the problems involved in keeping a horse in the circus. Transport. Stables. Pen.

'He can live in the stables with the other animals and he can travel in the big lorry with them.'

The traffic was still on the road. The coin was glinting and turning. Far away, through the window, I could see some horses grazing. They were like black steel animals.

At New Year we had supper in Grandpère's caravan. Anne Marie, Eva and I set the table. It was a large German caravan with a big table at one end, a kitchen in the middle and a bedroom at the end. There were African masks on the wall, and on the table there was usually a round biscuit tin with a clown's face and an old tapestried cloth woven with French hunting scenes. I used to sit in there with Grandpère, and he would make a cup of coffee and tell long anecdotes in French. I had no idea what he was talking about. He would laugh and gesticulate and point outside to the tent and say something about *les chèvres*, or a pigeon he kept that flew across the channel to France to join them, about the war, his sons, *le camion*. I liked the design on the tablecloth. I pointed to it. *La chasse. Oui. La chasse.* That evening, though, for New Year, Eva and Marie put down on the table a pink cloth and covered it with white plates and glasses, and plates of salami and gherkins and olives. There was enough room around the table for us all to sit down. I had bought some wine.

Suppers with that family extended right on through the night – it takes hours for plates of food to be carried from one caravan to the next, for bottles to be brought in from the cars. Supper was gradually assembled. It was warm and dimly lit: the gas heater flickered; under the shelves and behind the African masks were dark black shadows while on the surface of the masks the caravan lights gleamed and reflected.

Roget had been mending lorries all day and he looked tired. He sat down at the table and rubbed his face, which was red and laughing. His hair was black and full of frost. Anne Marie put slices of beef on the plates and poured some wine. The television was on, it always is in the circus, flickering away in the background. The door banged open and Eva came in from the dark cold outside. She was wearing a black sweatshirt that had 'WILD' written across it in sequins. She laughed, and her hair was falling over her shoulders.

We ate supper and watched Mick Jagger's *Rock and Roll Circus*. The crackers popped and we wore paper hats. Ruby played with some paper streamers, which caught and tangled in her blonde hair. Lucian slept in Anne Marie's arms. Her eyes were deep in the dim light and the candlelight from the table. Eva said that she never thought she would see in the New Year listening to Jethro Tull. Big Ben came and went. Ernest and Roget fell fast asleep, as they always did. Eva, Anne Marie and I watched a documentary about Elvis Presley. We all admired him. Eva said, 'Now, *that* is a real hero. They don't make heroes like that any more.' We drank some more wine and ate some biscuits Eva had made and listened to the voice singing. Both children fell asleep. The caravan was still warm and the curtains drawn to the night. I thought briefly about the horse. I would try to find a horse for next season. But that evening I was drunk and the caravan was close and hot and we were laughing – it was a suspended state and, in those moments, the future and the past didn't matter.

I went into Sidcup to buy some paper. I seemed to spend a lot of time in my caravan doing paperwork. As the day was ending I alighted from the bus on my way home, and walked along the edge of the main road, to the top of the lane. Soon I would leave Sidcup to go to Northumberland to look for this horse with my aunt. I walked down the hard little lane to the yard. The earth is spiked and waterless in the frost. The ground to my right slopes down the track where I am walking, and there is another path running up the field, along the side of a row of poplar trees. It is a black and white line in the landscape. Ahead of me is a pony on a tether. It hears my feet scratching on the ground and swings its head round to look at me. Behind it is the trapeze prop of thin metal, half against the ground and half against the white sky. There is a way to be navigated now, a horse in the future, somewhere, if I can find it, and deals to be done, people to watch out for. As I walk the painted lorries come into view, their white sides and coloured circus lettering, Santus Circus. There is a fire burning on the fields, the flames are orange and there is drifting smoke. The smell of burning comes through the frost, and the flames are orange in a monochrome world.

Horse

Look at the spotted horses, in white lordships' coats and with peppermint eyes, all spottered and plopped and studded and jetted and sprinkled and exploded all over with black. Each one is a Horse written out in a spotted language, with full spots and exclaims written all over them in Persian and Arabic, and with a Chinese poem written around their tails. If you could put all their black music together you could play a whole horse going Pom Pom, and call him Sonata, which is graceful like his neck. And all their red harness is doing them up like a Christmas. But they go by like the sea going away from the stones, and leaving only the stones tinkling in your ears and eyes.

The Circus, JUANITA CASEY

~

Horses are synonymous with circus. At first Astley's Circus was a horse show; clowns, human artists and wild animals were added later. English circus families, such as the Rossaires, are famous for horse training. In the past the presence of horses in the circus had enhanced blood lines and breeding stock throughout the country. Shows such as Bertram Mills' and Billy Smart's would carry up to a hundred horses. Many of the breeds that appear in the shows could not be seen elsewhere in the country: Billy Smart went to Shetland to find his Shetland ponies. Some people went to the circus with the intention of looking at the different types of blood horse. In the nineteenth century, the big shows, such as Sanger's Circus, where horses were used for transport as well as performance, would have had several hundred horses. The horse in the circus was an art form and an industry.

Today there are far fewer circus horses in England. This is because the majority of city councils ban all circus shows that contain performing animals. No other form of horsemanship is discriminated against in this way. The Lippizaners from Vienna may perform in Wembley Arena, you can see show jumping at Olympia, riders in Hyde Park, the household cavalry at Buckingham Palace. But circus horses are banned. Yasmin Smart, the daughter of Billy Smart, has ten horses. She has a Liberty act, and she does *haute école*, a form of dressage. Her uncle, Gary Smart, has a circus that does a short Christmas season every year in London. It is, perhaps, the best-presented circus in the country, and gives the contemporary audience a glimpse of what English circus was like fifty years ago. But there are no horses in the show, not even Yasmin's, because they are not allowed by the council. To see high-quality equestrian acts, large groups of Liberty horses, *haute école*, *la poste* – where two horses are ridden by one person standing on their backs – and all the pageantry and theatre that goes with these disciplines, it is necessary to go to Europe: to Alexis Gruss in Paris, Circus Krone in Denmark, Knie in Switzerland, Circus Roncalli in Germany, or to America and the Big Apple in New York, or Ringling Brothers. The large high-calibre horse acts cannot afford to work in England. The Bertram Mills' greys, Billy

Smart's famous group of jet black Friesians, all these horses have been sold abroad and the secrets of their training lost to English culture.

I left Sidcup at the end of January to drive to Northumberland and buy a horse with my aunt, Teesa.

My old red Sierra had broken down in the season. In the middle of the night when the circus was moving, the alternator stopped working and the car overheated. It ran for a week or so more, then early one morning it collapsed. We had been moving from Colchester to Basildon, and we had used the car to drive all the boys back to the old ground to pick up the second load of lorries. We left it by the side of the road and Ernest hitch-hiked back to pick up his car. That was a very late move – we didn't sleep at all that night. We towed the broken-down car on to the ground and I sold it that weekend at a car-boot sale in a field behind the circus. The two men who bought it were covered in oil, one had a beard, and they smoked roll-ups. They paid me the money and they asked if it would be all right to push it under the rope fence on to the track that led to the road. I said they could do what they liked with it. They asked for the key. It was pouring with rain, and my feet were soaking wet. The key to the car was tied to another key. The man with the beard shouted to his friend, 'Gotta knife, Reg?'

'What?'

He shouted through the rain. 'Gotta blade?'

Reg threw a knife across the path, his friend caught it and cut the string. Reg said that the police had arrested him before for carrying a knife. He said that they hated him. I didn't doubt it. They towed the car away and I didn't see them again. For the rest of the season Ernest lent me one of the show's vans to pull the caravan. It was a big red Mercedes with a clown's face painted on the side. Eventually I bought a new van in Sidcup from the man who ran the fruit and vegetable farm, an old Mercedes 608.

The day I left Sidcup for Northumberland, Anne Marie was practising the trapeze. It was rigged off a tall scaffolding prop. The air was freezing and the ground was rock hard. The children were buttoned up against the weather. Ruby was playing in a toy car and Lucian was in his pram. The trapeze was hanging from the prop, Anne Marie upside down on it, and Ruby screamed with excitement. Anne Marie hung by her toes. The trees in the far distance on the hill were ice clear and white at the edges. Traffic noise was coming from the road. Ruby was still screaming and running about. She wanted to hang from the prop by her hands. Anne Marie swivelled round, caught the bar with her hand and dropped to the ground.

Roget had a bag of props. Ruby was pulling at them. They were chrome rings and red velvet. They used to do a perch act, Roget explained. He worked off a metal pole, one foot in the loop and the other braced against the pole, which was hanging from the roof of the tent and Anne Marie worked off his hands. They spun neck to neck at the end. 'I loved my perch,' Anne Marie said. She lifted Ruby on to the bar, with the little girl's small red hands clasped. She hung there for a moment.

It was very cold and I was not looking forward to the drive north. I said goodbye to everyone and left.

Prince

Children nowadays would rather ride a pony than watch horses prancing in the sawdust.
Circus through the Ages, A. JENKINS

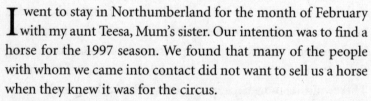

I went to stay in Northumberland for the month of February with my aunt Teesa, Mum's sister. Our intention was to find a horse for the 1997 season. We found that many of the people with whom we came into contact did not want to sell us a horse when they knew it was for the circus.

The day after I arrived in Northumberland, Teesa and I took two of her horses for a ride on the fell behind her house. I had not seen her since leaving Richie Richards' circus the previous Christmas. The grass was cold and wet and clung to the side of the bogs, the sheep scattered in all directions and the long irregular walls of bruised stones hugged the contours of the land. The sun was starting to set and burned very brightly on the horizon, the sky dark blue behind us and in front clear yellow and orange above the conifer woods, where yellow sap crept from under the bark and glowed in the light. We cantered up the field away from the farm. The horse I was riding pulled and plunged, it was fast and exciting, the noise of hoofs on the ground and the grass rushing away beneath me. I felt I could gallop for ever like that. Teesa was riding beside me, neck and neck, and she was still and poised on her horse's back. When we pulled up at the gateway at the top of the field I asked her if the horses frightened her, the riding, when she thought about Mum and that terrible accident. She said that once it did, she could hardly bear it. Now, though, she had got over it. She said you have to give fate a run for its money, and that you can't live your life in fear of an accident.

A lark was singing above the heather somewhere. There were no houses to be seen, not a road or a car or a shop, only these wide-open hills, valleys and heather. I rode behind Teesa along a stony track through the gorse bushes. I can hear the lark now, yes, I can hear it, I think, and I recognise the song, and this lark's song makes me think about Mum, and how she loved the fells, Northumberland, and being with Teesa, how they laughed and laughed together under the cold Northumbrian skies.

Teesa asked me what sort of horse I was looking for. I said it had to be eye-catching. It had to be a horse with presence. But Santus Circus was quite a small show, and the other animals were all very gentle. The public came round to look at them in the daytime, mentally handicapped people and children, and the animals all stood while they were stroked and went out on tethers in the daytime, so it had to fit in with this. It was a family show run by a family, kids everywhere, so a big energetic horse wouldn't be appropriate. It was getting dark. The evening was clear and some early stars were shining in the sky. A quiet, family-type horse, big enough to carry me, quiet but with a bit

of a sparkle. We rode down into a little valley, through a stream
and out of the dark shadows of the valley. We walked up the lane
to the farmyard, and by the time we got there, it was almost
dark.

Teesa's friend Liz came over and we wrote an advert for the
local *Free Ads* paper. Liz has big dark eyes and short black hair.
She is thin and moves elegantly, but she sends herself up. She is
a comic, she can do accents one after the other, posh then
Scottish then Geordie, and she splutters and slips reason, male
and female, leaving nothing standing on ceremony in the chaotic
wake of her satire. She outwits tragedy with comedy, and makes
sure that comedy triumphs.

This was what I wanted, a small flashy horse, a stallion or
gelding, with a bright eye and a long mane and tail – looks were
everything. He did not have to do anything athletic. He never
had to jump. I remember the small ring fence and the children
in the front row waving their sparkly wands and candy-floss
sticks. No, the horse definitely need not jump. In fact, it would
be better if jumping never crossed his mind. He had to look
good, unusual.

'Age?' asked Liz.

'Age not important,' I said.

'Well, you don't want an old horse, do you, Nell?' Teesa said.
'But you don't want a very young horse either. You won't have
time to bring it on.'

'Just don't mention age.'

'What about colour?'

'Spotted?'

'Checked, striped.'

'Not a black and white horse.'

'A brightly coloured horse.'

'An experienced horse.'

The telephone rang and it was a friend of Teesa's who dealt with horses. He said that he was off to Ireland to find the circus horse. The news of the hunt for the circus horse was spreading like wildfire over Northumberland.

This was the advert that we put in the Tyneside Supermart:

LOOKS ARE EVERYTHING. I AM SEEKING A FORWARD-GOING AND FLASHY HORSE THAT IS NOT NECESSARILY A NOVICE RIDE. BARBIE MANE AND TAIL IMPORTANT, AND THE MORE EYECATCHINGLY COLOURED THE BETTER, STRIPED, SILVER, SPOTTED OR CHECKED. THE HORSE NEED NOT BE A JUMPER BUT IT MUST TURN HEADS.

For a while there was no reply to the advert. Then a girl rang up from down the valley. She had an Arab for sale.

I drove to her farm to see the horse. The girl had a baby on her hip and long brown hair. The horse was standing in a long barn with a concrete floor. It was quite dark and a group of boys were eating sandwiches, crouched against the wall. The girl said that the horse was called Red, she never rode him as she never had time so he lived in the field. We took him out into the light and I rode him around a flooded outdoor school. He bent to the right and left and threw his head in the air. I think he had something wrong with his back. He wasn't the right horse. I thanked the girl and put him back in the field for her.

The next day a woman rang and said she had a high-stepping spotted horse, a real good-looker, and I arranged to have a look at it the following day. The same night a man called, sounding drunk. He said he had some nice horses in a field. He said he didn't charge for a look and hung up. A minute later he called back and asked if it was all a joke, then hung up again.

The next day Teesa and I drove to see the high-stepping spotted horse. The house on the hill where the woman lived was surrounded by white fencing. She appeared out of a stable door. She was thin and had blown-away dyed hair. She brought a small brown pony out of the stable and trotted it along a track for us, so that we could see it move. It tried to kick her in the face. We thanked her and left.

A few days later a man called Joe Mint rang. He said he had a quality animal, going well in any disciple, by which he meant discipline, just the job he said, and not an ounce of vice. I went for a ride on the fell. The day before we had seen some other horses at an immaculate yard in Edinburgh owned by a man who ran cruises in the Caribbean for old-age pensioners. He looked like a cartoon character in a huge yellow checked cap, or as though he was in disguise – he was even wearing a moustache. He showed us a unique collection of carriages, bright lacquer and fine spokes, kept carefully behind high sliding doors, the conversations of generations, passed between dead travellers, secret for ever behind the sealed black canvas hoods. He brought out a large spotted horse with a crazy eye. It galloped around the outdoor school, skidding into the corners and pressing on the rails. In my mind, the children in the front row of the circus waved their candy-floss sticks and sparkly wands, and the fat ladies who move slowly and love the front-row seats smiled and clapped, inert, immobile, and the horse in front of me slipped and snorted. It was nothing like a circus horse. Circus horses are highly domesticated. They are docile from constant contact with human beings. They often live to a much greater age than other horses – a troupe of Liberty horses may all be over twenty and still working because their work does not strain them. They do not jump, they do not carry heavy weights, they don't do many miles. The animals we saw in that yard were very fit, and in training for pulling carriages at speed in competition. I could hardly have taken a blind child for a ride on the spotted horse with the crazy eye.

A few days later we went to see Joe Mint's horses. The wind was blowing through his yard and leaves were collecting in little piles and pools, then blowing off again. Joe walked with a limp and talked with a grin. He banged open the stable door and a chestnut pony leaped out. He shouted at it and it snorted, raised its tail, and he raced it up and down the yard, its mane blown upwards towards the sky. I said it had a nice action, and Teesa explained that its action was all up and down, not moving anywhere. An Irishman who seemed to have appeared out of the wind agreed with her. Joe put the pony back in its box and Teesa and I followed him across the yard and over a gravel drive to look at some colts in an enclosure behind a high wire fence and some conifers.

Joe opened the gate into the paddock. 'Nice little colts these, mind,' he shouted to us. 'This one's just five hundred pounds.' He slammed the gate behind him. 'Five hundred pounds.'

'And not worth two,' Teesa said, and her voice carried to me then scattered on the wind.

'A very nice little colt,' he shouted, from behind the wire.

'Too much leg,' Teesa said to me, under the wind, and above it, loudly, 'Very nice.'

We didn't do a deal with Joe Mint.

It seemed to me that all the horses we had seen were perfect for the circus until you saw them, and then they were either too old, too young or too wild.

That day, on the way home from Newcastle we saw a Palomino horse, harnessed to a trap, being driven along the dual carriageway. It had a long mane flowing in the wind and a long tail, a short muscled arched neck. Teesa and Liz pointed to it at exactly the same moment.

'Isn't that exactly what you're looking for?'

'Stop the car.'

'You'll have to run to catch him.'

We pulled over and I ran back down the road after the horse. The lorries were going very fast and there were factories on either side of the road. Smoke and steam were coming from them. I shouted after the man driving the horse – they were moving away from me at some speed and I would never catch them. He didn't look round and I shouted again. A car blew its horn. The man with the horse glanced backwards over his shoulder but didn't see me. I shouted again, and again he looked round. This time he saw me and pulled the horse to a walk. I kept running and they stopped a few yards in front of me by the side of the road. I caught up with them. I was out of breath and the lorries kept overtaking. The horse stood stock still in the traffic. The man driving him was sitting in the little trap, laughing. I explained that I liked his horse, that was why I had run after them. The horse was shaking his head. He was blowing a bit and regarding me through his long mane with a corner of a backward-swivelled eye.

'Jump in,' the man said.

I did, and we went off at a fast trot down the dual carriageway, with this little curved sand-coloured shiny back moving in front of us, a blown cream-coloured mane and two small curved ears pointed forward to the road and framing the bland tarmac.

This Palomino was called Prince. He was a stallion and he was used for driving. The man said he was a grand little horse. He didn't need to sell him to me. I could see the stars and the tent

and the canvas and the people and the light and the ring boxes
and the sawdust behind him already. He was the ubiquitous
horse of the child's cut-out scrapbook, a horse of St Mark's
Square in Venice, a Swift horse, a tired horse on the Elgin
Marbles dragging the moon away from approaching day, a war-
rior's horse, a charger, a hero, a travelling horse, the favourite
horse, the horse inside at tea-time, a horse swimming in the sea,
an anonymous circus horse in an unsigned watercolour with a
clown handstanding on his back.

I bought Prince from the man and, at the end of February,
took him south to the circus.

Circus Horse 1997

In common with most modern circus animal trainers, my experience has been gained mainly by assisting and watching older members of my family and other experienced circus trainers.

Classical Circus Equitation, H.J. LIJSEN AND
SYLVIA STANIER

~

A friend of mine, who makes circus tents, built a small lean-to tent to come off the side of my Mercedes van. On one side it tied off to the roof rack and on the other it was supported by three six-foot-high poles. It had a pitched roof and stood about eleven-foot square. It was made of red and white plastic canvas. It contained within it an eight-foot square stable. I had this made up in Cheltenham, and it was where Prince lived at night. It was very heavy – it unbolted into nine sections. The lower half of the pen was made of marine ply and angle iron, and the top half was heavy mesh and angle iron. It had a door at the front and could be staked down at each corner. Prince was an exceptionally strong horse, so it was imperative that he felt secure and contained within the stable. I kept all the equipment I needed for him in the back of the van, and used the front half as a dressing room – Herbie had built a partition half-way down the inside of the van. In the daytime Prince would live on a tether, so that he could graze.

Andrew, my friend in Cheltenham, lent me his horse trailer to take Prince to the first ground. My caravan was already there as it had stayed with the circus throughout the winter and they had towed it to the first ground for me. We arrived in the evening at a sloping ground somewhere on the A12, just off the North Circular Road on the outskirts of London. The road ran along one side of the ground and there was no fence between it and the fast cars and lorries. The tent was up and caravans were parked around the outside of it. Jason, standing on the roof of his lorry fixing the satellite dish, waved as I approached. He saw the horse box behind the van. 'You're not going to have a horse this year, are you, Nellie?' he shouted.

I waved back. Ernest had asked me not to mention to any of the artists or workers on the circus that I was bringing a horse. This secretiveness is completely normal for the circus. Each season the changing elements of the show – artists, workers, animals, perhaps family, even the tent itself – are kept as strict secrets. This is to avoid interference from other shows, such as theft of ground or ideas, sabotage of artists' work permits, and troublemaking in general. I felt very nervous. I parked the van beside my caravan and the stable tent. I put Prince's little tent up. All the sections of the pen were on the roof of the van. I climbed up on to the roof rack, untied them, and passed them down to Roget. The grass was fairly level beside the van and the pen went up easily. The boys were putting the wallings on the main stable tent, whistling and calling in the half dark. Brian was there, and a new boy called Adam, who was going to be working in the stables, and a tall boy in a baseball jacket. I didn't recognise him. 'Who's that?' I asked Brian. He said that it was Robert, Ernest's nephew, who had joined the show for the season. I unloaded Prince with Roget and put him in the stable. Any variation in routine or expectation is a cause for excitement in the circus and people crowded around his pen.

'Lovely, isn't he?'

'He's gorgeous.'

'Nellie's new goldfish.'

'How much did you pay for him?'

'Strong-looking horse.'

'Perfect for bareback riding.'

Prince stared back with surprise and curiosity, a horse's own mixture of intrigue and threat communicated in the turn of his eyes and the flick of his ears. The boys continued to put up the wallings of the stable tent. The canvas was rustling and squeaking. The camels watched, with wisps of hay in their mouths, and the Shetland ponies were eating their feed. Adam came down out of the horse lorry with an armful of hay. Roget, a cigarette in his mouth, called to Adam to stand on Brian's shoulders, then climb up and shut the vents on the animals' lorry. They were banging and clacking in the wind. I was wary of Prince's reaction to the other animals and the constant movement of people in the dark and, besides, I felt self-conscious and quite alone standing in the uncertain darkness with a brand new stallion. Adam jumped down off the ramp, pulled himself up the side of the lorry and on to the roof, then made his own silhouette high up against the indigo-turning sky. He ran across the roof to the vents.

'Where did you learn that, eh, Adam?' Robert laughed. He was tall, with slightly hunched shoulders, and a loud laugh.

'Comes in useful being a cat burglar, dunnit, Adam?' Brian called to him.

Adam closed the vents, then swung down off the side of the

lorry on a length of chain hanging off the end. He laughed and karate-punched the air, and Brian was laughing and saying that he was a good South London boy. I could hear Claire calling to her dogs in the darkness. 'Skooby! Flossy!' The road was still very busy.

Brian was helping Roget with the hay in the stable tent, going beyond the call of duty, making himself indispensable because now the circus was all he had. Lights were going on in the caravans. Prince sniffed at some hay and watched the movement outside his pen – the tent was there, rearranging the landscape. It was cold early spring and the 1997 season had just started.

Claire and Elaina were happy to see each other again. They had decided last season that they were best friends. We resumed our duties: Elaina cleaned out the shop trailer; Claire and I did our shifts in the box-office. After Elaina had worked a couple of times, upside down on the trapeze, swinging and spinning at the same time she said that her back hurt – it was the same every year she said, it took a few weeks to get used to the hard work again. Claire had rested all winter and she was brimming over with health. She said she couldn't wait to wear her new costume. She said she was buzzing – she took it easy in the winter.

I sat in the box-office in the morning and sold tickets to the first customers. I could see Prince from the window, on the area of grass to the far left. He grazed quietly. Sometimes he trotted around at the end of his tether, neighed and looked around or shook his head, but mainly he just grazed. He was like a baby: there was no moment of the day when, consciously, or unconsciously, I was not listening for him, for a neigh or the sound of his hoofs on the grass. Prince's safety became my overwhelming concern.

Gypsies started to arrive at the circus – out of curiosity, or to try to buy things. One woman asked me if I had a nice little caravan for sale. Some bought tickets. The circus is suspicious of gypsies, because they steal generators; they come at crafty times, such as when the show is on and they know that all the circus people will be busy in the tent. Last season two gypsies had tried to break into Roget's van, but the dogs barked a racket and Roget chased them away.

A man parked outside the box-office in a Ford flat-bed. He opened the door of the lorry and stepped out on to the grass. He walked with a limp. A child followed him out of the cab, wearing a turquoise T-shirt. She had straight blonde hair and small eyes. The grass was shining with the oncoming spring and on the road the cars were glinting. The gypsy walked to the window. He had dark hair and a pink face. He had a slight Irish accent and he bought tickets for himself and the child. The wooden boards against the cab of the flat-bed were painted red. A car hooted on the road. They got back into the lorry and drove away.

Up to the right, a couple of hundred yards from the box-office, before a stretch of high chain-link fencing, there was a big lorry that sold fruit and vegetables. It was painted in high sign letters that said Bonzer Boot Fair. There was a little café in a caravan, too, and once I saw a rat, in the daytime, run right across the entrance to the ground. A girl walked past the box-office to look at the poster of the clown with the balloon over his shoulder. She was smoking a cigarette with absurd stiff fingers, her mouth a round circle of lipstick. She didn't buy a ticket, but a few minutes later some children came to the window. They asked for free tickets, then laughed like men and giggled like children and ran away.

I turned round in the swivel chair and through the glass

window of the door I could see the tent, coloured in broad running stripes of green and yellow, the sun lighting the colours and the shadows leaping underneath the flaps of the edge. There is a minute grain on the stretched ropes that anchor it to the ground, a pattern on the paint on the inside of a steel pole, grain in the steel, the sun catching one side of a blade of grass, darkness on the other, and variations yet within that darkness. The circus tent is immensely, spectacularly beautiful. The side poles come through the steel patches in the side of the tent roof and are held upright by stretched ropes, which pull down to the ground, on all sides. The king poles are way up in the air, coming down through the tent to the ring below from a higher point. They are hard silver and the blue sky is beyond, the flags blowing in the wind away from their anchoring poles. The king poles are held up by two tightly stretched cables, and two reach down to the coppolla, two across to the opposing king pole, and one down and away to the king-pole stakes, which are driven into the ground. This was the extent of the tent's geometry that I could see through the glass window. When a circus tent is set in a landscape the landscape seems to change around it.

Last night there had been some handicapped people in the show, and a lady in the front row who might have been Mum. She wore a neat shirt and a jersey. It made me so sad, and I could see the infinite suffering caused by such damage to the brain, the despair she must have had within her, and I was dismayed in contemplation of the gentleness of my mother's character still evident among the confusion of neural damage. 'Ladies and gentlemen, Elaina!' – and I wanted to throw down the microphone and run out of the ring and back to the tent and hide in the van. I wanted someone to come and comfort me, to be sympathetic, to feel with me the black and insurmountable nature of this type of pain. I did not want to be brave, to hold it back (don't cry); though I had to be brave and deal with it silently, behind a smile, with the sparkle and flash of fishnet, and I felt like a doll with a smile at the front of its head and a sad mouth when you turned it round.

Claire took over her shift in the box-office at lunch time. She had a cup of coffee in her hand and a pile of magazines under her arm. She said I seemed very tired. 'Why are you so tired all the time?'

'I keep worrying about Prince.'

'He'll be all right.'

'I'm going to practise him in the ring today. You can't rehearse an audience, though, can you?'

'Not really. Are you going to start training him?'

She looked me in the eye and I looked away. I said that for the moment I just wanted him to go into the ring in front of the people and be confident.

After that I went back to the caravan. I washed up, swept the floor and made my bed. There were a couple of hours before the show, so I went out and brought Prince in from his tether. The tent was empty, and we could practise in the afternoon.

Spring 1997

Don't be croth with uth poor vagabondth. People mutht
be amuthed. They can't be alwayth a-learning, nor yet
they can't be alwayth a-working, they an't made for it.
You mutht have uth, thquire. Do the withe thing and the
kind thing too, and make the betht of uth; not the wurtht!

Hard Times, CHARLES DICKENS

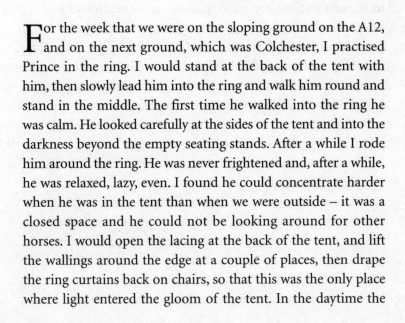

For the week that we were on the sloping ground on the A12, and on the next ground, which was Colchester, I practised Prince in the ring. I would stand at the back of the tent with him, then slowly lead him into the ring and walk him round and stand in the middle. The first time he walked into the ring he was calm. He looked carefully at the sides of the tent and into the darkness beyond the empty seating stands. After a while I rode him around the ring. He was never frightened and, after a while, he was relaxed, lazy, even. I found he could concentrate harder when he was in the tent than when we were outside – it was a closed space and he could not be looking around for other horses. I would open the lacing at the back of the tent, and lift the wallings around the edge at a couple of places, then drape the ring curtains back on chairs, so that this was the only place where light entered the gloom of the tent. In the daytime the tent smelt of crushed grass and plastic, it smelt of sawdust, and the sugary smell of yesterday's popcorn – it smelt of the circus. Sometimes someone would walk round the outside of the tent and I could see their clogs on the grass under the wallings, or the dogs would bark outside, and sometimes the boys would practise juggling behind the curtains, but mainly the tent felt empty and silent.

After that I would stand Prince at the back of the tent just before the show started, so that he would get used to the music and the lights and the motion of people around him. Again, he was quiet and relaxed. He didn't flinch. A balloon burst, the music crackled, juggling clubs turned and spun in the air. His eyes were looking backwards and his ears flickered, but he stood calm and still. I felt that we were being watched, not by Ernest and Roget, who wanted to see him going well for the show, but by the artists, who seemed to like him, and joked about him . . . but still, out of the corner of their eyes, they were waiting for me to make a mistake, waiting to declare him dangerous. The monotony of circus life and the pressure of living together makes for this type of response – support, yes, but edgy competitiveness, little plays of power in the turn of an eyeball.

At the end of one of the shows in Colchester I brought Prince into the back of the tent while the generator was still running and the lights were on. I did a rehearsal with him: through the curtain and into the spotlit ring. Of course there was no audience but otherwise the conditions were identical to going into the ring for real. Ernest said that I should practise it twice. Prince startled at the curtains, and raced into the ring, but he was not frightened, and Ernest said that he could work at the next ground. That evening I rode him around in front of the circus. The lights were on in big metal letters above the box-office.

SANTUS CIRCUS. Behind, the tent gleamed and reflected the light, and light drifted over the plastic, which shuddered and flickered in the wind. There was a wide, dusty piece of ground in front of the tent, surrounded on three sides by a motorway. I felt secure with Prince: he had accepted the new routing of life in the circus, he was petted and admired and he enjoyed the constant company of other people and animals. He was not frightened of the tent and did not seem alarmed by the ring. I had to admit to myself that he did not do anything in particular: he just trotted around the ring. That burned at the back of my mind: Prince was not an act. But, still, these were early days, and I enjoyed among these doubts the new freedom of the knowledge that Prince was mine and that I could do as I pleased with him. There was no screaming Richie Richards jangling his keys and lurking around every corner, and no one ordering me to muck out. I just looked after my own horse.

Prince was learning to be a circus horse. I felt a desire to compensate for my lack of experience with training horses for the circus by making sure that he was enjoyed by other people. The children in the circus would run after him and implore me to let them ride him. 'Ride Prince? Ride Prince?' they would beg, and I would lift them up and they would ride him a few steps over to the tent. Prince became one of the animals in their vocabulary. Prince, Copper the pony, the Shetlands – Bertie, Cesar and Spot, Snowy the goat, Rahnee the elephant, Bambi the rabbit and so on.

One morning in Colchester a woman came to the box-office and asked me if the circus would give a reduction for a blind child. The next day at lunchtime she brought the child to visit the animals. She was a tiny blonde-haired girl of about eight. She was completely blind and, lacking visual stimulation, chatted constantly. She wanted to know what was making this noise, where the tent was, and she wanted to know about the animals so that she could appreciate their sizes. We took her all the way round the outside of the tent and we took her into the tent and shouted so that she could hear the echo and sense the scale on the inside. We took her into the stable and Roget was there with the animals. I explained to him that the little girl was blind. He put down his pitchfork and lifted her up in his wide strong arms so that she could touch the elephant. In the background she could hear the chickens clucking in the wire pen outside Roget and Anne Marie's caravan and asked what that noise was. We walked over to them and Roget stepped inside the pen with her and let her bury her hand in a chicken's feathers. The circus was wrapping itself around her senses: she stopped chattering, listened harder, fitted the sounds together. After that I took her for a ride on Prince. She sat on him, and Roget held her there and we walked around the tent, within the guy ropes. 'Duck,' we said to her, 'duck now!' and she ducked her head under the ropes as Prince walked below them, and she laughed. Then I knew that I had found the right horse for the circus.

On the weekend just before we left Colchester the animal-rights protestors started to arrive. For the outsider the volume of aggression directed at the circus is surprising, and the animal-rights protestors were not the only example of the deep-rooted mistrust of travelling people that exists within Britain.

The situation with animals and the circus is not complicated; there are some instances of cruelty to animals in the circus, but from this we cannot deduce that all circuses are cruel. There are good and there are bad, as with all forms of animal husbandry. The animals at Santus Circus were domesticated, and they were cared for with sympathy and love. The animal-rights protestors who turn on the circus do so as a reflex, equating without thought the word 'circus' with 'cruel'. It is as if the animal-rights issue is used as an excuse rather than a reason to attack the circus. Boards are smashed, lorries vandalized, violent letters left anonymously at the box-office, and every conceivable authority summoned: health and safety, the RSPCA, local vets, the police, the trading standards authority. The men in suits walking daintily about the ground are bad news.

Circus people are not anarchists, but they are loathed and feared by society, and driven on to rubbish-tips and wastelands because no one else will have them. Their aged fathers are insulted, their property smashed or taken away by the council men. They cannot advertise on the road, the few brave shops who take the posters have bricks flung through their windows.

And direct action is not the only way in which the circus in England is painted black. Circus books and information about circus culture have been removed from schools and libraries. Circus no longer features in children's stories. The downgrading of the circus in England seems to reach out like ripples from a stone thrown into water. Circus words – clown, circus itself – are used in literature in a derogatory sense. The definition of circus in the *Oxford English Dictionary* is wholly prosaic and specific, whereas the French dictionary *Larousse* defines circus as a circular area for performance: it is a conceptual definition that allows room for the idea that a circus need not be travelling, and pinpoints the essential component of the circus – the ring.

The standard Soviet dictionary defines circus as a 'type of theatrical art' and, in correspondence with this, the Russians take circus seriously. The Moscow State Circus School is a prestigious institution with exacting standards. Only a few candidates pass their difficult entrance examination. There are circus schools in England but they are easier to join and have less cultural status. In general, English circus people are snobbish about the product of these schools and so, due to fault on both sides, a barrier is formed between potential new talent and the traditional circus. In my experience, talented jossers feed more easily into the circus system if they are from Eastern bloc countries, because there, standards are upheld. Circus is being ironed out of our culture, rubbed out, dropped: it is becoming the word that doesn't mean anything any more. The animal-rights protestors are the tip of a catastrophic iceberg. Long gone are the days when the people would visit the shows to see collections of horse breeds, to see quality craftsmanship of every sort. Like a church building, the circus should present ideal examples. The great European shows demonstrate ideal carpentry, lighting, vintage vehicles, athleticism. Such things don't exist on the shows in England any more, and the real sadness is that nobody cares.

The circus had put some boards up on the main dual carriageway outside Colchester. A council man rang and said that they must be taken down or the circus would be fined ten pounds per board. I walked round to Roget's lorry from the box-office to pass the message on. 'Under clause such and such of the highways and byways . . .' Roget was in the back of his lorry, mending something. I told him about the council man. The lorry had a brown carpet and dog kennels and coils of rope and the laundry. The back door sat at an angle when it was open as the bottom hinge had rotted away with rust. He looked tired. His eyes were red and his hair ran into them. He sighed through his nose with his mouth shut and swept back his hair with his hand. He looked me in the eye. He said that you couldn't do anything any more. He was fed up with it. He wanted to go back to

France. He said that the English people were hard to please. 'How can we be entertaining people when we have nothing left to feel proud of?'

Roget said that he had been down recently, so down that he just wanted to talk to someone who would listen to him or write it down himself. Ernest and Roget and their four brothers used to work as a big family troupe, until about ten years ago, with a juggling and unicycling act. Ernest would ride a unicycle and catch Roget on his shoulders, or Anne Marie would jump on a Russian bar and land head to head on Ernest's head. They are masters of circus arts. I remember Ernest's disgust when he spoke about the contemporary English clown, a silly figure running about in the ring making rude noises. His understanding of a clown was somebody who could juggle, tumble, play an instrument, improvise, mime. Clowning to him was a meticulous, complicated form of artistic expression, not an icon on a perpetual loop of hamburger sales.

I didn't know what to say to Roget: there was a gulf between us, as I had never been discriminated against in this way. I was with the circus, but miles away from the real feeling of their anguish. Eva said to me that I would never know the pain of the circus.

On the last Sunday at Colchester the animal-rights protestors arrived at the ground. They had their banners and their placards and they stood in front of the show and shouted at the circus. I knew they were there because all the boys were at the front of the show. I was just about to take Prince into the back of the tent ready to start the show. I heard Ernest shouting to Roget to leave them, and I heard more shouting. Grandpère had gone out on his fold-up bicycle to confront them. He makes all the boards that sit beside the box-office, cuts up posters to make a découpage of clowns and lettering, SANTUS CIRCUS SANTUS CIRCUS.

A girl in a green jacket was breaking one of the boards in half. He pulled it out of her hands and shouted in lost French swear words. She turned on him. 'FUCK OFF, YOU OLD GIT, YOU'LL BE DEAD SOON ANYWAY!'

Roget heard her shouting. He ran over and screamed back, 'LEAVE MY FATHER ALONE, YOU BITCH.'

She shouted back, 'YOU FUCKING CHILD MOLESTING BASTARD. YOU LIKE TORTURING ANIMALS, EH?'

In the summer Roget's little daughter rode the spotted pony to a car-boot sale. Ernest led it through the long grass.

Ernest shouted to Roget to leave them alone. I went into the back of the tent.

A few minutes later Roget and Anne Marie appeared in the back of the tent with the goats, ready for the show. They stood holding their leads while the goats grazed. Roget was shaking and his eyes were more red. He said that he couldn't let them say those things about his father. I asked Anne Marie if they would change their mind if someone showed them round the stables. She said that they didn't care. She said that they were totally mad. They would do anything. Last year they had tried to burn down the stables. Lucian was in his push-chair and Ruby was standing beside her. She looked frightened and hounded. She drew on a cigarette and shook her head. 'Christ knows what they will do,' she said to herself. Ernest walked around the corner of the tent and blew the whistle for the start of the show. Suddenly it was freezing cold. Through the wallings I could see grit and dust being blown across the ground. I picked up the microphone and unravelled the lead ready for the show.

Pigeons

The show moved from Colchester towards East Anglia. Prince did his début. The curtains closed behind us. I leaned forward and patted his neck, then jumped off and ran with him out of the tent and back across the ground to his stable. The timing was tight; I had to put Prince in his stable, then pull off the long skirt that I wore over the saddle, and put on my top hat and tails. Prince and I opened the show like this throughout the 1997 season. He was always well behaved in the ring, we were never late and he was always perfectly turned out. But at the back of my mind there remained a doubt as to the validity, in circus terms, of Prince's appearance in the ring.

One afternoon, Elaina suggested that I should wear a white skirt when I rode into the ring on Prince, with white feathers in my hair. She said that Prince could wear white feathers too. I asked Eva about this and she was quiet. Then she said that some people might seem to be giving me advice but in fact they were trying to make me look silly. She said that the *haute école* riders never wore feathers. She said that I would be better in a blue habit riding side-saddle and performing a few simple *haute école* movements. I remember that I reacted angrily to her suggestion. How could I do all this without assistance in training the horse? She said that she agreed, but she said I must remember that circus was an art and that like any other art it had rules.

I saw Elaina from the window of my caravan walking across the ground in some pink washing-up gloves. She was on her way to the tent to clean out the shop, the little trailer beside the seating stand where she and Anne Marie sold hot dogs, cups of tea and white candy-floss. She was wearing a blue tracksuit and trainers, and walked with her feet out and her arms swinging. Recently she had looked very ill and depressed. Before the show she appeared round the side of the curtains from the shop rattling her bunch of keys and pulling a cigarette from the pockets of her navy overcoat. It had a checked collar and she wore it over her costume for selling the hot dogs. Her face was disgruntled and in pain. 'You OK, Elaina?' I asked.

The broken Romanian flowed hard. 'No, I am not fucking OK. I have a pain here and I don't want to work. I am fucking knackered. Every day I just work and I am more tired when I wake up than when I sleep.' She pulled off her overall and hauled and snapped her fishnets. Every way she moved was aggressive. When she played pool the cue was a weapon, her body was an argument, and her voice carried far. If there had been softness in her personality it had all gone. For her act she entered the ring in a sparkly coat. One ground was wet, the ring flooded, and the damp air settled on our lungs like a leech. The boys laid down duckboards and as she entered the ring she lifted her cloak to avoid the water, like a lady in a rainstorm. Then she climbed the rope to the trapeze. She was attached to the bar of the trapeze by one metal cable, her 'longe'. (She called it her longe as her Romanian accent was very pronounced.) But she didn't care. She forgot her lunge one day and did the last and hardest trick anyway. If she had fallen she would have died. Ernest cursed her at the ring curtain, and as she left the ring I lifted my top hat to her, because I could not help but be in awe of her unremitting nerve and physical precision. She ducked under the walls of the tent, out of view, and into the darkness inside.

Prince was on his tether and his head was down, grazing. In a while I had to bring him into his pen to clean him for the show. I decided to go and speak with the new clown; he had arrived at the circus at this ground. I walked across the grass and knocked on his door. It banged open and his broad face looked around the side. He was sitting at the table, just to the left of the door. 'Come in.'

I kicked off my clogs and stepped into the bare clean caravan.

'Sit down here, at the table. You want coffee?'

'Yes, please.'

'Here is a cigarette.' He slid a sawn-off beer tin across the table to me. It was full of cigarette ends. 'My wife has to buy many things for the caravan.' He wanted to know if there were many problems in this country for the animals. I said there were many problems like this for the circus in England. He stared at me, right in the eye, not taking his from mine, even when he was smoking. He tipped his head to one side. 'It is a very shit situation.'

He stubbed out the cigarette and looked down. Very shit for the circus. His wife was putting the kettle on the gas. There were no ornaments, except for a photograph of a clown in a frame, a clock, and a calendar on the wall with the times of the shows written on it in biro. His wife picked up a lighter off the table and lit the tip of a toothpick; it burned black. His daughter was a small child and she was sitting beside me. She twisted round in her seat and looked out of the lace curtains behind. 'Horse,' she said, and looked at me.

'That's Prince,' I said.

She repeated slowly, 'Prinze.'

'You from a circus family?'

'No,' I replied. 'I just love the circus.'

The clown laughed and shook his head. 'You are like me, my friend, you are not normal.'

'What is your name?'

'Marine. This is my daughter Maya and my wife Benni.'

Maya touched my arm and stroked the wool of my jersey. She sat round on the seat and ate some crisps from a bag.

'You have a very nice horse.'

'I want to make an act, though.'

Marine nodded. The child beside me rolled a marble across the table and he caught it before it fell off the edge, and held it in his fist. He leaned forward, holding the marble between his forefinger and thumb, and looked through it with one eye. A twist of colour spiralled through the glass centre.

'Must make your own way. Must follow your own way.'

He stopped and lit another cigarette. He started to explain about an act in Bulgaria but I couldn't understand what he was saying. I thought he was talking about a girl who rode a horse with wings. He sighed, leaned back and addressed his wife, who was stirring three cups of coffee. He said something to her in Bulgarian and she replied without turning around. He said something else. She nodded. She started to speak slowly, in

English. 'This girl she had a horse and she would ride around the ring, and she, on her arms, you know, these birds, like the ones for carrying the letters, you know, these white birds.'

'Pigeons.'

'Yes, these peejens. She would sing a song for the circus, for the ring.' The R was lost in the word, curling down into the dialect. He nodded.

'It was a very lyric number.'

'Lyric?'

'Yes, a lyric number. You must think of something then practise every day. Make plenty practice.'

Benni put the coffee in front of us and sat down beside Marine. She put her elbow on the table and lit a cigarette. There was a television on the shelf beside the table and it was on, though nobody was watching it. Marine explained to me that he had trained in the circus school in Moscow for seven years. He said that he had had to practise hard when he was there. He always wanted to be a clown, though. It was the only thing that interested him. Marine communicated in statements. He said: 'The circus is not theatre. The clown is not an idiot.'

The child laughed beside me and Marine rolled the marble back across the table. Benni said something abrupt in her own tongue and the child sat quiet. 'I have to go and bring the horse in now. I have to go.'

They nodded seriously and said 'Thank you for the company.'

'Thank you for the coffee. See you later on.'

Outside a fine rain had started to fall and the wooden soles of my clogs outside the door were damp and glistening.

Night Time

'I am an idiot but I am Marine.'
                        MARINE, CIRCUS CLOWN, 1997

~

The day was ending. I had done two shows and was finishing Prince for the night. He had settled into a routine. As the show was ending, he would hear the music of the last act and start to neigh and bang on the sides of his pen. In the stables the animals were eating their hay. Some light came through the gaps in the wallings and from the coloured lightbulbs at the top of the tent, but there was more shadow than dark. The tent was laced up and I had in my arms a pile of hay for Prince. The camels followed my movements with their heads, then leaned over the railings to catch at wisps of hay with their lips.

As I went back under the wallings Adam, the boy who worked in the stables, was coming the other way with a bucket of water. I saw a dark shape against the plastic and heard him swearing to himself. He appeared under the edge of the wallings, and put the bucket he was carrying over the railings for the camels, and stroked their noses. He was tall and thin and wore a baseball jacket all the time. He ate Twix bars for supper, about eight of them. He said that Roget bought him croissants too, and he had them as well, two a day. He was eighteen. His face committed him to nothing. Yesterday we were standing in the back of the tent waiting for the show to start. I did up Prince's girth and set the cassettes for the show. Adam brought in the donkey and the goats, and tied them to the side pole. The geese were waiting in their crate. 'Make a lovely fur coat, wouldn't you, Prince?' he says.

'Piss off, Adam.'

'No, he would, lovely fur coat, and his tail would make a lovely hat for an old lady in the hairdresser.'

'Best horse in the world, this.'

'Lovely fur coat,' and he walked over to peer round the side of the curtain at the audience. 'A whole fucking tribe of pikies in there tonight. They'd love your horse, pinch him in the night, burn off his freeze mark.'

I don't like to think of anyone touching Prince, and I know the dangers of those people whistling and calling on the other side of the curtain.

He walked over to Prince. 'Yep, burn off his freeze band and say it happened in a fire.'

I turned round and hit him. He ducked and laughed.

'Fucking court case in two months, ten-thousand-pound fine, like what I was telling you about yesterday, caught driving a car seventeen times without a licence. Now my mum's going away and I've got to go home and look after my little brother, fucking little sod he is too.'

'Where's your dad?'

'Dunno. I'm adopted. Well, not adopted. Found in a phone box when I was a baby.'

I turned down the music a bit and made the five-minute announcement into the mike. The people on the other side of the curtain knew that the show would start soon, ladies and gentlemen no flash photography, no video recording during the performance, and ditto, no smoking in the big top (again), and could the audience refrain from running about on the tiered seats for their own safety and other people's. Thank you. Adam mimicked my voice, no smoking in the beg torp, and he stroked Prince's nose. Prince shook his head up and down and shifted his weight from one foot to the other at the back. That is what I did every day, stood behind the curtains and swapped joked insults with Adam. In the stable tent the camels dipped their noses into the water. 'Good night, Adam,' I said. 'Going to the pub tonight?'

'I've got eight cans of lager in my caravan. I'll just have them and listen to music.'

'What music?'

'Soul.'

'Can you lift the walling for me a minute? Else I'll drop this hay everywhere. It's for my fur coat, for the night, greedy, he is.'

Adam lifted the wallings, and just before I went under them and into the indigo evening he told me to look out for the big cloud across the sky. He said, 'There's a big cloud. First of the seven signs,' he was laughing, 'the end of the world, Nellie.' He lifted the wallings and followed me out underneath them. Outside a heavy thick black cloud was being dragged over the darkening sky, bringing with it curtains of rain and its own cold winds. Adam was wearing a baseball cap, his eyes were wide open and his lips pulled back. 'Look at the cloud,' he said, 'the first of the seven signs.'

The sky was growing darker and darker, and the puddles were

reflecting the light; they looked ice cold and bright white. The wind was blowing and a child was rattling the gate of the caravan door and laughing The sky seemed to be sealing itself up with darkness and the wind threatened to carry unwelcome rain.

I took Prince his hay. He ignored me as I went through the flap into his tent and opened his stable door because he had his head in his feed bucket. I dropped the hay in the corner and took his water bucket to fill. As I was standing beside the water barrels Marine and Maya appeared out of the dark.

'You want drink whisky tonight?' Marine asked. Maya was standing right beside him, looking up at him. Her stature was identical to his, very upright, arms slightly out from the body. She skipped and bounced when she walked, and she could do a handstand in the palm of his hand. He lifted her like this, upside down, right above his head. He said that he was feeling very nervous because of the public tonight, no good public. He said that the public had made him nervous.

'OK,' I replied. I knew I had a full bottle in my caravan.

At that moment, behind Marine, three figures were walking towards us. I vividly recognised the gait of the first: it was a friend, Vladimir, whom I met at Oxford, who was more or less my best friend while I was there. I was happy to see him and gave him a hug. Marine was still standing beside the water barrel, looking at Vlad with curiosity. I introduced them. 'This is Vladimir,' and Marine said something to him that I didn't understand. They laughed and Vlad replied, also in Russian. The rain was falling heavily now. I thought we should go inside. The two others with Vlad were Plum and Giles, who were also at college with me. The rain gusted and Marine took Maya's hand. He said he would be five minutes, and something else in Russian. He vanished round the side of the stable tent.

I had to finish Prince for the night, lace up the tent and give him the bucket of water. The surface of the water in the barrel was breaking and circling with the falling water drops and it had an orange light from the lights on the road fanning across it in crescents.

'Where is your caravan, Nell?' Vlad asked, and I pointed to it across the ground.

'I'll be two seconds with Prince. Good to see you two as well.' Plum was grumbling in the rain and Giles was smiling. 'Two seconds, help yourselves to whisky from the cupboard.'

It seemed strange to see these people I had known at university in the circus. I thought of my first few weeks as an undergraduate: I had been miserably unhappy and had lain in my bed crying and listening to people carousing along Holwell Street. The doctor prescribed me anti-depressants and I took the first one after drinking heavily. I woke up in the morning with a mouth like sandpaper and unable to walk straight or focus my eyes. It was cold, mid-October, and I put on the synthetic fur coat Mum had bought me, and walked out along the road to Blackwell's. I stood at the back of the shop looking at the books and I remember being excessively hot and unhappy. I started to cry, for morose self-pity and confusion. Vlad, a fellow first-year English student, was in the shop looking at books too and, although I was looking at the ground, he peered into my face and asked me if I was all right. He said to come to the pub for a drink, and we walked out of the shop and down Broad Street. Vlad has a long stride and bowed legs, and he looks forward, his eyes narrowed, as he is short-sighted; he squinted to look down the street. From that moment on we were best friends. In the first year we had rooms on the same staircase; in the daytime we used to sit and drink black coffee, and at night whisky. Vlad never

really did much, apart from drink pints of coffee and read intel-
lectual books or comics. There was a kind of listlessness to life in
Oxford; but this was probably due to personal laziness than the
atmosphere of the city, although when I think about Oxford I
can just remember dark streets at night, high stone walls, the
sound of parties coming from indiscernible windows and people
sitting in pubs. We shared a house in the second year, and when
Minety was sold Rick bought for me and Clover a house in
Marlborough Road, which is in South Oxford, where from time
to time I lived again with Vlad and a lot of other people. Vlad
used to spend the day sitting at the table in Marlborough Road,
drinking his strong coffee and playing chess. By that time we
knew a lot of people in the town, through my restless attempts at
a busy social life and Vlad's unremitting conviviality with anyone
who called round. I made friends with a boy called Simon, who
was reading microbiology. He was exuberantly energetic, and
built a pyramid with a glass apex at the end of the garden. 'Vlad
just loves chatting, doesn't he?' he said, and it was true: people
would come round and Vlad sat at the table chatting and chatting, about anything. For all his laziness, he was clever and
learned, and could discuss quantum mechanics easily.

We made friends with a boy called Jo, who was half Irish, a
guitarist and singer. During the second year he lived with us for
a while, and only on some nights; he used to drink in the bars
on the Cowley Road and sing Irish songs, sometimes with his
band and sometimes on his own. Vlad said that it was as if Jo
knew a secret about the world that nobody else did. The girls in
the pub used to sit and watch Jo, or dance to attract his atten-
tion, and every single one of them thought they could win him
over and make him their own. He looked about twelve years old
and was deceptively endearing. I had a birthday party in a bar in

London for my twenty-first. Jo arrived, wearing a crumpled blue jacket. He had been in Kilburn drinking whisky for the previous twenty-four hours. After supper he sang 'Danny Boy', drunkenly, a slurred voice but a magic voice none the less, and his face was in agony as he sang. He sat down beside Vlad and poured a glass of wine. When he is drunk his voice is more Irish.

'You're looking after this one, eh, Vlad?' he said, and Vlad nodded, resigned, and Jo slugged the glass down. A few minutes later I saw him behind the bar pulling pints of Guinness, momentarily unnoticed, then seen angrily by the barman.

I thought of these times as I watered Prince. Life then seemed, by comparison, leisured and without routine. It was dark now, and in Prince's stable the rain was pattering on the plastic of the tent roof. He had finished his feed and was lazily eating hay. He looked up when I came through the entrance to his tent, then carried on eating. I put the bucket in the corner. I patted his neck, just behind his ear where his muscle protrudes. He shook his head and put his ears back. He wanted to be alone with his hay so I left him.

In the caravan Vlad, Giles and Plum were sitting at the table. There was a bottle of whisky on it and they hadn't opened it. They had all been to Russia together the year before and they were talking about an evening there. Plum wanted to ring a girl he had met there who lived in Cambridge. The curtains were drawn and it was warm. The rain banged on the roof and the light above the table swung slightly with the movement of the caravan. In that light, faces are hollowed out and half seen. I put some onions in a pan and lit the gas. Soon the caravan smelt strongly of onions cooking and cigarette smoke. Giles and his brother, Tom, had been to visit me in the Chinese circus. We had sat in the back of my little van. He said he had a new job in London. Vlad said he was heading for a fast car and a flash girl-friend now. Plum still wanted to ring the girl. In Oxford he used to watch cartoons all the time. He loved cartoons.

'This is better than the van in that Chinese circus, Nell.'

'It could hardly have been worse.'

Vlad was living in one of the colleges in Cambridge, where his father was the president. The circus was a few miles down the road. 'Vlad's practically living in a stately home now,' Giles said. Plum rang the girl from my telephone but she was out. He looked annoyed. I put some tomatoes in the saucepan and boiled some pasta.

There was a knock at the door. It was Marine, Benni and Maya, with a bottle of whisky. Giles, Plum and Vlad moved round the table and they sat down.

Marine said, 'Hello, Nell,' and shook hands with the boys. 'This is my wife Benni.' They spoke to each other in Russian and I couldn't understand any of it.

Benni was sitting at the end of the table. She stood up and looked in the pan. 'You cook for everyone?' she said, and I said that I might as well. Did she want some?

She said, 'Sure,' and she would get some bread from their car-avan. 'Maya is so happy to be coming here, she is very excited.' She looked at her daughter who was sitting beside Marine and playing with an empty cigarette box on the table. 'All the time she say, "We are going to Nellie's caravan," all the time, she can't stop talking. I think that she must be tired but she is awake all the time.'

Maya was bouncing the carton on each plate, and chanting the words from the show. She was learning English fast, through mimicking what she heard. 'Ladies and gentlemen, Meeese

Alayana, on the *corde leez*, Meeese Elaina, an' Meeese Claire, an' aerialduo.'

There were not enough glasses on the table. Vlad reached up to the cupboard above his head and took down three more. Marine poured whisky into each and gave everyone a glass. 'OK, boys,' he said. 'Good company, up!' He drank the glass empty. He always said that – 'Up!' It is a signal in the circus, when acrobats are working together. 'Up!' they say, to give the command that they are ready for the next movement. 'Up!' I can hear Marine saying it now, emptying the glass, never sipping.

Benni gave Maya a glass of Coke. 'An' now, from the Santus Farmyard, pleeeze welcome . . .' Her words got mixed up. She gripped the glass in her little hand, and drank the Coke.

Marine was talking more Russian, leaning one elbow on the table and gesticulating with his hand. Giles nodded and said something. They seemed to be in agreement. Benni said to me that Maya just talked and talked, all the time, like a radio.

There was a knock at the door. I shouted to come in. It was Roget. He said, 'Hello, everyone,' and laughed. 'Who are your friends, Nell? You having a party, eh?' He always said that, and burst out laughing again. He stepped into my caravan and wiped the rain off his face. He said that he had to go back because dinner was nearly ready but he had come to see if I had any salt – they had just run out. He wouldn't have a drink . . . well, a very quick drink. 'Your friends live in Cambridge, eh?' He stood at the end of the room with a drink in his hand. 'I can't stand the rain,' he said, 'I am full of water.' Yesterday there had been wasps in his caravan and at least the rain washed them away. 'I can't stand wasps either.' He says wasp with a hard 'a' and a 'z', wazp. 'What are you cooking, Nell?' he asked. 'Pasta. I love pasta, I always cook it. My wife gets fed up with it. You like cooking. Are you cooking for your friends too?'

'Where Ruby?' Maya asked.

'She is in the caravan, darling,' Roget said. 'She having her dinner now. You can see her in the morning.'

He said OK, he had to go now, and I gave him a bottle of salt from the cupboard.

Marine poured more whisky. The fresh air that had come into the caravan with Roget was filled again with smoke and heat from the gas rings. I burned my fingers checking the pasta, but it was ready. I mixed it with the tomatoes and onion and put it on to plates, and in a little bowl for Maya. Marine never ate his food right away; it sat on the table in front of him while he carried on drinking and smoking. He didn't start it for half an hour, maybe longer. They went on speaking in Russian. Benni asked anyone for a five-pound note. Giles gave her one, and she told him it was for a magic trick. Maya ate her pasta, then ran to the end of the caravan and sat on the bed. On the shelf above it there was a silver horse my godmother gave me, and she stood on the bed and lifted it down to play with it. On the bedspread there was an old toy monkey that played a tune when you wound it up that Mum gave me when I was small. Now, if I listen to that tune, 'Rock-a-bye Baby', and hold the monkey right close to my ear, so that I can hear the little machine inside whirring – his mechanical heart that has never seized up – I can see Clover's and my bedroom in Rawlinson Road where the gas fire used to flicker and hiss in the grate and the light filtered through delicately patterned curtains, and Mum was never ever far away. The monkey and the horse cantered round the bedspread, ladies and gentlemen, the Santus Ponays.

Maya was laughing and her fringe was in her eyes again. Her teeth at the front were black. Benni said it was because of Chernobyl.

Marine poured some more whisky. He raised his glass. He looked around the table and, through the smoke in the little room, he smiled the way he always smiled, with his lips together and twisting to a grin. 'Up! To new friends.'

Everyone agreed, to new friends, and Marine carried on smiling and tipped his head downwards but looked forward. At last he ate a mouthful of pasta. 'Very good pasta, Nellie,' he said.

'Why Marine?' I asked him. 'Like the sea marine, you mean?'

He said, 'I very much like the sea. I take one bottle of wine and I sit alone in the dark and I look at the sea. I am nothing. Do you understand? I am nothing, only very small.'

Maya danced back over to the table. She knew that we were drunker now and she knew that she would be funny. Benni's sharp manner with her softened and she looked at Maya as a mother looks at a child she loves. She had the singing monkey in her hand and she had put a little sparkly top hat on him, a Christmas present that Clover had given me last year. She mimicked Marine's magic top-hat gag. 'Ashina bashina, pirichona asyoula!' These were Marine's invented magic words. She waved her hands over the hat, then lifted it from the monkey's head. She turned it over and pulled from it a silky headband. Everyone burst out laughing and she smiled.

'One day she will be number-one clown, you see.' Marine smiled.

He poured more whisky. Giles said 'This one is for Maya,' and lifted his glass. It was very close in the caravan, there was nowhere to move to, and nowhere else to look, just at the circle of faces around the table and the glinting glass of the bottles and glasses, the plates of food. Vlad would be thinking about coffee. I got up to put on the kettle. Benni asked me if it was OK for Maya to play with all these things. She had found some paper streamers; the bedspread in the dark at the end of the caravan was covered with them, and she was winding them round the monkey and the horse. I said it was fine, nothing could break. It sounded as if the raincloud had passed over. I stepped outside the caravan to listen for Prince and to wake myself up.

Prince was quiet. I didn't go into his tent as he would wake up and perhaps become agitated. It was much better to leave him, once he had gone to sleep, once he was quiet. I could see the shape of the elephant through the walls of the stable tent, as the lights were still on in there. Its silhouette looked like a sculpture. I could hear the others in the caravan, laughing, and the clinking of glasses. It was cool and damp outside. Once, years ago, my friend from Oxford, Michael, had found a big rock on a beach. Only he would know the stone inside its dull exterior. He took it back to Oxford and carved a snake from it: the snake is curled up, like a concertina, and its head rests along the top of its body. It is compact, and the stone is dark oily green. I kept thinking about that snake. The rock had contained a snake. Now the white light of the tent contained a sculpture.

One of the ponies neighed in the stable and I could hear Prince turning round and snorting. He neighed loudly, and was then dead quiet, listening for a reply. I told him to go to sleep, and not to be so noisy. I went back inside the caravan.

There were trails of coloured streamers across the floor. Maya was sitting on Benni's lap, opening and closing her eyes. The kettle was boiling and I made some coffee. The music was playing loudly, someone had changed the tape. Benni picked an apple from the bowl on the table and cut into it. She put Maya on the seat beside her and Maya leaned against Marine. Benni stood up and put the knife back on the table. She pulled open the apple and Giles's five-pound note was folded into its core.

Marine stared at her, his eyes half shut, smiling, the boys were laughing and I think Giles said he thought he would never see the money again, he had forgotten about it. Maya was falling asleep. Benni said that she had to take her home. Marine said, 'OK, I come too. Thank you for the company. OK, boys, we see you again, you come to the show.' He stood up and leaned over the table and shook their hands.

'Do you want some coffee, Marine?'

'No, I go home now, have to have energy for the show, to move on Sunday, must keep energy. Thank you for the food, very good pasta.'

Vlad, Plum and Giles stayed for a while. They were going to get a taxi back into Cambridge. They said they liked Marine, Giles said, 'That's the thing about whisky. When you drink whisky you like everyone, everyone is good.' Then I started to wonder, drunkenly and to myself, as to how Marine really saw these strangers from Cambridge, and how they saw Marine and his family. Privilege lay between them, a wide space that seemed to have been crossed. Marine, Maya and Benni had a caravan and that was all, and Marine, though good, was not the number-one clown in the world. These boys were going back that evening to a Cambridge University college – a fortress, by comparison. The table was piled up with glasses, plates and coffee cups. How had she put the five-pound note in the apple? Easy, when people are drunk, to do tricks like that, no one notices . . . Hadn't she gone outside earlier to get some bread?

Marine is a good man. He had been saying that Maya had been cast to do a Coca-Cola advert, and he had said that it was dangerous for children to become famous when they are little, either they go up too much, in their own heads, or down. He is very sound, a very intelligent man.

Vlad said Marine reminded him so much of Russian men, the way he stood, with a cigarette, and sometimes with his hand in his pocket. Marine, like the sea. I told them he made seal noises while he worked, whistled and chirped like a seal. 'Maybe that is because he likes the sea.' I felt depressed. Was I making of the circus and circus people an exhibit for middle-class friends? This was a bad thought. But we had all drunk together, genuinely laughed. I couldn't figure out who was making me feel suddenly guilty. There was no reason for it.

Outside the generator went off and the lights in the caravan dimmed as they switched to the battery. The music stopped. The little radio set in the wall of the caravan above the cooker worked off the battery. I switched it on and tuned it: it was very crackly and indistinct. I found a local radio station. I had done some publicity on the radio a few days ago. I had to be anonymous and people called in to ask me questions and had to guess what I did for a job. Pearl from Saffron Walden thought that I was the town-crier and Pete from Huntingdon thought I was a strippergram. Someone guessed it in the end but it was a circus fan who lived nearby who put two and two together and gave the game away. 'Why don't you come and work in the circus, Giles?'

'Because I want a fast car soon.' He was laughing.

Giles is going to get a fast car. But I want a fast car too, one day, a fast lorry.

'Why are all the people in the world so delicate now?' I asked Giles. They are trying to phase out hop-on-hop-off buses because someone considers them too dangerous. The conversation was drifting and we were falling asleep. 'But that just makes people even more useless at looking after themselves. The more danger you take away then the more hopeless people become.'

Giles was laughing, and Vlad and Plum were starting to look dizzy. They fell asleep for a bit.

'What can you do, though, Nell? Make life more dangerous by law? An EEC regulation that cars are to have no doors. Ban MOT tests.'

Now I knew I was too tired, and I started to laugh and laugh. I had forgotten to take off my makeup earlier and I could feel the eyeliner stinging in my eyes. I stood up and looked in the mirror on my wardrobe door. There were black streaks on my cheeks and on my temples. 'OK, I have to go to bed now. I'm so happy to have seen you. You will come to the show tomorrow?' That is what happens when I've been drinking with people who don't speak English; I start to speak broken English to everyone.

The battery lights were going dimmer and the radio was more crackly. I felt dizzy. The others woke up and I walked out of the caravan as there wasn't room for everyone standing up inside at the same time. The grass was wet and shiny outside, and the lights had gone off in the stable tent. 'Good night, good night, thank you, thank you for coming, see you tomorrow, good night, sleep well, OK, good night . . .' I stood and watched them walk across the ground and round the side of the tent. Their silhouettes disappeared into the dark and it sealed up again. I went back into the caravan and wiped off my makeup then fell asleep fully dressed.

Night Masks
May 1997

Once such ideas began to torment him, would they ever quite leave him alone? Would they rather not increase in urgency? Would they not threaten his very existence? And indeed the manager believed he could see, during the apparently peaceful sleep which had succeeded the fit of tears, the first furrows of care engraving themselves upon the trapeze artist's smooth childlike forehead.

First Sorrow, FRANZ KAFKA

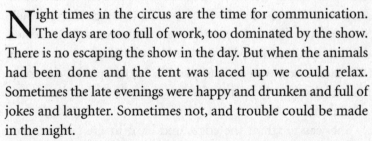

Night times in the circus are the time for communication. The days are too full of work, too dominated by the show. There is no escaping the show in the day. But when the animals had been done and the tent was laced up we could relax. Sometimes the late evenings were happy and drunken and full of jokes and laughter. Sometimes not, and trouble could be made in the night.

We were somewhere in East Anglia. Elaina was becoming increasingly demoralised, and frequently voiced her dissatisfaction – her unhappiness was evident in her face. One night after the show she knocked on my door. She looked forlorn.

'Come in, Elaina.'

She sat down and started to cry. 'My body is fucked,' she said, crying, 'my body is broken.'

There was a singer on the tape that was playing; she was singing a road blues song and the lyric intermingled with Elaina's lament.

'Never, ever, ever end up like me,' Elaina said. 'My body is fucked, and I can't carry on. It hurts all day and all night. Not even millionaires can get their health back. I could have married a millionaire, he did want me real bad, but I want to earn my own money.'

There was a jug of flowers on the table and their petals were strewn all over it. I listened to Elaina. She didn't want a reply. She said that she couldn't have a child now, she was too messed up for that. I watched her miserable eyes and wondered if I was being manipulated. But this wasn't a joke.

There was a racetrack beside the ground and they raced cars all night under floodlights. Who cares if circus people have contaminated water, or no water, and who minds if the ground is too noisy to sleep, and the children scream all evening, and around the trailers is full of broken bottles and rubbish? Sometimes I hated the romance created around the road life. Look at Elaina to see what the hard knocks of life can do to you. She would never apologise for herself. 'My aunt did stick needles in me when I was young,' she said, and she showed me some scars on her wrist.

She was rough at the edges and hard in the face, but you would be too, and you, too, would lie and betray if you had to survive in a life that offered nothing. She was sitting at my table, smoking a cigarette. Her hands were pointed in the fingers and lined, her face was a painted mask, she was drinking wine and her eyes were red. That is all the emotion you will ever see.

Her husband has tattoos and affects a wide East End drawl. He told her to shut up sometimes when she was speaking. He was not from the circus but in marrying Elaina he married the circus. One time she was helping me make a new skirt to wear on Prince. We were trying it on after the show. She had a cigarette hanging out of her mouth and she was arranging the folds. She is very good at making costumes, sews sequins by the thousand. He walked around the corner of the tent. 'You're late, babe. Where's my supper?'

'OK, Speary, I'm coming.' But his face was hard. She had picked up the sparkly material, and followed him home.

Elaina left my caravan and I went to their lorry with her. It was a single room conversion, with a big telly and stereo, and the roof was full of plastic flowers. Speary was lying on the bed half clothed. Elaina stood by the gas cooker and drank some wine. She didn't say anything, and still the mask was there. The curtain was blowing in the night through the open window, and there were ears outside in the dark. They said they had to leave. I have told you a dream of love and it comes to this: just surrender and hate and a longing to give up. I couldn't figure out if their demoralisation was cause or symptom of a wider demoralisation that ran right through the show at that time. There were tales of love (on the wall there was a photograph of Elaina in her wedding dress behind the circus tent) but they had all gone out of the window and away into the darkness.

Speary swivelled round on the bed and leaned down to the table for some tobacco. There was a plastic jar of sequins and their reflected light spots the table. The tobacco dropped shreds on to the table, and with the very ends of his fingers he reached for the cigarette papers. I felt too tired to move, my legs hurt, and I could see my reflection in the mirror on the bathroom door opposite. My face looked swollen with tiredness.

There was a bang on the door. 'Look,' said Elaina, 'we have got a drunk Claire.'

The mood in the lorry lifted. Claire was drunk and her only care in the world was her man, Jason. (Lovely Jason. The girls from the audience bang on the caravan door for his autograph and Claire sets the dogs on them.) She looks after Jason and holds on to him, and he loves her true.

Yesterday Jason, Speary and I were putting the foyer tent up. We were just having a laugh and taking the mickey a bit. I lifted one end of a piece of metal on to the back of the lorry with Speary. It banged on the side of the lorry as I lifted it. 'Don't get excited now, Nellie.'

'You're the one getting excited, showing off your biceps, Jason. Look at that big cloud with the orange edge where the sun's going down.'

'Don't get all poetic on us now, Nellie. Can we be in your book too, eh?'

Across the field Claire was walking her dogs. Jason stopped for a moment and wolf-whistled to her. She laughed, looked across at him, tossed her long black hair and threw her torso back on her hips as she walked. He wolf-whistled again and it seemed he loved her true.

Behind her mask Elaina was drinking more wine, and I wondered if she had another purpose. There were other voices in other caravans and I could hear many conflicts. I was too tired for this sort of talk. It would go on all night. For now, all there was to do was go to sleep, shut my eyes to the caravans' bright windows and drift out to unconsciousness.

Jaywick

'But I felt it all the same; I felt often it's mysterious stillness watching me at my monkey tricks, just as it watches you fellows performing on respective tightropes for – what is it? Half a crown a tumble.'

Heart of Darkness, JOSEPH CONRAD

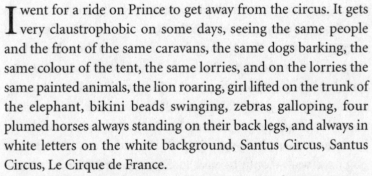

I went for a ride on Prince to get away from the circus. It gets very claustrophobic on some days, seeing the same people and the front of the same caravans, the same dogs barking, the same colour of the tent, the same lorries, and on the lorries the same painted animals, the lion roaring, girl lifted on the trunk of the elephant, bikini beads swinging, zebras galloping, four plumed horses always standing on their back legs, and always in white letters on the white background, Santus Circus, Santus Circus, Le Cirque de France.

We stood on a ground on the north side of London at a place called Harold Hill. It was a solid concrete ground – it was said that the concrete was eight feet deep. The boys worked all day to put in the stakes for the tent and they didn't finish until the evening. The surface of the concrete was hot from the daytime sun. There is a B&Q at the front of the ground and the circus sign, above the box-office, glowed in front of commerce's bright neon. Ernest said we could finish for the day. It was Monday and the show didn't open until Wednesday. The stable tent was up, and Prince's tent. I couldn't get a stake into the ground to tie it to, so I had piled up some blocks of concrete I found on the other side of the ground. Roget said to Rick, who visited in the afternoon, 'Look, your daughter is making pyramids.' All around the ground there was a bank of earth and rubble, against the chain link fencing. Strands of wire stuck out of it, shattered lumps of concrete and broken toys, old nappies and trailing strands of clothes. Right in front of my caravan there was a round hole in the concrete full of dirty water. A doll's head, with waterlogged eyes, floated in it.

In the evening I rode away from the ground through a housing estate. There were kids on mountain-bikes and Spice Girls standing in driveways, and they turned to stare at Prince. Sometimes the younger children ran across the tarmac towards him, horsey, horsey, horsey. On the horizon I could see fields and trees. A boy was walking along the pavement on the other side of the street. I crossed, just before a T-junction, and asked him how you reached those trees in the distance. He told me the way and said he was going there himself, to his house, he lived near there. I walked along with him. He was called Len, he said, and he walked with a long springy gait. He said it was like taking a dog for a walk – only, he said, and he sounded unsure, a horse was bigger than a dog. He said that the horse would like it on the fields as it was softer for the hoofs. We crossed the road and went down into a subway under the A12.

'Where do you keep the horse anyway?' he said.

'I'm from the circus opposite B&Q.'

'The circus – I know, I saw it today after work. You know, I work in B&Q. I couldn't believe it when I saw the elephant today after work. It was mad.'

'Come and see the circus.'

'Do I get free tickets?' He laughed.

'I don't know. Maybe. My name's Nell.'

The subway was low. Prince walked sideways a bit.

'There's a bit of trouble on the estates, but I've seen other people riding on the common near my house.'

We came out on the other side of the A12 and the road went alongside it, past a few takeaways, pubs and hairdressers. Then we went down a road to the left. 'Thank you very much for showing me the way.'

He had jeans and a blue shirt and a strange, long, turned-up nose, wide-apart eyes, a long fringe. ''Bye, then.'

''Bye. Nell, isn't it?'

I was turning into the road that led to the common, and I said, yes, it was Nell, his name backwards.

'Oh, yes.'

And we waved goodbye.

The circus moved away from Harold Hill eastwards towards the coast. We stood in a suburb of a seaside town called Clacton-on-Sea. The suburb was called Jaywick and was situated about two miles around the coast from Clacton. Across the car park from the circus, towards the granite sea wall that slopes to churning grey water, there is a pink amusement arcade and an indoor market. It said on the outside that it sold designer clothes, and it had a huge roof with red tiles, which dropped nearly to the ground. I went in there to buy a cup of tea and a very fat woman was slowly sweeping the wet floor. Her clothes hung about her huge body and she looked tired, dirty and despondent. The indoor market sold cheap canned food and dishcloths, and T-shirts for fifty pence. I stood while some bacon was cooking and watched the woman sweeping. She stopped and looked right at me. 'All right, love?' she said kindly.

'Well, yes, just·about.'

I was tired and cold, and quite lonely, and it was as if that was a mutual feeling, and it bonded us together. Just about. She nodded, and she knew what I meant and she knew that I knew. That is the very edge of exhaustion, and something was communicated between us without words.

Jaywick was inhabited by people who had forgotten about work. On either side of the circus there were shanty towns of tiny concrete and wood houses, built for holiday-makers and now either empty or lived in permanently. On the first day in Jaywick we built up the tent. The shanty town was to us just roofs, all hung about with wires, so many wires, like a scratchy black mist. Two men came from these houses to help us with the stable tent. They were called Dave and Bill. Bill had broken teeth and a shred of a Scouser accent. Dave said that he helped in an animal rescue centre. He said he had found two dogs tied up on the beach: someone had put them there to drown. Their friend Geoffrey appeared from the houses.

Dave and Bill whistled to him. 'Look who's here!' they shouted. 'Geoffrey, OI, GEOFFREY!'

Geoffrey had a tiny unshaven face and a huge foam baseball cap. It was filthy, engrained with dirt. His clothes were all black and when he walked he bent at the waist. Claire called him the dirty little man. He talked all the time, in statements and questions. He talked like somebody who had never heard a reply. He came over and spoke to me while I was putting up Prince's stable tent. 'Hard old life, isn't it? Eh, know what I mean? A hard life. Still, nice to see the animals, real animals. I looked in the back of that lorry there, well, blimey, what a big elephant, and that bison, bison, is it, with the big horns, that big thing in the back of the lorry with the big horns? Blimey, wouldn't like to see them when they're angry. Hard life, isn't it, all this work, look at you with this big heavy pen, you want to lift that corner a bit, that's it, blimey, what a hard life, all these people Italian, are they? Marvellous really, that they can speak all these different languages, when you think about it, no, I wouldn't do it myself, oh, no, I'm a man on my own. What do I do? I make bicycles, I made a unicycle, only I can't ride it. I expect some of these could, though, eh? Juggling and all that. From Suffolk, I am. My dad made engines for lawn-mowers and we lived in a house with an acre of fruit trees. I'm a man on my own, though, wouldn't do all that work myself.'

Geoffrey watched the circus every night. He sat in the front row looking out from under the peak of his baseball cap. One night he was standing on the grass bank at the back of the tent with a nylon bag full of hats. It was his mad-hat collection, top hats and bowlers, Stetsons and sombreros. He had a Mexican hat and he put it on his head and almost disappeared under the brim.

I saw the roofs of the houses from the top of my van, where I had to stand every week to tie off the stable tent, and I saw the wasteland at the back of the ground. There were piles of burnt mattresses and broken tables. Once I went down into the main street of Jaywick, past two fish and chip shops with lonely tables in the windows and Sweet Tina's lace curtain shop, which was closed as Tina was on holiday for a week, and along to the amusement arcades, synthetic bleeps oh-my-darling-oh-my-darling-Clementine-thou-art-lost-and-gone-for-ever-oh-my-darling-Clementine. The arcade was empty, but for a woman pushing a pram with a baby in it. Then I saw that the woman was not a grown adult but a little girl, and the baby in the pram was a doll.

The first show of the week had ended. It rained throughout the whole of that week, and Prince's stable flooded and I had to cut a drainage ditch around the side of the van. At the end of the show I stood by the curtains as usual and took the money for the people going through to the stables to look at the animals. The show had been packed and they had been a good audience. One man asked me how much pony rides were – there were pony rides after the show – and I said they were fifty pence, only for the children, though, as a joke. It was obvious that they were only for the children. He laughed and grinned, only for the children. He had a can of beer in his hand, he was grinning, nodding, half cut, only for the children. The last people to go through the curtains were an old couple.

Claire was standing just inside the curtain, waiting for Jason to finish the pony rides, and the red lights from the ring were lighting the side of her face and dramatising her makeup, as she knew, and there were sparkles round her face. She had a tiger's claw on a gold chain around her neck. Circus people often have that, a tiger's claw mounted on a gold clasp. The animal-rights protestors won't let them keep tigers any more but they carry the claw as a secret symbol of their forbidden culture.

The lady was holding the arm of the man and they were both smiling. They were neat and dapper, dashing-looking. The lady said she used to work for a circus, she stood for a knife-thrower. She was living with a Chinese magician at the time. She said she had only had this for one year and patted the hand of the man she was with. He held her arm carefully. The knife nearly hit her in the left breast, just missed. Luckily it just missed and she patted his hand again. She said she loved the circus, and when the music started she nearly cried. The man with her said she had tears in her eyes when the music started. As Claire was standing right beside the curtain I introduced them. Sometimes I thought that Claire didn't like to speak with the public too much, but she stepped right forward and looked into this lady's eyes, her face still illuminated by the red light. 'This is Claire. Claire, this lady used to work in a knife-throwing act.'

'Did you? When did you? Who with? Bad, isn't it, when you get stabbed?'

'Lovely show, thank you, good night, dear, good night, then, take care my love.' They went through the wallings at the back of the tent and out to the stables.

Within minutes of their departure I had a row with Robert about something. He was treading on the lead of the mike as I was trying to coil it up. He was standing on it on purpose – I could tell because he was looking at me and laughing. I felt annoyed. I overreacted. Perhaps there had been a row in the offing. For a while I had felt he'd been putting me down. For example, when we pulled on to a new ground on Sunday evenings I always waited in the cab of my van while Ernest set all the caravans in position. Sometimes it took a long time, an hour or more. Ernest directed the driver of each load with a flashlight. Coming on to the Jaywick ground Robert walked over to my lorry and said, really hard and aggressive, 'Turn your engine off. *You* have got to wait for everyone else to go on to this ground.' I switched off and fell asleep in the cab – I couldn't work out why he was like this. Anyway, after the show I seemed to feel this same bullying. I said, 'Fuck off Robert,' and he turned on me. 'Don't tell me to fuck off! I don't take any shit off anyone.' Then walked back through the curtains to the ring.

There was no public in the tent then, though for sure there were some keen ears behind dark curtains: any barney, as Claire said, was entertainment of a kind. I walked after him. 'Don't talk to me like that, Robert. I'm sorry if I swore at you but I just want to get home and get changed at the end of the night.'

'Get back to your caravan, you bitch,' he said.

As I usually do when I get angry, I started to shake all over. The thing is that the tiredness makes things worse. I was always so tired – everyone was – and that exhaustion was eating away at morale. You can't laze about when you are with the circus, and let time drift. There are specific times for relaxation, short moments between the long working hours. The exhaustion cannot be dealt with by a couple of good nights' sleep. The exhaustion becomes part of you. That was why we rowed like that – that, and the relentless pressure of living so close all the time. The circus is an isolated, tight community where you live with only thin walls between you and the outside world staring in. Eva and I were reading *Heart of Darkness* one night in her trailer. She said that Marlow's descriptions of going down the river seemed to her to describe the life in the circus – the longing to give up, the loneliness, the sense of being a voyager travelling through violent, hostile people who invisibly observe the traveller, from within the jungle, from behind the curtains. I was sitting on the chair just to the left-hand side of the door to her caravan. She read a section from the book: '"The fascination of the abomination – you know. Imagine the growing regrets, the longing to escape, the powerless disgust, the surrender, the hate." That is like being in the circus,' she said. 'We are the boat going down the river, even in Gravesend itself, the people outside, it makes me shudder, to think of Sasha, and all the people that you are among but not with. The circus is the boat on the river.'

I carried on flicking through the book. I read one passage at random. I saw a description by the narrator of the jungle. I could hardly believe what I was reading, in the light of Eva's sorrowful comparison. 'But I felt it all the same; I felt often its mysterious stillness watching me at my monkey tricks, just as it watches you fellows performing on your respective tightropes for – what is it? Half a crown a tumble.' But that is typical of Eva. She is perceptive, more than anyone else I have ever met, and though perhaps she is fixated more than most on the black planes of life, this reaction to Conrad's work occurred to me again and again while I was on the road in England with the circus. People on the outside imagine the circus to be a haphazard, footloose gallivant across the country; they do not see it as it is, which is a rigid daily and weekly routine, remorseless, exhausting, demanding everything and taking more than you have; and the loathing for the outside world that sets in as you are forced to face it, every day, from every aspect, and feel its hostility. Anne Marie said that there were good people and bad people everywhere, 'But, then,' she said, sighed, flicked a cigarette, looked to the ground, 'after all these years, I think that there are more bad . . .' Her voice trailed off and it was an admission that was a window to too much pain.

I went into the dressing-room section of my van, and pulled open the door. Prince was standing in his stable waiting to be fed. My wardrobe had been made by a friend in Cheltenham called Rocky. Cheltenham seemed a long way off. In that world you don't live right up close to your friends as you do in the circus. You see people in the pub or pass them on the road, and wave, and pass. People become the vehicle that they drive. Fast tractor waves to scaffolding lorry waves to the big black circus van waves to the old tractor waves to the skip lorry on its way from the rubbish-tip waves to Rocky's white van waves to Ben on his way back from a liquid lunch in town waves to Andrew clip-clop down the road on his pony and cart. In the back of my van I pulled on a pair of jeans and a T-shirt. I opened the door of the van. Prince neighed, banged the side of his box and nodded. I led him out of the stable and behind the stable tent. I didn't know where Robert was and by now everyone would know about the argument or have heard it themselves. It was stupid to have had a row like that and I wished that I hadn't, but for the moment the best thing to do was to ride away from the ground, along to the beach, maybe on to the beach, breathe a bit of air from the sea and calm down.

The track with the burnt mattresses at the back of the ground ran along the edge of a marsh and past the back of the shanty-town houses, further along. The narrow roads among the small houses did not have pavement and tarmac streets but were rough tracks, with potholes and puddles. The houses were askew and each one bore the different stamp of the occupants. Some were empty and boarded-up, or the windows were smashed and the rendering on the outside stained grey. A house on the very edge, beside the marsh, had lobster pots spilling out of the back garden, a shell of a Land Rover with a piece of blue tarpaulin stretched over it and some boats lying in the longer grass. Some houses had verandas, and green and white plastic strips blowing in doorways and Alsatians barking on chains in the front garden. Others were neat with fresh paint and lace curtains blowing in the windows – from Sweet Tina's, I guessed. There were old estate cars with flat tyres at the side of the tracks, Jack Russells behind pink picket fencing. One of the first bungalows we passed on the right-hand side, after going through the iron gate, was decked with Union Jack-coloured flowers; they were all over the roof, the garden and the window-ledges, with a dozen or more white ornaments, of unicorns and Peter Pan and horses and horses' heads. There were roses on the archway over the front gate and along the fence. It was pretty and the house was painted white with black window-frames. We paused, for a moment, outside to admire it. Some of the houses were so run down, and some were pride-and-joys, perfectly pretty. A couple came out of the house and admired Prince. 'That is a lovely horse,' they said. 'I used to have horses when I was younger,' the lady said, and she tucked in her chin and smiled at Prince with her head on one side a bit. 'Where do you come from?' they asked me, and I said that I was with the circus, over the field, and pointed to the tent, just visible across the marsh. The lady said that when she was a young girl she used to work as a trapeze artist for Bertram Mills. I tell them to come to the circus, if they want, 'It's a nice show, a family show, a French circus.'

'Maybe see you later, then. Goodbye. Take good care of your beautiful horse. Goodbye then. Goodbye.'

We went further through the houses. People hung out and talked to each other, leaning on car bonnets or out of windows. The good thing about Prince is that people always want to touch him and admire him, so you fall into conversation everywhere. In fact, sometimes I found it turning dark and I was chatting to someone – three women with peroxide hair and East End accents, whose friends came over to chat too – and the dark started to come and Prince and I were still away from the circus. All the streets interlocked in a haphazard kind of grid. They weren't exactly streets either but rutted lanes with houses all along them. Some of the houses had steps running up to the front door, then a porch with blue paint on the door. Some kids were sitting, chatting, on the steps of one, two younger girls and a black girl with dreadlocks, and an older woman who had scabs on her face. The woman shouted to me, asked if she could stroke the horse, would he bite her? 'No, not unless you stick your finger out right underneath his nose.' A boy of about sixteen wheeled on the track on a mountain bike. He asked how old the girls were in the circus, not eighteen, no, no eighteen-year-olds, and the girls screamed with laughter and pulled faces at him, fancy a nice bit of trapeze, their faces were scornful and dirty, they were taking the piss, sending him up. They fell about, and nudged into each other, and he grinned and turned on his bike.

We rode along the sea wall. At the end there was a huge camping-park. There was no one to see on it. It was bleak, blank deserted tarmac. There was an entrance through the concrete sides of the sea wall on to the beach. We went through. The sand was very soft and deep and dry. I thought Prince had never been on a beach before because he floundered, snorted, broke into a canter. We cantered along the beach until we were level with the circus again. It was low tide. There was no way back to the circus so we cantered back down the beach and I felt the wind and the salt and Prince's rocking-horse gait. After that I went back to the circus.

That evening Ernest came round to say that I shouldn't worry about Robert. He was being very rude, but don't worry. I didn't worry too much and felt tired. I sewed a few sequins on to a new leotard and listened to the radio. I went to the chip shop for some food, as I couldn't be bothered to cook, and drank some whisky.

I fell asleep at about midnight. I had had the heater on as there was quite a cold wind coming off the sea. But the wind seemed to have dropped and it was too hot in my caravan. I jammed open the window and pulled back the curtain a bit.

Through the lace curtains I could see the lights still on in Anne Marie's caravan; they were awake, drinking and watching television, with cigarettes and glasses, and murmured sleepy talk as the day drifted to late night. The noise of the geese and Anne Marie calling to her dogs would wake me in the morning. I just lay there for a while and listened to the cars in the far distance and some voices from the marsh and the sound of Prince banging about in his stable. I started to fall asleep and was woken by Prince, banging harder. I got up to have a look at him. The grass outside the caravan was damp and my clogs were cold. I walked round to the entrance to Prince's tent and crawled under the wallings, which were laced up at night. They were white so the tent was not pitch dark inside. Prince was standing, wide awake, and staring at me. 'What do you think you're doing, Prince?' I scolded him. 'Go to sleep, you nutter.' I flashed the torch around the stable to see that he had some water and that nothing was tangled around him. He had trodden his straw into a soggy mess and pawed a muddy scratch on the ground. I had left the door of the dressing room open before so I pulled it back. Prince was still looking at me but his ears were more relaxed and he turned away to pull on his haynet.

I didn't wake up again in the night, though I'm sure that Prince had his own restless thoughts and night thoughts, which were the drifting smells of the other horses and their noises, then the start of the dawn, illuminating the sides of the tent and the sounds of the birds on the damp air. I dreamed I had left all my clothes at Minety. I couldn't get them myself as I was doing a handstand and I had to hold it for a few hours. I was on a little platform in a field, and across the field there were some large oak trees. Jackie, my old schoolfriend, was there and I asked her to find the clothes for me. She went away to Minety and returned with an armful of clothes, all the clothes I had mislaid over time and forgotten about.

'Was it very beautiful at this time of year at Minety?' I asked her.

'It was very beautiful as it always was.'

'Can you remember it? The long grass and the quiet of the fields, the grass coming right up to the windows and the air coming into the rooms with the peaceful light from outside? Where did we sit outside to have tea? It was somewhere in the garden. Now I can't remember. I can only remember it from the air as if I'm hovering over the house.'

'Under the nut tree in the corner of the garden, beside the church wall. The table had a slate top and cast-iron legs, it was an old sewing table.'

'Did you love it at Minety?' and I kept asking her, 'Can you remember how beautiful it was? We were only teenagers when we sat at the top of the front stairs at a party, on the landing beside the window-ledge covered in dead flies where the light came through the stained glass, and we watched the people down below. You were sitting there and I hardly knew you then. Can you remember it? Will you remember it? Can you recall my mum sitting in the garden having tea, surrounded by damp roses with falling petals and tangled forget-me-nots? It was so beautiful and I can only just remember it.'

In my sleep I was ensnared in the melancholy of it. It came right to me and caught me in it. I started to cry. I wanted to cry. The crying woke me up as the dawn was there, birds were starting to sing and I could hear them through the open windows, and the lights were still on in Anne Marie's caravan.

Party

If only one were an Indian, instantly alert, and on a racing horse, leaning against the wind, kept on quivering jerkily over the quivering ground, until one shed one's spurs, for there needed no spurs, threw away the reins, for there needed no reins, and hardly saw that the land before one was smoothly shorn heath when horse's head and neck would be already gone.

The Wish To Be a Red Indian, FRANZ KAFKA

The circus moved away from Jaywick and the argument with Robert was left behind. We moved back into East Anglia for a few weeks. Elaina's depression surrounded us and she constantly voiced dissatisfaction.

In East Dereham there was a bar opposite the ground, in a squash club. The landlord was hospitable to the circus and didn't mind the children going in there in the evening with the grown-ups. One night I went in for a drink. It was a high red-brick building with bare walls. Marine and Benni were at the bar. Elaina was sitting behind the pool table speaking Spanish with the Moroccans while Jason and Speary played pool, wheeling around the tables, eyeing up the order of the balls, with drunken cool, and calling out in their overblown bravado. Maya danced between the adults, first pulling at someone's hand then climbing up to a bar-stool-high knee, receiving wide arms from Adam and Brian, who scooped her up and held her, hello, Maya, hello, Maya, hello, Maya, and disdain from her father – acted – who did not look right at her or help her up on to his knee, but kept his elbow on the bar and half acknowledged her. She curled her lips and shook a little fist at him. He swivelled his eyes to look at her and she ducked behind him out of view. He looked on the other side, and she swung round the stool again to hide behind him again. His face softened, his eyes shone, he smiled and you could see his teeth. He grinned, swung his arm round the back of the stool, caught Maya and lifted her into the air. 'Mine daughter.'

Marine bought me a pint of lager. 'Are you having a good time here, with this show, do you like it?' I asked, for the sake of conversation.

'Every circus is the same,' he replied.

Jason and Speary came over to where we were sitting at the bar. Jason was smiling with his lips pressed tightly together, his front teeth were knocked out by a turfer handle when he was sixteen, and one of the false teeth had just fallen out.

'Go on, Jason, give us your best smile.'

He smiled but he did not open his mouth. He was quite drunk and walked like a little boy-man, looking quickly to right and left, carrying his arms slightly bent at the elbow and held away from his body a few inches. Speary was lazier, more indolent, he didn't walk quickly or carry himself straight, he swayed and lurched.

'Hello, Nellie, bit late, aren't you?' They grinned, and put their arms round me. 'Hello Nellie, your round, Nellie, buy us a drink, Nellie.'

I'd heard this before and I'm not a soft touch any more, I

hope. They saw that I wasn't going to buy them a drink then so they carried on playing pool.

'Do you play pool, Benni?' She said she did sometimes. She was sitting opposite Marine on a bar stool and she looked as if she didn't want to talk. Marine announced grandly that he only played pool for money.

'How much do you win?'

'None, I never win, I am an invalid.' He smiled, and Maya wriggled out of his arms and jumped on to the floor. 'I am an invalid. I spent much time in the circus, it is not good for me. When I was young I wanted to be the best in the world. Now I am thirty-six, how much longer must I spend in the circus? I don't know any other life or speak with any other people. Listen to me, you must follow your own way only. You understand me.' His face was serious. This was the thing he insisted upon. 'You must follow your way only. For now don't think of this person and that person. Don't try to be with others. Just follow your own way and you must believe that you are a genius.'

Brian's new girlfriend was standing beside the wall. He said that he had had enough of waking up beside someone else and having to think about them, and he was going to get rid of her soon. Claire was talking to her. She was being drawn into the circle but it looked impermanent. Elaina was playing pool now and walking round the table like a hustler. Speary arm-wrestled the Moroccans, and the good-looking one took off his top and bared his teeth. Speary beat him as he beat everyone. Marine jumped up and said he would wrestle the Moroccan, and the Moroccan bent his arm to the table. Jason and Speary played pool again together. They shouted to me: 'Nellie's got a goldfish that she looks after on build-up day. I wish I had a goldfish to look after.'

That's what they called Prince, Nellie's goldfish. Speary cut in,

'Yeah, Nellie's got a horse and she DOESN'T KNOW HOW TO TRAIN IT.'

It went a bit deep, that one, and I could feel the annoyance flickering in my stomach.

Maya hit Brian with the pool cue and started to cry. The Moroccans were shouting for the next contender, taking off their T-shirts and putting them on again. Elaina's walk was getting harder, she stopped to say something, then bent backwards at the waist and gestured with her hand in an open cup. Her face was livid. 'Cam an,' she shouted. Nellie's got a goldfish and she doesn't know how to train it. Adam was standing beside me. He was pouring a pint of lager into his mouth, and he half finished it and put it on the bar. He said he was going home now. My impressions of that evening are of aggressiveness around the pool table, the sweaty arm-wrestles, Maya's childish hyperactivity and that depressing statement at the centre of the night: 'Every circus is the same.' It was as if our relationships with each other, that night at least, were simply a way of passing the time.

The next night Brian and Adam left. Nobody saw them go, and when the circus moved the following week, Elaina and Speary and all the Moroccans left too. Some say that Elaina wound up the two boys to go; and certainly, through the night, there had been restlessness outside the caravans. One time, at Richie Richards' circus, Polly had said to me, solemnly, that in the circus nobody is indispensable. You can lose the centre and the heart of your life, the person who is life, who is everything and everybody, who has taught you the world, explained the universe, set all the scenes, created your ideas, and yet life will carry on, the fear of other bad things and the gleeful expectation of good things that will happen, come what may.

We moved down out of East Anglia. The weather changed for the better. Jaywick had been very wet for the whole week. I looked at the photographs of the mud-drenched Glastonbury Festival on the front of the newspapers. All my friends would be there. Still, in the circus we were threading about all the time through mud and over boards, and the idea of a weekend pop festival in a quagmire seemed silly. Times change.

The circus arrived somewhere near Dagenham. Usually the first load – the caravans, the children, the animal lorries – pulled into a new ground at about midnight. Ernest waved everyone into their positions with a torch. While Roget set his caravan and moved Ruby and Lucian from the cab of the lorry to the caravan, Anne Marie walked her dogs and made coffee for Ernest and Roget. I unpacked my caravan, polished the table, cleaned the mirrors, dusted my pictures, lit the hot-water boiler and laid an electric cable.

Once, last season, I had gone round to Sara's caravan just after we had arrived at a ground. She was dusting her entire caravan. I said it seemed a funny time to be doing the cleaning and she said she always did it then so that it was clean for the morning; it was a good time to do it, as you were unpacking. From that moment I resolved that on every move day I would clean the caravan when I arrived in the night.

It is hard to explain what you feel like on move night. We would have done a show, taken the tent down, started all the lorries and then driven up to fifty miles, so you feel tired, dishevelled, your face dirty, perhaps still made-up, too many cigarettes, too many cans of Coke, tired muscles, wide awake, exhausted. But it became a ritual, finding the can of Mr Sheen and polishing the pictures and the table. If the caravan was set and unpacked in the morning, the build-up day was easier somehow. The more organised you are, the easier life is, the nicer it is. When there is a break in the day you can go into the caravan, sit down, make something to eat, read a paper, listen to the radio. These patterns become overwhelmingly important.

That move to Dagenham, however, was very late, and the first load did not arrive until seven or eight in the morning, in broad daylight. I had to drive all the boys back again in my van to pick up the second load of lorries. After I had unpacked the caravan I pulled Prince's stable from the back of the van then climbed up on to the roof to undo the heavy boards of his pen. Jason and Robert were joking about outside Anne Marie's caravan. Roget was walking about in his big red check jacket and waxed hat. I called to him from the top of the lorry that the boards were ready. There are so many good views from the top of that van, across fields or into the windows of factories. In Thetford we had stood in the grounds of an old zoo. From the top of the van I could see high oak trees and through the branches of oak trees the grand roofs of pinnacled buildings, the walls of an old kitchen garden, a view slowly obliterated throughout the day as the big top arose, though from the woods behind, when I went back up on top of the van to tie off the stable tent, I could hear the elephant trumpeting through the undergrowth. Now, in Dagenham, all I could see was a main road stretching into the distance, the empty field where the tent would stand, and beyond that some allotments. I passed the boards down to Roget, sliding them off the edge of the roof rack. They were very heavy and we moved slowly. I braced my foot against the vertical supports of the roof rack, and as I slid the boards off the edge to Roget waiting on the ground, I ducked down, to keep my centre of gravity low. I did not want to fall off the top of the van and under a sheet of inch-think marine ply.

Two boys had followed the circus from the last ground, and in Dagenham they had pitched a little two-man tent at the edge of the ground. They were called Nick and Woz; Nick had shaved hair and tattoos, and Woz had long dreadlocks with tattoos. They wanted to work in the circus. The circus people regarded them with mild suspicion, and the easy tolerance that has no particular outward manifestation but whose subtext is simple: if you can keep up with the work, you can stay. Boys like this will come and go. At first nobody talks to the new boys particularly, certainly nobody is overtly friendly to them. I have seen the point in this. It is a devastatingly hard life and bonhomie from the first moment would be misleading: in the circus, if you are not resilient enough to take the initial coldness, then the work, the hours, the conditions (climbing under a lorry dripping bitter oil in the pitch dark, through mud, to hook a cold chain to a blind piece of metal when you have not slept for twenty-four hours or eaten) would cripple you. There is no point in being soft; they might as well get used to it. But if they stay, then over the weeks they will become part of the circle, know the jokes, buy a round, with their open eyes see the outside world differently, find a companionship that is not one-to-one but is one to a whole small tribe.

'OK, Roget, this is the last one.'

'Ya voile,' he called back, cheerfully.

I slid the last section of the pen off the side of the lorry. It was a warm morning and the sun was out. 'Can I unload Prince now, Roget?'

'Course you can, darling. Just put the stake out and I'll give you a hand.'

'He might be a bit lively with all those horses right there.'

I unloaded Prince, and put him on his tether. Across the

ground, behind a barbed-wire fence, a field of mares called to him. My heart sank: I was feeling too tired to cope with him if his hormones played up. I did not want to leave the ground, and I had a feeling in my stomach that he was going to be trouble that day. I stood on the ramp and watched him cantering around at the end of the length of chain. Ernest walked over to where I was standing. He looked very tired and was walking as if his back was hurting. 'You ready to go now, Nell?' he asked. 'We go back for the second load now.'

'I don't want to leave Prince today, Ernest. I think he's going to be worried by those mares. You know if I wasn't here, and he got off his tether . . .' I wasn't flatly refusing to go back for the lorries but I felt worried, which was made worse by the tiredness. I could see Robert's sister, Yoyo, with her poodles. She had just joined the circus. The poodles looked like bright white cut-outs against the green grass.

'OK, maybe it is better you stay here. Jason can drive your lorry. He is insured for anything.'

'I'll help Anne Marie with the stable tent in the meantime. It is just that the fence is made of wire and those horses are very close.' Prince kept stopping, neighing and shaking his head and then cantering around again.

'No, that is fine. OK if we take your lorry?'

The tax had run out, and we had been stopped the other night. But it would be all right. 'The documents are in the glove box.'

'OK, see you later.'

Ernest went back over to the caravan. I heard him calling to the boys and the noise of the engine starting. The van pulled out. All Prince's boards for the stable lay in disarray beside my caravan.

*

Anne Marie and I unrolled the heavy plastic of the stable tent. Woz and Nick took a corner each and dragged it into position. They had slept in their tent, but Anne Marie and I were exhausted from the open night. She was very thin and very strong; her hands were like cold steel when she tied the ropes around the stakes, a half hitch, round twice, going downwards, back up through, pull the rope tight and press the knot downwards into the base of the stake, and make sure that the tail of the rope runs out in a straight line from the point where the descending rope meets the stake. If you know how to do this properly you can tie a rope without losing any of its slack. The two boys were sweating and grumbling. They kept wanting to sit down and drink some lemonade. Anne Marie sighed and raised her eyes to me. She would work all day and look after the children and cook for the men when they arrived back from the second journey. She is hard and tough, looks like a dainty beautiful Swiss girl, but she is steel underneath. She wears a leather jacket and jeans and only eats salty food, drinks neat whisky and loves the very hot weather, when working is difficult, sweat saturates your fishnets, fills the tent with oppressive hot air. Lucian was in his push-chair by the elephant lorry. He started to cry loudly. Anne Marie took him back inside the caravan for his breakfast, and I started to unload the boards that make up the animals' pens in the stable. The two boys began to knock in the stakes. I lowered one of the heavy boards from the back of the lorry. I was strong then, from the work, and could carry these big boards on my own. But the night had taken my energy. I could move only very slowly and had lost reflex co-ordination. I kept forgetting what I was doing. I let the board slip. It crashed on to the ground. I knew I had to go to sleep for a few hours. I jumped off the back of the lorry and walked over to Woz. His top was off and there was sweat on his face. His tattoos said Mum and Dad, that he loved a girl. I forget the name of the girl, love, hate, snakes, swords, daggers.

'All right? You looked fucked.'

'I'm knackered. I'm going to go to sleep for a couple of hours. You see that caravan there, with the funny door? That's my caravan. If the horse gets off his tether then please, please, come right round there straight away and wake me up.'

'OK. No problem. We can do the stakes anyway.'

I'm usually quite careful not to take any mud or dust or dirt into the caravan, but I felt so tired. I took my shoes off and lay down on the bed in my clothes, a T-shirt and a pair of sawn-off leggings. My hands were black and smelt of metal. It was very hot so I opened the window at the back of the caravan, beside my bed, and propped it wide with a cushion. The flies kept landing on my bare legs and face so I pulled the embroidered shawl that lies on my bed over my body. Before I slept I remembered Prince again, and although I couldn't hear his chain rattling or his hoofs on the hard ground I sat up and looked through the window at the end of the bed. He was still looking over to the field of mares. If he was going to be trouble then it would be better if I had a bit of sleep behind me. He is very strong when he gets excited. I lay down again under the shawl and fell fast asleep, hearing neighs and the rings from the end of the stakes, and traffic on the road across the ground. The night before, when we had been waiting to leave the last ground, an old man had appeared beside my van door in the darkness. He said that he had been told to see me as he was a musical clown. He had a beard and a red shiny face and small, bright teeth. He wanted to work next year. I didn't think he was a clown. I couldn't help. Come back to this ground next year. He smiled then went away into the darkness. In my sleep I kept thinking about the musical clown; he was riding Prince around in the field, playing a harmonica. The sleep deepened, saturated right through me, and I didn't think about anything.

There was a loud banging on the door of the caravan and I could hear someone shouting my name. 'The horse is off! The horse is off!'

I just knew it, that that day there was going to be trouble. I woke up, fell off the bed, banged open the door of the caravan. Woz's dreadlocks were shaking and he was pointing to where Prince had been tethered. I could hear thundering feet, all the dogs were barking, and people were running out of caravans, Yoyo with her poodles and her mother, Yolande, who had bright blonde hair. She juggled huge dice on her feet and was called Mademoiselle Yolande. She had a thick French accent and bright eyes, and she laughed loudly and cooked rich food for her children.

I ran out of the back of the caravans, and saw Prince at a flat-out gallop circling the large field, his head down and his mane flowing. He turned and charged for the fence where the horses were, accelerating. Everyone seemed to be running in different directions, with head-collars and buckets. I thought he was going to go through the wire and could see the big smash-up, the tangled wire, kicking horses, cut legs. He stopped dead by the fence and leaned over it, his neck arched right up, his nostrils quivering. I walked up beside him and caught hold of his head-collar. 'Stand still, Prince, steady, wait.' That is what I always say to him at the back of the ring doors, 'Wait,' very loudly with a loud T on the end.

He dragged me away and I was forced to let go of him. He turned back into the field and circled again. I kept shouting at him, but I was losing my breath. He stopped again by the fence, and I caught him, and again he dragged me away. I fell and ripped my leg on a strand of wire trailing out from the fence. This kept happening – catching him then being dragged away. He ran down the side of a building, I think it was an old cricket pavilion or something. As I tried to hold him I scraped my arm on the rendering on the building's walls. I had to get his bridle on or a rope around his nose; otherwise it would be impossible to hold him. The next time I caught him I shouted to Woz, who grabbed the other side of the head-collar. Between us we held him long enough to pull the bridle over his head. We led him away from the other horses, and tethered him against the wall of the building. The dogs were still barking and everyone had crowded around, exclaiming and scolding. Yolande looked quite alarmed by him. She said, 'How can he ever work in the ring like that?' But I knew it would pass, that he would become docile again when he forgot about the mares. He is just very strong and wild when be becomes excited. He couldn't see the mares around the side of the building.

Woz said we should stake him with an elephant stake but Anne Marie laughed and gave him some food from the bucket. 'No, he is OK,' she said. 'He just like to run around.' She had seen animals escape and be caught again, and had had strong horses and late nights and tired days. My dreams of a horse in the circus were in a state of disarray, and the gentle ponies of my childhood a million miles away. Dreams came to this: a struggle to control a highly overexcited horse with my own strength. But I felt reassured by her lack of surprise.

Prince had broken his tethering collar – the stitching had ripped right through. I attached the chain to the head-collar for the moment. My hands were sweating and the black dirt in my palms had turned to a pasty liquid. There wasn't any point in going to sleep again. I was wide awake and I wanted to keep an eye on Prince. 'Thank you very much, Woz.' He was shaking his dreadlocks and saying that that was a strong horse. Thank you for waking me up, don't worry about it, I just saw him running over to them horses.

After that Anne Marie and I put the stalls into the stables, with the help of Woz and Nick. We did the whole lot, elephant boards and partitions and the pen for the goats, long before the others arrived in the lorries from the last ground.

Ernest and Robert had to go back again for another load. In the evening Anne Marie and Eva, who had just arrived from her house in Whitstable, and Roget, Ruby, Lucian and I sat outside my caravan in the sun eating crisps and drinking beer. Gradually the entire company came over, Claire in a tight, cropped top and platform shoes, and Jason, Marine, Maya and Benni. The last load of lorries pulled on to the ground. Ernest and Robert climbed out of the cabs and came over and sat down at the table. Ernest looked exhausted. He drank a glass of whisky and talked about the journey with Roget.

Eva regarded the company. The lorries stood still around us and the dogs were quiet. 'This is a very difficult club to join, an exclusive club. You have to drive eight hundred miles in twenty-four hours, and then you can join,' she said.

The eight-hundred-mile club. Ernest had driven about that far in the last day, as there had been a breakdown too, and he had had to put up the poles, the king poles, the skeleton of the tent. No wonder he was exhausted. Up there, in the sky, the stars were starting to shine.

On the Friday night of that week we all had a barbecue after the seven o'clock show. I took off my costume and did Prince for the night. He had forgotten about the mares and was quiet in his stable. My dressing room is in the back of the van, behind the cab, and the door to it is inside the stable tent. It is a sliding door and he knows the noise of the metal hinges sliding on the runners; it means the end of the day, hay, his feed, and he neighs when he hears it. I hung my costumes in the wardrobe and gave him his feed bucket, then went into my caravan. I felt very tired that night, but through the open door of the caravan I could see the blown flames of the barbecues, and the children running about, chasing each other, captured and set free. They had been playing a game earlier where one person stands with their backs to the others, they have to creep forward, and when the person at the front looks round they all freeze: Clover and I used to play it in the garden in Oxford, it is called Grandmother's Footsteps. Eva watched them playing. 'Do you still play that game?' She laughed, 'There must be a renaissance in children's games.' The flames were rising and jumping from the little metal stands and there were bottles on the table, the light shining through at their centre and dark around the outside of the glass. The other light came from the lightbulbs hanging on cables around the caravan, and through the lace curtains at the windows and the open doors. The generator was still on so the whole ground was distantly floodlit by the light on top of the tent. It looked like a film-set, half real, half there.

I wanted to wake up, stretch out, relax. The show is very tiring, two hours long and two a day. I was not supposed to sit down during it, because I was constantly backwards and forwards through the curtains, announcing acts and filling in the gaps, smoothing things over, making the right timings. For example, the boys had to move all of Mademoiselle Yolande's props and take up the ring mat before the elephant came in, and she was the

next act, so in that space I had to speak slowly, add things in, perhaps a cheer and a few wolf-whistles, thank you, boys, and now,
ladies and gentlemen, trained and presented by Roget Santus,
will you please welcome, Rahnee the elephant. I stepped to one
side and gestured to the ring curtains. Sometimes nothing happened: there had been a delay behind the curtains. Rahnee the
ELEPHANT. Nothing happened. I hated those moments, when I
had to think of something funny to say on the spot – well, she
must have fallen asleep in the stables, the late RAHNEE.
Occasionally the clown ran through and we did a quick banter:
Marine, what are you doing? What are *you* doing? You have to
give your balloon to a young lady? OK, is there a young lady
who wants a balloon from Marine? And so on. Never, ever fall
asleep. An accident is about to happen around every corner, a
prop tangled in the rigging, a child running across the entrance
to the ring, a power-cut, an escaped pony. One time one of the
Shetlands, just before their act, escaped and ran out of the tent
and round the car park. Anne Marie and I chased him, in our
high heels and fishnets. I could hear the music changing and any
minute now I would be due back inside the ring. We caught him,
though, in time, and I was out of breath for the announcement.

I put on a pair of shorts and went out behind the caravan to
the trapeze prop. It is a high, scaffolding structure from which
the trapeze bar hangs. It was the perfect light to practise in – you
could see what you were doing but were still relatively hidden by
the dark. I gripped the bar and hung, felt the skin pull and
stretch on the inside of my fists. I pulled myself up once, and
again, no more, the strength went and my arms tensed ineffec-
tually. I regripped the bar and stood on the ground, then
jumped a bit and tipped my body back so that my legs swung up
and through my arms. I hooked my knees over the bar and

hung down, letting my arms drop and dangle towards the ground. The bar is not properly wrapped and is very hard: it pinches the back of your legs. I could see my shadow clearly to the side of the prop and my hair hung down like a wig. The kids came running over. 'Nellie trapeze, Nellie trapeze,' and they stood about pointing and clapping their hands and jumping on the spot. I reached up for the bar and went through my arms and hung like that, with my arms inside out, then dropped to the ground again. Claire and Jason appeared from the dark. Jason took off his top and reached for the bar. He swung round then hung in a perfect planche, his body suspended horizontal to the ground from his inverted hands. He dropped to the ground. Claire practised the planche. She is strong and sure on the bar. She pulled herself up on it and sat on it like a swing. The children stood about, watching and laughing.

We ate cooked chicken and salad, and Benni made some sausages, from a strong spicy meat. We drank wine and grappa and whisky. Yoyo and I made cocktails with peach schnapps and vodka. The liquids were thick and sweet. The music played on a stereo outside Robert's caravan, whose door was split and the top half was open. One of the poodles stood with its front paws on the top of the door, watching the barbecue. It looked like a lady with fluffy hair and a big nose.

Jason, Claire and Robert talked about going to a bar called the Circus tavern just down the road, but the night held us.

The food was eaten and the bottles emptied. It was very hot and still. Marine and I funny-danced, showing off, grand gestures and slapstick. Marine fell over and the children screamed, delighted. The grown-ups were getting drunk, and when they were drunk they were silly and didn't scold, but were like children again. Ernest went to switch off the generator and, as the noise of the engine died the ground fell dark, save the caravan lights and the light from the fire. Robert danced with Claire. She was dressed in a straight tight white satin skirt and an emerald top, and her long black hair fell back. She is superbly confident of her own body, she is quite large, but beautiful because she thinks beautiful. Yolande disco-danced: she is a good mover and good fun, smiling and making jokes. Jason never dances, ever, and he sat at one of the tables with Yolande and smiled. Roget just laughed and clapped and danced in the light from the barbecue, while Anne Marie danced barefoot.

The night deepened. A fog came down in the glowing distance. Ernest said that it was too foggy to walk to the Circus tavern, and Marine said it was always a mistake to leave the good parties. The ground we were dancing on was worn and dusty, the grass scraped away. Everyone seemed to lose their shoes. I sat down for a while and talked with Ernest. Maya sat on my lap. The music carried on, Robert changed a tape – some Caribbean juggling music. It was late now. Usually Ernest and Roget fall fast asleep at parties, in their chairs, their heads nodding and rocking, and they snore loudly. It is no wonder, by the evening, that everyone is exhausted.

Last season, after build-up, we had gone to the pub just down the road from the circus. I remember it distinctly as Elaina had been telling Ernest about an artist who had perfect white cuffs and collars, 'He did make me ashamed, Ernest, they were white, perfect white, always.' Roget fell asleep in his chair with a cigarette in his mouth. That night in Dagenham, however, an enthusiasm for the night spread through the entire company. Nobody went home early to their caravan, but danced and danced right through the night to morning. The problem of the artists leaving had passed: the Santus family can expand to fill a tent at the drop of a top hat. Yolande did her foot-juggling and some other cousins, a brother and sister called Tolly and Nina, arrived from Leatherhead with a hand-balancing act.

The move had been hard and long but by the end of the week energy had been regained. The night was warm and the business was good, the road busy and the ground not overlooked by houses. If our affection for each other had been undermined by Elaina's aggression, then that party reinstated the friendship that existed between everyone on the show. Claustrophobia was replaced with a deep sense of freedom. There were no conflicts, no problems, just the dark shape of the tent and the music, carefully watched by the poodle. In the light of the fires they seemed to be a multitude of good friends, with whom I would not be for ever, with whom I would lose touch, though never forget, and that was the point, the electricity: it was the moment then, passing, never regained, never forgotten.

Summer
Whitstable, August 1997

And I must borrow every changing shape.
To find expression . . . dance, dance
Like a dancing bear.

Portrait of a Lady, T.S. ELIOT

Throughout the fortnight that we were in Whitstable, the weather remained very hot. It was almost unbearable for working: we all sweated hard and it was impossible to keep makeup on for more than half the show – it just ran down your face and into your eyes. I developed a loathing for fishnet tights – as I woke on a hot morning I would dread the moment, later, in the sweltering afternoon, when I would have to put them on. In the afternoons I washed Prince, held the end of the hosepipe over my head, or ducked my head and shoulders into the big plastic barrels of water outside the stable tent. Sometimes, when Roget was washing the elephant, I would climb up on to her back and help him clean her. I would be covered in mud and drenched in water, but it was so hot that it didn't matter – you could drench yourself in water from the hosepipe (which ran warm all day) and within minutes the sun dried your clothes crisp again.

For the show, however, such abandon to the conditions was impossible. This was how I dealt with the heat when I was getting ready: I would open all the windows of the caravan so that a breeze ran through it, then have a cold shower and, still cold from the shower, put on my tights and leotard. Under the fishnets we wore shiny dancing tights. That is a terrible feeling, in the sweating heat, to stretch on thick, elastic tights. I would sit down at the table and put on my makeup. It was so hot that a layer of foundation on my skin felt like wool and my skin sweat and the makeup ran off. I carried my coat to the back of the tent and wore a cotton shirt over my costume. Then I would lead Prince across the ground to the tent, and we both stood there, in the hot oppressive air of the tent, sweating, standing very still, trying not to overheat. The hot weather made Prince very docile, and he loved standing under the hosepipe to be washed; I would run it right over his head, and he drank from the end of the pipe.

The evenings were magic, though. The air never moved and the heat didn't go away. We would sit outside the caravans eating and drinking. Candle flames stood still and tall. The grass was very long and brown. I had become good friends with Robert. Sometimes, after the show, we would walk across the fields at the back of the ground and swim in the sea. We walked back one evening quite late. Everyone had gone out, except Roget. He was sitting in the fold-up chair outside his caravan with Ruby on his lap. The chair had a pink crocheted blanket on it. Roget said that he had had it for fifteen years – it is an aluminium picnic chair – and he showed me where he had mended it. That is typical of circus people: they bother to mend things, keep things, make the old things work and live on. Ruby was leaning back against his chest, and they were both looking at the stars. Every few minutes a shooting star fell across the sky, and Roget pointed out to Ruby the falling stars and the patterns he knew, the Great Bear and a Dolphin and Orion's belt. Robert and I said a few words to them, but Roget didn't really move. He said he loved looking at the stars. Another shooting star fell, across the top of the dark tent, and behind its familiar silhouette. Ruby saw it and pointed to it.

After one of the shows at the weekend we were to go and eat with Eva. Her house is about five minutes from the ground, and faces on to the little road outside the Oyster Bar in Whitstable. I was standing in the dark behind the curtains during the Western act. Eva appeared out of nowhere, as she always does, gliding around the corners of the tent. She was standing beside me and she had her camera round her neck. She said, 'Join me for dinner after the show, and I've asked Robert as well.'

I was pleased to leave the ground for the evening, and after the show, on the prompt of the closing noise and the silence of the generator being shut down, the darkening of the tent's surface as the top lights switched off, I left my caravan and walked across the ground to Ernest's car. Roget was standing outside his caravan; he had just finished putting the elephant to bed and his bow-tie was undone and hanging around his neck. There were chairs outside his caravan and the children were crying inside. Beyond on the turning road an empty bus passed, each window lit up. The night was clear and there were shooting stars again. It was hot and still and Eva was already at her house. I was looking forward to seeing her.

Talking to Eva is always a pleasure to anticipate. She is a meticulous cook, and cooking is itself a drawn-out process, and finely done, but she is never without ideas, always attuned to the present moment. She is a comic, she was born in showbusiness and breathes it too, vitally clashing the most morose Irish pessimism with a sharp blade of wit and insight. Although she doesn't live on the show full-time, Eva organises all the paperwork for the circus, and deals with its bureaucratic problems.

'Let's stop for a break,' the lawyer said to Eva, during a meeting.

'I feel broken already,' she sighed.

I wait beside Ernest's car; the doors are locked and he is in his caravan. I knock, he said two minutes. Sorrow, the little brown collie, circled at the end of its chain, pulled towards me then turned and fitted into the little wooden kennel. I crouched near it and whistled and the little dog came out again. Eva loved that dog, loved it, and Sasha took it for long walks in the deep grass. As I stroked the clean head and looked at the dog's black eyes somebody was standing behind me beside the car. It was a tall person, with a familiar large frame – not elegant or uncomfortable, affably clumsy, a powerful body – someone capable of generous affection when reservations are overcome. I suspected, a kid turned into a man without protest but without much understanding either. I could not see his face clearly but I could see his mouth smiling and I saw gold in his ear and round his neck.

'Robert,' I said, and that was his father's name. His father had married into the circus and Robert's strongest connection with it was through the dynasty that constituted his maternal family. Robert was a Santus.

'I've just knocked for Ernest and he's coming in a second.'

'I know,' he said. 'I saw you walk past the door of my caravan a few minutes ago. Can we stop at the off-licence, do you think, to buy Eva some wine? Will it be open? What time is it?' He was like a child sometimes, asking questions.

'Gone ten, I should think,' I said, and I had to go back to the caravan to fetch some money. I said, 'Can you ask Ernest to wait for one minute if he comes out?'

I ran back over the ground. Roget's dog was still out on its chain and it barked as the wood of my clogs banged on the pallet outside my caravan door. I went inside quickly and found my wallet in the cupboard above the table. We had been paid the night before and it was full of money. I pulled out ten pounds and put it back in the cupboard, flicked the door shut and switched off the light. My older sister had made me a wooden clown that hung from the light cable and it was swinging slightly with the movement of the caravan. There was a knock on the side of the caravan. I turned and saw Robert standing in the doorway. He was still smiling and his eyes had a question in them. He stepped through the door and he was taller than me, seemed to fill up the caravan. Outside, Anne Marie was standing on the steps of her caravan and calling to Roget, that voice that was always the same, always despairing, desiring, tiring, '*Mon cher, mon cher,*' and beyond, in the darkness, fixing a pipe, wiring a plug, Roget calls, '*J'arrive, j'arrive.*' Robert said that Ernest would meet us at the gate. He turned round suddenly. 'We had better go now,' he said. 'The off-licence will be closed.' We left the caravan. I pulled the door shut and we walked away from the tent and the other caravans to the gate.

Sasha was sitting in the passenger seat. They had just pulled up at the gate. I got into the back seat while Robert opened the gate. My money was in my pocket and I was holding a jersey for if it got cold later on.

Ernest, Sasha and Robert went to the pub beside the house. Whitstable is busy and cosmopolitan. Eva loves Whitstable. 'I think Whitstable is like San Francisco,' she said. People were coming and going from the pubs. She has a very rare way of seeing, and valuable: she prizes an object that is original, that is not a copy or an imitation. A particular rag doll from a second-hand shop, a delicate clock made of driftwood, a thirties lamp with glass beads hanging from the edge of the shade. She never does anything without thinking very deeply as to the right decision. There is a wooden picture frame on the wall and two pictures propped in the frame.

Eva opened the door. Her hair was down and she was in the middle of cooking. She moves delicately. She went back through the house to the kitchen, and she was as she always was: the smell of burning garlic and opened wine, the thin rasp of her voice and the promise of long conversation. 'He would go to the pub,' she said of Ernest. 'Honestly, Nell, take my advice and never marry into the circus. Look at me, cooking all night, the fellas in the pub.'

I sat down in the chair beside the door to the kitchen. I was so tired. The smell of the cooking food and the wood of Eva's furniture, the window open to hot summer air was a sensory reminder of Minety and all of life before Mum had her accident, and I thought that that, perhaps, was all of life's objectives, to create the sensory experience of childhood. I wondered about the long years of their marriage, Eva so cultured, never losing heart in talk – I mean that no subject would bewilder her, there is no subject she cannot consider brilliantly, nothing is beyond her – and Ernest preoccupied unequivocally with the circus. The world outside, so meaningful to Eva, to him is nothing.

'Ernest thought that Bob Dylan was one of the Beatles,' she told me, and she was still laughing, still disbelieving, twenty-five years later. I opened a bottle of wine and poured two glasses. The others were at the door; I could see them through the frosted glass. I went to open it and they came in, admired everything, took seats, lit cigarettes. Eva came through from the kitchen, kissed Robert and Ernest and asked Sasha to find another chair upstairs. 'Dinner isn't quite ready yet, guys,' she said.

The house was full of books, bought by Eva and inherited too, from circus fans now dead. Two shelves are full of circus books. Eva had lent me some when I first joined the circus. Robert pulled one out, saw a picture of his family, and more, who were cousins, and friends, all the way back, dead and alive, people passed and loved and lost and never seen again.

I stood at the door of the kitchen. Eva was dropping sliced potato into hot fat. There were bright knives and salad scattered on the side. She gave me a bowl of strawberries to slice. 'Do you still love the circus?' she asked me.

I said I did, and she said I was mad, leaned hard on the mad.

'It's nice to fall in love in the circus.' They were well into the circus by now next door, and the hissing of the fat drowned our conversation from them.

'But think of it in fifteen years' time, screaming kids, a pile of laundry, never allowed anywhere near your typewriter. Don't make my mistake.'

'What about Robert?' I asked. I had become closer to him than I had meant to.

'He is very fond of you.' Eva took some potatoes from the pan, put them on a plate, with chicken, and passed it to me. I took it to the table with a bowl of salad. Sasha was upstairs playing computer games and Eva called him to supper.

We ate a large meal, close up as the house was small. The television was on at the other end of the room, behind a bookshelf that jutted out into the middle of the room. Robert and Ernest talked of their family in France, how bit it was, everywhere, even in restaurants in Spain they know of us, know of the Santus family. Robert said that he had stayed on a campsite in France for a bit and there were some gypsies staying there as well. In England the gypsies and the circus are entirely separate, but in France it is different. The circus and the gypsies intermarry more readily and help each other along the way. I can't remember exactly what it was but the gypsies had helped Robert in some way at this campsite, perhaps with a part for a lorry or moving a caravan. Robert looked at his uncle for confirmation. 'That's right, though, isn't it, how they see the circus? *Le voyageur*, eh? *Le voyageur*, the same as them.'

Le voyageur. I was never to be just like them, always on the outside, but deeply seduced. I felt drunk and tired, and I shut my eyes. I heard French and English, and Ernest was calling my name, 'Nellie, Nellie, don't fall asleep, Nellie. Eva is making coffee.' I gave Ernest a cigarette. He chewed it in his mouth and shut his eyes: he was starting to fall asleep too.

'You guys look tired,' Eva said. We are always tired. There is not an evening in the circus when someone is not falling asleep. Robert is saying something in French again.

'Better we go back, eh?' Ernest said. 'We have some coffee and go back.'

We drank black coffee and Sasha was still playing computer games.

When we got back to the ground Ernest said goodnight, banged shut the door of his caravan. For a few minutes the tiredness lifted in the fresh air. Robert and I looked at the moon and the falling stars. It was bright and clear and silent. The tent was its own dark shape, rearranging the landscape. Inside, it would be pitch-black and sweet-smelling. The moon is a night-time sun and lit up the sides of the lorries: zebras gallop with heads perpetually twisted to the sky. I couldn't forget that *le voyageur*, nor fail to be dazzled by his bright white teeth and gold. He was saying something in French to his grandfather, who had opened his caravan door, hearing the noise. Grandpère waved an old man's wave and laughed, and shut the door again. Robert and I said goodnight, and I walked towards my caravan. In a quiet world the animals were still restless on the lorries.

Leysdown
August 1997

This is what you shall do . . . take off your hat to nothing known or unknown or to any man or number of men . . . and your very flesh shall be a great poem and have the richest fluency not only in its words but in the silent lines of its lips and face and between the lashes of your eyes and in every motion and joint of your body.
Preface to *Leaves of Grass*, WALT WHITMAN

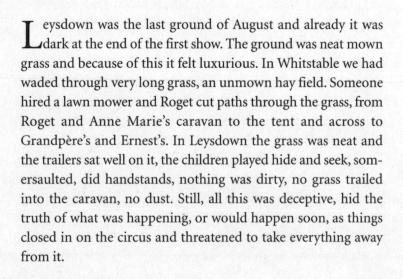

Leysdown was the last ground of August and already it was dark at the end of the first show. The ground was neat mown grass and because of this it felt luxurious. In Whitstable we had waded through very long grass, an unmown hay field. Someone hired a lawn mower and Roget cut paths through the grass, from Roget and Anne Marie's caravan to the tent and across to Grandpère's and Ernest's. In Leysdown the grass was neat and the trailers sat well on it, the children played hide and seek, somersaulted, did handstands, nothing was dirty, no grass trailed into the caravan, no dust. Still, all this was deceptive, hid the truth of what was happening, or would happen soon, as things closed in on the circus and threatened to take everything away from it.

Eva sat in my caravan after the show. 'They will be here by the end of the week, you know, and we can't stop them coming. The VAT men. They know how hard it is, to exist, to make a living. But they will still come. There is a woman in the VAT office who thinks that we are cruel to the animals, and so she is making a problem where before they left us alone. There is vindictiveness in their action.' One afternoon, last winter, when we were parked in Sidcup, Anne Marie had shown me some pictures from the year before, of Ruby's christening. There was a boy who looked after the elephant. Anne Marie said he was ever so dirty but for that day he put on his one clean top, which was a thick wool jersey. 'You know,' she said, 'he didn't take it off all day, even though he was boiling hot.' She was smiling, remembering the boy and the day. They had had a service in the tent and Eva and Ernest were godparents. She showed me a photograph of Roget outside the tent holding Ruby. Ruby is wearing a blue and white gingham dress. The sky is blue and the tent is yellow and green and Roget looks very handsome, the little daughter smiling. In those photographs they seem more themselves than ever, strong, sure, making time for family ceremony in their relentlessly hardworking lives. That is why I think about those photographs when people try and hurt the circus. Eva said it was not my problem, though, 'Don't worry about it, Nell.' Outside the caravan we can hear the funfair. 'Let's go up the road to the bar and enjoy ourselves, right?' she said.

An old alarm clock was lying on the table. Eva picked it up and shook it. The hands had stopped. She looked over it with her glasses and turned it so that it caught the light, which curled around it.

'Anyway, a miracle will save us at the last minute. Things always work out all right in the end, don't they?' She shook her head. 'Why do you like all this so much, Nell? You're far too romantic about it. You don't understand that a life in the circus will leave you time for nothing else.'

I stood up and opened the door of the shower. I pulled some cotton wool out of the plastic bag hanging on the shower fitting and wiped off my black eyes and red lips. Some of the sparkly eye-shadow went into my eyes and stung. The bags under my eyes and the spots on my skin were revealed as I wiped off the makeup. My eyes looked red and were smeared all around with black. I wiped it off, again and again. It sat on the inner rim of the eyelid and was impossible to get off, so I left it. I thought that I did understand, and many times I cursed the exclusivity of my circus life.

'But, still,' Eva said, 'fall in love in the circus. That is very nice, but don't forget the screaming kids in twenty years, and the mountain of laundry. Listen to me. You will thank me one day.'

I carried on looking into the mirror and wiping my face. I could hear some voices. I had talked with Marine the other night. He said, 'You must follow your own way, believe me, your own way, you understand me?'

I felt I was with family. I didn't want to be far away from the tent, but I could hear those voices loudly in my head, go your own way, don't fall under, don't be seduced. I wanted to feel the circus as it really is and yet I couldn't, or didn't dare. And something else was creeping up on me, tiredness, the thief in the night that takes away all energy for the day. I felt an acute need to live in one place for more than a week, for my caravan door to hold the same view for more than a few days. Bricks, mortar, a garden, local shops where I could become a familiar face. I felt that I was learning what it really is to be itinerant, and I realised with dismay that I was fighting myself. I did not belong on the road.

'Look at me,' Eva said. 'I am still amazed to find myself in the circus. I can never feel that it is home.'

I remembered her sitting in the cab of my lorry one night, earlier in the season, on a move night. She had leaned forward on the steering wheel and said that she couldn't quite believe it, that she was still here, twenty years later, in the cab of a lorry, waiting on a circus ground. Even now she thought, What on earth am I doing here? 'Let my life be a warning to you, Nell,' she added. I listened to her advice, and I wondered silently how much longer I could keep going in the circus.

'You must follow your own way, believe me.' That was in the back of the tent, before a show, and Marine's lips were pressed tightly together and he wasn't smiling, and his eyes, which had a cloud of white greasepaint around them, were locked into mine.

The bar at the top of the road in Leysdown had a low roof and red carpets. It sold alcopops, lager, cheap cocktails. The walls were covered in hand-drawn notices. Disco on Saturday Night! Happy Hour! Karaoke! Men sat at the bar and families at the tables. Children ran about and teenagers skirted the pool tables, drinking Coke. The East End go to Leysdown for the bank holiday, out through the East End to the Isle of Sheppey, and the long muddy beaches and late-night karaoke, fish and chips for the kids and bumper cars and popcorn and every variety of kiss-me-quick, and beers outside the end of the Las Vegas arcade strip that runs from the supermarket and the novelty stands and the junk shop (the girl selling novelties had long blonde hair and long legs and dark glasses and she watched the whole town go by) to the sea wall and the beach screened by high litter banks. Sunny Leysdown on Sea. Leysdown village.

Couples drove past the circus on the way into town in Cadillacs, listening to music loudly. There are caravan parks, acres of chalets behind big gates, sign-written and guarded by boys in Cortinas with packets of cigarettes, and in front of the circus, right opposite, was the funfair. Prince looked up and neighed when they first fired up their music. 'You've got to move it, groove it, shake it, baby, who do you think you are?' On the rides they gave us free tickets and laughed innuendo: 'Come back tonight, baby, and you can have a free ride, it goes much faster.' Claire and Jason were on the bumper cars and Roget malleted the test-your-strength machine and nearly broke it, and Ruby won a toy panda, and the boy with the goldfish and black eyes was half Swiss. We went to the fair almost every night after the show and then to the bar up the road. That was where we were heading that night, not to the fair, though, not that night.

A girl was standing on the platform at the end of the room singing Whitney Houston. She was a very good singer, young, and her hair was long and blonde. She was fifteen, the star of Leysdown on Sea, the mini-priestess of the empty-orchestra, the kid with the honey voice and the grown-up body. On cabaret nights she wore a velvet dress and sang in the disco hall. At the bar they said she was a great singer and she ran the karaoke too. She seemed sullen and bitchy. Sasha adored her and her picture was in the windows of the pub on the outside.

Eva, Robert, Sasha and I sat at one of the tables. Ernest is over by the bar with Yolande, buying some drinks. Tolly was another of Ernest's nephews and he had come over for the evening from Leatherhead. He was very noisy and funny. He looked half Mexican and he was quite short, with big lips, piss-taking eyes, and a croaky, joking voice. Eva said that you would come to Leysdown if you were a celebrity trying to hide away from it all, or if you were on the run and wanted a place to hide.

Leysdown is a very poor place. At the car-boot sale people try to sell bundles of broken coat-hangers and kids play with discoloured Barbie dolls in muddy puddles, and there are no pet dogs to be seen but fighting dogs. Nevertheless the bar draws you into its seaside melodies, and I relaxed for a bit – vanilla alcopops, cigarettes, crisps.

A boy with muscular dystrophy, caught in a wheelchair, was at the front of the stage. He could only just move forward, his head was locked to one side, his mouth was open and his eyes looked in different directions. He lived in the care home beside the circus. Some of the other patients had been to the circus already to look at the animals. A woman with a long skirt and a complicated jersey had stood on the other side of the barbed-wire fence and put her hand on the wire. She was clearly very disturbed: she had painted her face bright red. She looked over to the box-office where I was sitting speaking with Eva. We both saw her over the fence and went outside to hear what she was saying. She wanted a ticket for the circus so Eva gave her some ringside seats. She said, 'Thank you. I will come tomorrow.' She walked back to the care home. The boy in the wheelchair was called Chris. He wanted to sing on the karaoke machine and he did, slowly, croaking, agonising, the words only just there, but there. Eva was sitting to my left and the karaoke stage was to my right. She had her hand in her hair and her head was resting on that same hand, and she was watching the boy singing. Suddenly I felt overcome with embarrassment at his singing, the worst kind of embarrassment. I said something to Eva, to distract myself from it, but she urged me to listen to him. 'That is just so moving, isn't it?' she said. 'Listen to him. That is really brave.' Everyone in the bar supported him and cheered at the end of the song. It was a love song. After that he sang 'You'll Never Walk Alone' and everyone joined in, but it was the love song that was moving. That is what Eva always does, though: she makes one look more closely; Eva stares at the minute fabric of life. She once found a painting in a junk shop of an old shed beside a railway line, in the middle of nowhere, anywhere, in the middle of who knows what, but in an empty, gloomy landscape. On the wall of the shed was a ripped, faded circus poster. If you looked very closely at it, you could see the lettering and the clown's face. It was very intricately and finely painted. Eva found a magnifying glass, and peered right at it. 'It is a miniature,' she said, 'perfect, a gem.'

That was her word, gem, and it was a gem, precious, difficult to find, brilliant when you looked very closely at it. Eva paints miniatures too, and when you look at the tiny expressive faces you can't believe that they are reduced reproductions; they are like tiny faces seen through a telescope, far away, but the detail remains.

We drank some more alcopops and there were peanuts scattered on the table. The star of Leysdown was singing one of her songs and Sasha watched her from under his baseball cap with an expression of dismal resignation. He wouldn't talk to her, was mortified by the idea, rather drank the Cokes that everyone bought him and walked back to the circus. Tolly and Robert sang a song together. The man introduced them as clowns, circus duo, the boy who drops all his clubs – and Robert blushed. They sang 'Summer Nights' from *Grease*. They were very funny, Tolly indignantly refusing to sing anything love-wise to Robert, Robert slightly serious, singing properly. Tolly was wearing a baseball cap back to front, almost a beret. He knew how to stand on a stage, turning his body but not his head, making eye-contact with the very back of the room, never turning his back to the audience, not even a bit.

I was finding myself falling for Robert. I saw after a while that his bullying came from anxiety. He had bossed me around at the start of the season because he was worried about his own position, and did not have the maturity to deal with that worry: it seemed to me that he was a boy who had turned into a man without much understanding of the transformation. He had grown up with the Santus Troupe and had told me how he could remember as a child being shouted at for touching the bright chrome unicycles. They had always had perfect costumes, perfect hair, they were real professionals. He was excessively proud of his uncles – me uncles, he called them. He worked very hard for them, drove all night, and when he arrived at a new ground he would run up and down the road waving in the lorries, uncoupling the Atkinson, Ernest's favourite lorry, recoupling something else, backing up trailers, helping his mum and sister. I could hear Ernest and Roget all the time – Robert, Robert – calling to him in the darkness for help with something. As the season progressed he lost a lot of weight and he relaxed, as he saw that he was as invaluable to the show as he wanted to be.

Robert took me out to dinner and he bought me flowers, but he insisted that he had a wandering eye and always would have, which annoyed me. He was transient. That was in his bones. He would not form a strong attachment to people whom he knew instinctively would pass by. I would leave the circus eventually, and although he and I had quite similar personalities we were from different cultures, and this difference stood as a barrier between us. Or maybe the plain and simple fact of the matter was that he didn't fancy me and, puerile as it sounds, this was annoying.

Robert started to undo all the independence I had found for myself along the way. I like to think of myself as totally independent and going my own way. I have heard those voices and have listened to their advice. But he was messing with my head and I was infuriated. I drank a few more alcopops. A man called Roy was heckled on to the stage and sang swingingly in a great baritone, 'Delilah'. That is the chorus, 'My, my, my Delilah'. In the song a lover is stabbed. The bar is swinging. 'Delilah'. His voice was great, the song perfectly sentimental, tragi-comic, a big song sung well, and everyone cheered. The queen of Leysdown Karaoke Club sang as well. I got up to buy a round. The man at the bar was the landlord. 'She sings well,' I said.

He was watching her. 'Yes, she is a good singer.'

I think my emotions were being spun out along these songs. That always happens. The truly tackiest songs spin you right out. I remember, when I was nineteen, standing beside my friend Andrew's pick-up in the drive at Minety. He had come over from the farm at the back of the tip in Cheltenham for the Minety festival, a big village fête that took place on our fields. The last year before the accident, Mum had organised it: she got the farrier to come and shoe the horses as a demonstration; she asked a man who lays hedges to come and lay a section (this left a hole in the hedge that never grew again); someone else built a length of dry-stone wall; the local foxhounds came for the day and Mum set up a terrier-and-lurcher show; she gave the children rides on Brian, a Shetland pony. There is a photograph somewhere of Mum with the pony: she is running with it, her skirts blowing, laughing, and there are three children all laughing too, running along beside her. There is a child on the pony, laughing. Mum has got her head back slightly. She was very excitable, I remember that, she would laugh and giggle and jump up and down sometimes, and she loved it when people were having a good time at her expense. She used to bring out bottles of whisky at the drop of a hat. There was nothing stingy or half-hearted about her at all. She was exceptionally well liked. Now, when I talk to people about her who knew her from the days when we lived at Minety they speak with unreserved affection. Charlotte. She smiled with her eyes, as they say. Why did it have to happen to such a goodun when there are so many badduns?

The next year they held the fête again. Mum was there with a lady who looked after her as a nurse. They wandered about the stands, but Mum looked confused, rubbed her forehead, and hissed, because she had lost the power of speech. It was utterly miserable. She had to be changed every few hours, and she was too tired to join in, too tired and too ill. I didn't know what to do and I felt as if I was going mad. I stood beside Andrew's pick-up, then sat down on the ground and cried. We were just outside the house, and beyond, in the fields, the fête was still going on. The whole event had been shot through with tragedy. Andrew and I had had some laughs, yes, like when his collie sat on the trailer during the tractor-and-trailer reversing competition, obediently doing what farm collies do, but it was too sad to be happy. 'Come back to Cheltenham with me,' Andrew had said. He put out his arms and I stood up and gave him a hug.

At that moment from the fields we could hear on the old Tannoy that someone had rigged up that they were playing the song that goes 'I am your lady and you are my man', an eighties classic. I was sobbing. 'The music doesn't help much,' said Andrew drily, but he was nearly crying too. That is what I mean. Your emotions get spun out along the lines of the song.

I laughed to myself at my own boundless sentimentality. The

seats were worn red velvet. I would not look at Robert. It was sweet, though, and the beach where we swam was lit by the moonlight. You said you had a wandering eye. I will have a wandering eye too, then.

The boys in the fairground screamed for the punters on the last few minutes of the rides. SCREAM LOUDER. That was what they chanted over and over again. There were lightbulbs in the eyes and loud music in the ears. A girl in a nylon T-shirt and leggings was singing 'Wild Thing', almost just saying the words. She had a thin face. 'Wild thing, I think I love you.' Robert was staring at her. He was undoing the whole lesson I had taught myself. But that was OK. I could do it up again, in time, and maybe a bit of feeling, torn this way and that, was as interesting as it was superficially painful – and, in any case, that is the point, the game, the laugh, and before long, in sober day, there would be more serious things to think about, and when they came to hurt the circus, no one would think of these seaside amusements.

Raid

A show coming in over a country road comes right out of the land of pure imagination and vanishes as mysteriously as it came.

'Big Top Rhythms', IRVING K. POND

~

It seemed as if the week darkened. It had been so hot when we built up the tent. On Tuesday morning, as I was lifting the canopy on to the box-office with Ernest, the boys had called from the fairground across the road, as the heat was starting, '*Bonjour!*' We had waved from the front of the box-office. I sold tickets over the wooden counter, through the hole in the window, and while Grandpère carefully wired his circus boards to the hedge they uncurled green tarpaulins from the waltzer chariots.

That evening, at the start of the week, there had been no show, and the sky was clear and blue and the sun was shining hot. I took Prince to the beach. The figures on the shore were little stick men and nobody seemed to mind that I was riding along there. I saw a family wave from the shore and I rode inland a bit, across sands that were shiny or wet. I waved back and a little girl in a yellow dress started to run across the beach towards me and Prince. I could hear the parents shouting to be careful of the horse. I shouted back to them that it was all right, he wouldn't hurt anyone. They stopped shouting and I could hear them laughing with each other. I rode towards the child and she ran towards me. Then we were standing beside each other and I jumped down off Prince.

'Why have you got a horse here?'

'I'm exercising him.'

'Does he like the seaside?'

'He does now.'

'Can I ride on him?'

'Well, you can sit on him.'

'Will he bite me?'

'No. Don't put your hand out. Here, pat him on his neck.'

I bent down, lifted her up and put her on Prince's back. She held on to the front of the saddle. Behind me, the sun was against the rocks in the far distance, although the rays were still touching the water. That was the last hot summer day I remember distinctly.

Later in the week Clover came to stay. On Thursday afternoon we walked up to Leysdown's Las Vegas strip and bought solid sugar doughnuts from the man I had met in the pub the night before. We watched the bumper cars in the big concrete building – the bumper-car man had a broad bare chest and a shaved head. Then we sat on the wall at the end of the strip and looked at the stony shore below. There were gulls painted on to the sky and a high blowing bank of multicoloured rubbish, and all the children ran out from the chalet park and through the rubbish and rain and on to the muddy sands. There was a continuous noise of electronic music from the arcades and high shouts from the children. Clover came to the circus and helped me with my jobs, washed up and cleaned Prince. All the kids in the circus loved her. They ran and caught her legs, Clover, Clover, Clover, and in the show-time she sat on the low wooden trolley at the back of the tent and they all sat round her. She turned and leaned on the sea wall and looked at the sea. She said she was working hard now, for her exams. She liked it, her work, but she liked this too, living outside and being with the children. She said that when she had children Mum's accident wouldn't matter so much any more. Things would have come full circle. I said I felt pulled back to stationary life now; more than ever I missed the stability of our childhood. She brushed the sand from her hands.

That night after the show we went up to the bar for a drink. Claire and Jason were there, and Marine, Benni and Maya. They were all sitting around one table. No one from the Santus family was with them. They had pints of beer and crisps. Jason was talking quietly to Claire and she was looking at the table. She glanced up as Clover and I walked over to where they were sitting. The bar was full and the stools at the bar were crowded. Claire looked at us and smiled her closed smile – mouth shut – and tossed her hair. We bought a pint of beer each and drank it with them. Something seemed to be missing from the conversation. After that we walked across the road and bought some chips for supper.

I felt that we should get back to the ground quickly. That night something was not right. The quiet that rests on the circus ground at the end of the day, when the circus is not moving, when the animals have been put to bed, the dogs have stopped barking and the public has gone home, did not seem to be there that evening in Leysdown. By the end of the day in the circus everyone is knackered, dog tired – many times I have sat in the trailer with Anne Marie while Ernest, Roget and Grandpère sleep in their chairs. The circus takes every last drop of energy, hides it away in the heavy walls of the tent and in the rough under-neath of the seating planks, along the taut ropes that hang the curtains by pulley blocks from the inside roof of the tent, and in the straw of the animals' pens. The string of coloured lightbulbs in the roof of the stable tent illuminates tired faces, and the grass behind the curtain is trampled by exhaustion. Roget and Ernest are fit and strong, masters of endurance and hard-living, long hours, dead weight, freezing rain, but by the evening the circus seems to have overwhelmed them.

That night the doors of the caravans were open. The ground was dark as the generator had been shut down. Clover and I could hear people talking and moving about in the darkness. There were no raised voices and we could not hear laughter, only a steady noise of wood against metal falling from a low height. The noise went on all night. Clover and I sat around the table in the caravan. I went outside to see if I could help. Around the other side of the tent Robert and Roget were lifting a heavy crate from the back of a lorry. They were speaking French. I saw the glint of an eyeball or the cast shadow of a body but they seemed, and the voices, to become interchangeable. I thought that they didn't want any help, that they wanted to work alone. Through the darkness I could sense deep anxiety. What was occurring was strictly family business, and I went back inside the caravan.

In the morning I went to the box-office as usual at nine thirty. All around the still lorries were huge piles of old props and crates of props, seating stands, heavy iron stringers and wooden seating boards, costumes, bales of hay, coils of rope and coils of metal cable, scaffolding bars and signs, tarpaulins, stakes, strips of plastic, metal railings. All the lorries were empty. The back of the seating truck was open. Roget was standing on the dusty floor and he looked exhausted. He was unloading the last pile of metal chairs. 'Goodbye, lorry. Good lorry, this. Ten years I work to keep her going. Now what is happening?'

Every week that I had spent with that circus I had followed that lorry into a new region late on a Sunday night or early on a Monday morning. Now I can't forget the sight of them, a string of coloured lorries winding away in front of me through new unfamiliar early countryside, church steeples over the hedges, or brand new industrial estates, or small towns, still asleep as the circus arrived (only the milkman would see us or a farmer with cattle, or a drunk on a bench), and I can't forget the sight of the lorries in the coloured line making their way forwards, backwards, the pioneers in reverse, unprotected museum pieces.

The painted clown's face that had been bolted on to the side of the Mercedes van was lying face down on the grass. The circus had never looked untidy like that. Ernest had never allowed equipment to lie around on the grass or the lorries to stand with their doors open. But now the circus looked like the scene of a disaster, or as if someone had been searching like a burglar through the contents of the vehicles, and thrown things all over the grass.

That morning the VAT men arrived in brand new shiny black Land Rovers. They all wore dark glasses and hats, and they had the efficiency and manpower of money. Their drivers sat on the grass beside the gate to the circus and waited for the negotiating to finish. Ernest persuaded them to leave him one lorry. After that they drove the rest away to be sold at auction the following weekend. Anne Marie sat on the steps of the box-office with the children and watched.

'You OK?'

'I can't believe all that work is gone, taken away.'

'It's terrible.'

I didn't know what to say. Ernest, Roget and Robert had faces that had been up all night and none of them was smiling.

Eva explained to me that previously the tax men, realising that the circus was struggling hard to survive, had put them on a back burner and had taxed them according to what they were able to pay. If they were behind on their tax payments I do not think that the way they were treated could be said to be fair or humane. Money was clearly short and the family were working round the clock to keep the circus going. They are an art form, and as such are surely eligible for financial support. She had told me about the woman in the tax office who had taken against them because they had animals: they were being punished for being cruel. I felt that the word cruel had been torn from its meaning, abstracted, thoughtlessly applied to these people who lived for their animals, lived for them more than anyone else I knew. If you pass by Santus Circus, call in and look at the stables: there will be a few camels grazing in the field, some rabbits in hutches, ponies on tethers, and there might be a blind child laughing in delight as it buries its hand in a chicken's feathers. But the tax man took their lorries away, made business even harder, and in doing so were satisfying the small-town prejudices of the politically correct.

Ernest's will was stronger than that of the VAT men. They left him one lorry. He had a day to move the entire circus, and he did it. I could not believe it. Secretly I had given up hope for the circus. I thought they would have to stay in Leysdown for another week, or move slowly back to Sidcup and lose the back end of the season. It was crucial for business that Ernest stood at the ground following Leysdown. And in the face of these massive logistical problems he did it. He moved the circus. He did over ten trips backwards and forwards with that one lorry. The following weekend he went to the auction and bought back some of his lorries.

Santus Circus continued to tour right through to the late autumn, and the blessing of an Indian summer allowed them a long back end and good business. I visited them twice and the tent was full on both occasions. The circus went back on the road for the 1998 season. I am amazed by the willpower of people for whom nothing seemed easy. They are formidable people.

Shortly after the VAT raid I handed in my notice, and left Santus Circus at the end of September. I had been with them for a year and felt an unequivocal need to move on – which is the wrong phrase. I felt a need to stop moving on, to settle in one place, even if only for a few months. It was they who were moving on.

Ernest and Eva, Roget and Anne Marie did not seem to hold it against me that I had left before the season was finished. They said they understood – and I suspect that what they meant, benignly, was that they had expected nothing more from an amateur. I was a josser, all right. I can only thank the Santus family for their humour and affection.

I believe that Santus Circus is perhaps the only circus in England where the true spirit of the circus survives. The circus happens as a reflex. It is not a customer-care consumer product. I would have thought that Santus Circus will probably never have an e-mail address. It is just a circus. Yet it is a precious object. It is fragile and vulnerable. It fights like an army. Don't ignore Grandpère's wooden boards. Don't tear down Eva's posters. Don't sign petitions against them. Don't smash up the lorries or blow the car horn or scream insults from your car window. There can be no greater dedication to art than the lives of the circus people. Think about it. They do not go to and from offices or galleries to home or to studios. Their entire existence, for ever, their family life, their upbringing, their relationship with their children, husbands, wives, in-laws, animals, all these things are an expression and a result of their dedication to their work, their art, and their own particular, peculiar, precious culture.

Epilogue

'Amateurs?' said the old clown, looking over the top of the steel spectacles that gave him such a severe look when in plain clothes. 'No, you won't run across many amateurs in our business. You see . . .' he shook out the shimmering silk folds of a pair of vermilion pantaloons on to which he was sewing gold and silver stars '. . . ours is a job for what you might call specialists. Even to make a clown's dress like this so as to hit the public slap in the eye needs experience. And, you may take it from me, you can't become a rider – what we reckon a rider – nor yet an acrobat, nor yet go on the wire or the trapeze without you've studied from the first days you can stand. That's why circus people will tell you that all this fancy education is ruining the business; takes the kids away when they most need to be learning something useful. I'm speaking of what I know.'

He paused in his sewing to gaze for a moment at the yellow flame of the Beatrice stove on which his tea kettle was beginning to murmur. 'Of course,' he went on, 'there are just one or two lives you can take up later in life with a fair chance of doing well. There's the haute école, for instance. I've known handsome girls who had the luck to find a good teacher and could afford to buy horses ready made for 'em leave the stage for the ring to show their looks off in a long habit and a tall hat. I'm speaking of years ago, but I dare say it's done still. In Paris they was all the rage at one time. You'd find young women of good family who had been used to the horses from childhood *posing as* haute école *stars, and collecting the rich young fellas around them like flies over the treacle pot. In my eyes, of course, they wouldn't compare with the girls that had belonged all their lives to the circus. I used to think it was their horses that really earned the flowers and the bonbons, while they just sit still in their saddles ogling the front rows, and I couldn't see that did any good to business, teaching the public to swallow fourth-rate work like that.' He let his sewing billow over his knees and ruminated. 'No,' he declared, 'I never knew but one amateur do us a good turn and that was a very queer case indeed.'*

'The Understudy', D. L. MURRAY

For the winter of 1997 and the very early spring of 1998 I went back to Cheltenham to stay with Andrew at his farm on the tip. I took Prince there too, and he spent his days in the paddock with Andrew's pony. I believe he missed the show and the company of people, for as the drivers came and went from the offices on the ground floor of the farmhouse Prince would stand by the gate and watch them, and when I went to see him in the field he would follow me to the gate.

I continued to live in my caravan, and spent the days writing and looking after Prince. It was not so easy, though, just to leave the circus. I had become accustomed to the constant presence of other people, colleagues and friends, to the barking of Anne Marie's dogs, the shape of the elephant outside the caravan window, the sound of the show music – and I missed the spotlight. In the circus my life was private, because I was constantly moving, and so hidden – and yet a part of each day, the show, was lived in front of the public. I missed that. The structure of my life had changed profoundly. There were no long nights of driving. On Sunday afternoons, when in the circus we would have been coupling up lorries and caravans, packing away the tent, Andrew and I would go to the pub. Then I started to become a local again.

Ronnie the old builder sat at the bar in the Gloucester Old Spot pub and fondly contemplated the loneliness that had not left him since his wife ran off with the green-eyed horse-dealer. He sits there like that every night and tends his feelings, and above, pinned to the black rafters, last year's hops drop dried leaves. He drinks pints of cider. Richard the ferret man was telling him a tale from the hedges, and Rich's dogs lay flat on the floor beside him, tired from long runs after rabbits. Richard has brass rabbits pinned to the lapels of his waxed coat, and he wears a broad-brimmed leather hat.

I tried on the hat. 'Good for the low-lying sun, isn't it?'

Rich nodded, lifted the hat off my head and put it back on his own. He looked through the window right into the sun to the hedges beyond the main road. He narrowed his eyes. He had an idea that he was a cowboy. 'That's right, Nell, you can look into the sun when you wear this hat.' He turned as he heard the door open and shut – everyone turns when they hear the door open and shut: it clicks, swishes and slams, and whichever figure was seen through the frosted glass appears in true detail.

'All right, Andrew?'

'Hi, Ferret, hi, Nell,' Andrew said, and nodded to Ronnie. He had his hands in his pockets and was wearing his clothes from the farm.

Over by the fire Ivor sat with his terrier. He is old and his jaws collide toothlessly. Soon the landlord would be back. Craig

Brown, the landlord of the Gloucester Old Spot, had walked right the way across the south coast of Australia in record time, and when the door opens and closes and the flames leap in the fire the newspaper cuttings on the wall of the pub, above the map of Australia marked with a slow line of coloured pins, flutter and shudder. Craig Brown organised a pantomime for charity. Richard the ferret man was the Fairy Godmother. The pub stayed open late that night and the police came. Craig was charged. He was given community service.

Further down the road, in the village of Bishop's Cleeve, the old pubs have been gutted and replaced with countryside decoration, which includes made-up poems in made-up italics painted on to the walls. Dogs are banned. The old roads have been stamped by a ring road. The land has been dug up and the houses converted into offices. The old communities are still there, defiant with their binder-twine and corrugated-iron sheds. There is a butcher, two bakeries, a post office, a jeweller and a gift shop, with plate-glass windows and dull-lit dried flowers. Soon a giant supermarket is going to be built in the village, and there is a petition in the bakery that you can sign if you object to the supermarket, beside the bread face that warns young customers not to climb on the basket rail as they might hurt themselves.

The tip is the same as ever, though the holes of rubbish are more full and the mountains of it have grown and more holes are being dug for further tips. The men come and go in high-visibility jackets and muddy boots. There is Cat Man who feeds all the cats that live in the farm. Wash-bay Ray loves cleaning his lorry and hogs the wash-bay. James Herbert runs the workshop now and he drives a different sports car every week. He has a number-plate that says 'Herbie'. An ash-processing tower has been installed and ash coats the surface of the drive. Andrew and I wonder if it's coating our lungs. I sold my caravan to a boy called Lee, who works on the ash tower. Andrew refers to him as Ash Lee.

Some time in December 1997 I flew to Germany to meet a woman who trains horses in a famous German circus, Circus Roncalli. She is called Yasmin Smart and she is the granddaughter of Billy Smart. I had begun to see that I could learn to do *haute école*, a genuine circus discipline in which the ridden horse performs elevated dressage movements. It seemed like a way finally to embed myself in the fabric of the circus world, not as a passenger but at last as an authentic component of a show. As with all circus skills the act is the product of many years' training. Few people still practise *haute école*. When properly executed it should be as brilliant as the Spanish Riding School. Roncalli was the first show I had seen on the continent and I started to understand how deprived England is of high-quality shows.

Dancing girls and a brass band entertained the audience as they arrived at the show. The foyer tent was laid with polished wooden boards and there was a brass bar and popcorn spilling out from brass funnels behind stained-glass windows. The clowns threw confetti and the artists gave out sweets from silver hats to the children. Gold cherubs and red velvet decorated the inside of the tent in a baroque frenzy, and the audience, coming up to the seats from the passage below, were lit by white spheres of light. Boys in red and gold military uniform, fluent in four languages, showed them to their seats and there was a bandstand that someone told me was the work of four carpenters, reconstructed at every ground. There was a twelve-piece orchestra and four perfectly co-ordinated spotlights. In England the best shows rarely have a band, and they certainly never have a dazzling bandstand reaching backwards into the shadows of the tent in shimmering light, all hung with figureheads and mouldings.

Yasmin's horses were the first act and they were preceded by the dancing girls in bright costumes, parodying the shape of the horse and rider. It was humorously done, the girls skipped and slow-marched in time to the music, then the curtains went back. Yasmin and two others rode into the ring and the horses seemed to dance in time to the music. I was sitting quite far back in an audience of over a thousand people. Yasmin sat straight and still on the huge black horse, which waltzed and side-stepped about the ring like a sprung machine, like a ballet dancer, magic clockwork. She did not appear to move in the saddle and smiled throughout. The music was exact, violin staccato noises, and the horses corresponded with mathematical precision.

There was a boy who did an act with a life-size puppet in a black top hat and dandy tails, and the puppet had a painted, glossy plaster face. Only half-way through the act, when the puppet was standing on a pedestal in the ring, and moving with jerky, animatronic movements, did I realise that it was a real person. A man and a woman did a beautiful aerial act with cords hanging from the roof of the tent. He grasped them with his hands and turned his body inside out around his shoulders. He hung like this, crucified, and she pressed a slow, immaculate handstand on his back as they both rose high into the roof of the tent. There was deep organ music playing and blue light.

The next morning I rode Yasmin's horse in the ring. A man raked the sawdust into lines between horses and the deep red velvet chairs beside the ring were covered in dust sheets. Yasmin had led the horses through the complicated curtains of the back doors. I had followed her in the darkness, and then we had emerged in the ring. I rode the horse as an audition. She wanted to see how I sat on a horse, how I looked and whether I had a deep enough seat. She needed another rider for the 1998 season. The horses flexed perfect supple necks and eased in a soft trot over some poles she had laid down. Around the ring people came and went. Several languages were being spoken at once, and I recognised some of the people from the show. There was a beautiful woman with long black hair who practised on a Palomino horse. Yasmin said that I was not a *haute école* rider but my seat was all right. She could teach me. She still had to renew her contract with the circus for next season. She said that she would contact me in a month and tell me what was happening for definite.

I had time to stay and see the start of the afternoon show that day, then I would have to rush off to catch the aeroplane. The Roncalli trailers, which are like thirties railway carriages, painted in cream, embossed with the Roncalli sign and a number, formed a sort of courtyard at the back of the tent. I waited there for Yasmin. A man was warming up on a grey Andalusian horse. The earth was gritty and the noise of the orchestra was coming from inside the tent. The leather shone and creaked and the metal on the harness gleamed. The man riding the horse was concentrating hard. The horse curled its neck and side-stepped. Two clowns were standing beside one of the trailers in dressing-gowns. One was drawing a picture in the air and the other was watching his hands. The horseman was watching the movement of the horse's legs underneath him and the whites of the horse's eyes were glinting.

Yasmin saw me from the back of the tent. She came over to where I was standing. 'I have to go now and get ready for the

show. You can go in whenever you want. They know who you
are now.'

'Thank you very much for everything.'

'I will ring you before Christmas, OK? Then we can talk
further.'

'OK.'

'Nice to meet you. I have to run now.'

'Goodbye.'

'Goodbye.'

She turned to go back towards the tent. She looked over her
shoulder at me and waved, her eyes looked very large and very
bright, made larger by the show makeup.

In that same autumn I went to see a show in Paris called
Alexis Gruss. Yolande, Ernest Santus's sister, had told me about
him. We were standing outside her daughter's caravan. The
white poodles were lying beside the caravan wheels. We were
talking about horse acts. 'You know who you should see,' Yolande
had confided. She opened her eyes wide. 'He is the best in the
world.' She spoke in a half-whisper. She leaned towards me,
dropped her voice and tilted her chin upwards. 'Alexis Gruss.'
She closed her lips and leaned back and looked at me. 'He is the
best in the world. Hard,' she said, and clenched her fist. The
poodles started to bark at a figure walking around the back of
the caravans. 'Hard but very good.'

I went to Paris for the weekend with Vlad, who is not unre-
servedly enthusiastic about the circus. We went to the winter
circus in Paris, the Cirque d'Hiver. There was a café beside the
circus building called the Circus Bar. There were photographs of
artists on the wall. I felt that Ernest and Roget, Eva and Anne
Marie, younger, newly in love, bravado, perfect makeup, tired
after the show, meeting with other artists – I felt that they were

in the café, their imprints in the air. (Later, when I went to visit them, they asked me what I had been doing. 'I went to Paris to see Alexis Gruss. I went to a bar beside the Cirque d'Hiver called the Circus Bar,' I said, and they all nodded and laughed. 'The Circus Bar – that was our bar! Did you go there all the time?' Of course, every day.)

We looked up Alexis Gruss in a directory, found a number and called it from a clear glass payphone. They were playing that afternoon in a park, in the Bois de Bologne. There were two circuses in the park and someone had been tampering with the signs. Vlad and I walked round and round a huge wood looking for a tent. A man was sitting with a hundred bicycles, reading a newspaper.

'Come on, Vlad, let's hire a bike each. Come on.'

'No. Someone will steal them or something.'

'Well, ask the man if he has seen a circus.'

The man with the bicycles looked annoyed. He said that there was a circus in the children's playground. Not Alexis Gruss. We walked in the opposite direction. We walked back through a wood and along another road. It was the afternoon and the show was due to start in ten minutes. We walked along another main road. There was no sign of the circus, no sign of the top of the tent or of a lorry or of a caravan. We came upon the man renting bicycles again. He looked over the top of his newspaper and frowned. We turned round and walked off back down the main road. We didn't turn to the left or the right this time. We walked past a municipal pond. There were ducks swimming in the shallow water and winter-yellow leaves floating on the surface, and the shadows of the ducks drifted across the bottom of the pond. The water was clear. There was some smoke from a bonfire and we saw the occasional walker in the park. The cars went past very fast. We walked in silence. Then, about a hundred yards ahead of us on the left-hand side of the road, we saw a sign that said 'Circus Alexis Gruss'.

The tent at Roncalli, the foyer and the front of the show, the high fine walls of perfectly glossed picket fence and wrought iron and stained glass and running lights, the lines of vintage trailers, are presented to the audience as a complete, seamless product. It is very German: no element of the show is neglected or fails to correspond to the look of the whole. It seems to be perfectly well organised. I have begun to think that a country's standard of circus will relate to the way in which that country sees itself. The form and content of the show is an expression of the people that create that show. The Chinese circus acts unfold like a lotus flower and consist of an obsessive focus on balance. The Mongolian acts are the product of a race supremely accomplished in fighting. American circus is a celebration of scale – the largest and most successful American circus, Ringling Brothers, has three rings in which there is a constant movement of artists.

Alexis Gruss's tent was large, dark and dusty. It was decorated by one string of fairy-lights around the quarter poles and the band were tuning their instruments on a high bandstand, behind some rusty wrought-iron fencing. An old man slowly put a velvet cover on the ring fence and the faces of the people entering the tent were lit only by the fairy-lights and by some yellow bulbs around the popcorn machine. Vlad and I were given seats in the front row. The noise of the band tuning up persisted for about twenty minutes. Then we realised it was taped music. Someone was having a joke. There was a huge illuminated horseshoe at the ring doors. That was the only decoration. I saw a girl put a microphone in the microphone stand and then, a few minutes later, another girl came and took it away. There was a sort of guileless humour in the air. It reminded me of Santus Circus, where the best artist effects, the blue light under the seating stand, the scrolled painting on the ring boxes, the white face of the indigo clown, seemed to have been done by accident. Circus culture seems to be a deep-rooted instinct with the French people. They create circus and they react to circus as easily as breathing.

The taped music stopped and the lights went down. A man's voice spoke philosophically about the circus over the microphone. Vlad translated a bit of it and I half guessed the rest. He spoke quite quickly. Then the curtain drew back and a man walked into the ring with a huge grey shire horse wearing a plain brown-leather harness and pulling a chain harrow. Slowly they harrowed the ring, leaving circles in the sawdust. When they had finished everyone clapped. You see, in England you wouldn't see that. It was a wonderful piece of showmanship, and at the same time poetic, intellectually complicated. The harrowing of the ring prepared it for the show. The act of harrowing the ring crossed the clear boundary that lies between itinerant showman's culture and the static agricultural community. The pulling horse, the plough, heavy harness: they are the unequivocal tools and symbols of graft, a working and reworking of the same piece of land. The circus turns over minds, lives in the air between the artist and the audience, but is graft none the less, and the image of the chain harrow in the ring seemed to me to be a showman's hand reaching out to shake that of a farmer to verify a mutual understanding of hard work. Plumes and sequins did not decorate the act. It was a rude, simple statement, a loaf of bread on a wooden table, a wheel turning in the mud.

The show lasted three hours, and Alexis Gruss, his sons and

daughter and his wives worked continuously throughout. It was the most brilliant circus I have ever seen.

The show was based on horse acts. A spotted pony pulled a huge wooden tumbrel. Alexis Gruss's children jumped out over the high sides and juggled and tumbled. One of the boys star-shaped his body on to the wheels of the cart and as they turned his body rotated. The humour between the family was evident throughout the show. It was almost like watching them practise together. One of the daughters rode into the ring on a big black horse wearing a classical ballerina's outfit with a wide net skirt. She sat on the horse sideways, as if she were sitting on the ground, and smiled. The horse walked around the ring. Then she left. A tiny black Shetland trotted in carrying a doll identical to the girl. Two of the sons played cards, drank cassis and laughed together. They were lit by a spotlight and a dim light from the king poles. They started to play boules. They were laughing together and clowning a bit. We were drawn into the conviviality between them. We forgot we were in a circus. The circus was making pictures in our heads. It had taken up a line of thought. It was a cat's cradle in the brain, shapes dropping, being picked up and rearranged. We forgot we were in the Bois de Bologne and we forgot we were in Paris. I forgot I was with Vlad. The two figures, with their clear eyes and smiles and pre-cise movements, fluid humour, were all that existed for those moments. Silently, through the curtains, an elephant walked into the ring. That is an artistic achievement, if a circus can present an elephant as a genuine surprise. I turned to Vlad. 'Look, an elephant!' He glanced to one side and his mouth opened and he laughed.

They made many good pictures in the ring after that. The elephant played boules with them. They produced some giant skittles and a giant wooden ball and she knocked the skittles down with the ball and they all applauded. One of the boys jumped up on her back and stood on her neck. The other boy was standing on the ground and they passed white clubs between them. It was a big old dusty tent on a slow winter afternoon in a Parisian park on the west side of the city. The tent was only about a fifth full. Something very brilliant was happening in the ring. It was not theatre and it was not circus as people imagine it – there were no sequins and fishnets – it was like nothing I had seen before. I think that it was representative of true circus, which is a family performing for money and executing certain recognised disciplines to a very high standard. (It seemed that all the children could tumble, juggle, contort, play a musical instrument, ride, balance, sing.) At the same time as they were playing in the air, they were inside the audience's heads and making new pathways. They were inventive, artistic, exuberant, and the entire show was underpinned with humour. There was none of the sickly Disney iconography that English circus has inadvisably borrowed from American shows. One of the sons ran and jumped on to the back of a horse galloping around the ring. He landed true on the hindquarters. Someone threw him a flag, and as he galloped around the ring it uncurled and blew about behind him, almost forming a secondary circle, and the flag was dark blue and it had the European star icon on it. At the very end of the show the black-haired daughter rode into the ring on two huge black horses. She had a foot on each and she rode round the ring at a gallop. There were bells on the horses' harnesses. Then an Arab horse galloped into the ring behind her and ran between the two black horses and under her legs. She leaned down and caught a lunge rein attached to the harness of the third horse. All three horses continued to gallop about the ring and she remained standing on the two black ones. Another Arab came through the curtains and again it went under her legs and between the two black ones, and again she caught a lunge rein. This happened eight times until the ring was full of galloping horses. The brothers were cheering from the ring doors and the bells were ringing. The girl was standing on the two black horses and she was holding eight white reins in her hand.

When I returned to England I could wait no longer to hear from Yasmin. I called her on her mobile. When she answered the telephone she was out of breath. She said that she was just standing in the school running the horses. She said it was 100 per cent definite. I could join her next season. 'You will have to work as a groom as well if you want me to train you to ride.'

'OK. But I'm taking the job as a rider not as a groom. I am taking the job to work in the ring.'

'I understand, Nell. You have to get on, don't you?'

'Yes, you have to get on.'

'You must arrive at my farm in Belgium at the end of February. We will start the training there, then go to the circus in April. I will write anyway and give you all the details.'

I could not believe my good fortune. I could not believe that I was going to be working in the ring at Roncalli next season. A circus person, a josser made good, a chronicler of the circus – I had no idea any more what I was. I had bought and sold and lived in trailers, had a wardrobe full of costumes, a box full of sequins, and I had lived with and loved and hated circus people for three years. Germany, Circus Roncalli, *haute école*: this was another path through the circus that I had no reason not to follow, and every reason to be excited about.

I bought an almost brand new American caravan. It has a

freezer, a microwave, air-conditioning, a separate bathroom and bedroom – it is big enough to have a corridor! It was with very deep regret and sadness that I decided to sell Prince. I could not take him with me to Germany and he would not have suited that circus: none of the grounds are large enough or rural enough to tether a horse. I sold him to Ivan and Phillip. They had left Richie Richards' show and were working on their own truck-riding act. Where Ivor is the talented athlete, Phillip is a true horseman. I went to see them when the circus they were with was somewhere on the north side of London. They had a black and white horse that lived in a lean-to tent between their two caravans. Phillip showed me a book where he kept all the horse's records, a cart on the back of their lorry that they were intending to drive it in. Clearly they were both working hard to make their act a success. Prince would be happier with them, I decided, within sound of circus music and the constant contact of people, than he would leading a lonely life in a field somewhere. Phillip came down to Cheltenham and picked him up. We shook hands and hugged. I wished Prince luck. I wished those two boys luck – they are battling away to do what they are best at and to sustain their art. I know that their wages will be poor, and I have heard that the show they are with is doing badly so they are on half wages. They deserve better.

Grande Finale,
Roncalli 1998

~

I remember now Elaina's snide accusation that I was running
away, and I remember feeling guilty as she said it. I don't
think that I was, in fact, guilty of anything; nor were my reasons
for joining the circus particularly mysterious or complex.
Happy normal family life had been replaced first of all by a
nightmare composed of all the most depressing episodes from
Casualty, and when we woke from the nightmare we found
our childhood over, and the narrative of the nightmare continuing in real life. What I had grown up with and found
familiar did not exist for me any longer so, on leaving the struc-
tured world of university, I submerged myself in the thing that
intrigued me most and that had perhaps offered some relief
from the problems at home during the first terrible year of
Mum's accident. The circus. In a world turned upside down by
tragedy, the circus became a new fixed point, an opportunity

for a brand new identity. I wanted to change my spots. I wanted to be authentically a part of a life that had nothing to do with my own – the only connection with the circus that I could claim were a few childhood games of dressing up. No, I was not running away from the past, I was in pursuit of a future.

Life in the circus was at times challenging. It was difficult, but never so hard as sitting in Intensive Care holding my mother's inert hand and praying that she would come back. And never so hard as the drip-feed of understanding that came to me over perhaps two years: the truth that she would never come back. It is as if she has been taken away and made into another person, who tragically shadows the old. If I have hidden in the circus, then, perhaps I have hidden from her, from my mother; and now I know that I want to say goodbye to the circus, for the moment, hang up my top hat, and go and find my mother again. I must return with the love of my childhood. And perhaps I am being too hard on myself, and hardening the past, knocking the fun out of the circus memory. I was often in awe of the picturesque quality that exists in the routine of circus life, and the vibrancy and flippant humour of circus people. I was certainly drawn towards the ring itself, a place where I aspired to be, finally on the inside looking outwards, finally real, finally able to claim the authenticity that must surely be mine.

The figures in the circus whom I had met over the last few years had emerged from their puppet surface and become real friends and real enemies, the crisp outlines of their circus characters blurring and melting into the world they inhabited. In Roncalli we seemed to remain as our plaster showpiece counterparts, pretty toys in a glorious toy box, trapped in a world where we were perpetually on show. There was a god there worshipped by all and that god was called Ego and Ego was worshipped by the religion of vanity. At Roncalli I came into contact for the first time with the spirit of lusty, prosperous showbusiness.

Circus Roncalli is closer to Disneyland than it is to Santus Circus: it is a large-scale entertainment business in which every element of the show corresponds to the whole. It is a meticulous and infinitely picturesque re-creation of a 1930s circus, celebrated by the public and the circus community. At the present time all circus artists want to come and work at Roncalli. The German magazine *Stern* declared that 'Circus Roncalli is for our decade what Woodstock was for the 1970s.' Living at Roncalli is like being a moving figure in a sentimental painting of the circus – sit in the brown lacquered café wagon, where black-and-white photographs of old circus artists line the walls, and one's face, looking through the window, staring out over a cup of hot chocolate, is the painted face of an off-duty showgirl relaxing between shows, glimpsed through grey cut-glass windows and reflected among strings of lightbulbs with subliminal jazz floating past in the air. No element of our lives was private, save for the space on the inside of our own caravans – and even then I once looked up to see the face of the director pressed against the glass of my window staring at me as I did my makeup. Santus Circus is the most unselfconscious place in the world, doing itself for real, just a circus. Circus Roncalli is the most brilliantly contrived place in the world, a perfect re-creation of a circus, not a circus. We were like exhibits in a museum, watched and photographed as we worked, ate, relaxed, performed, dressed, made up, chatted, practised. I was sitting at the back door to my dressing room. A thin muscular girl called Natalia was strapped into a huge circular frame, and the frame was revolving across the grass. She was practising a new act and she kept trying to tip the frame so that it would revolve against the grass in a series of arcs like a dropped penny. The balance was wrong and the frame persistently came to a face-down standstill. She released her hands and feet and stood up, rubbing her hands, frowning. I was watching her practising, and from my left a man appeared with a camera, angled round the practising figure, turned and pointed the camera at me, smiling guiltily, then slipped off towards the back of the tent.

We warmed up the shiny *haute école* horses behind the tent, their long manes blowing and flapping around their knees, bits jangling, the bright red and gold of the saddlecloths glorious in a low summer sun, the horses curling and turning against the cream sides of the trailers. The man who walks around upside down in the roof of the tent walked past with three legs and three silver juggling clubs and shouted greetings in Italian. The Moroccan groom leaned against the side of the stable and watched the horses moving. There were eight girls in skintight costumes in eight electric colours, with feathers on their heads and Barbarella High Priestess of the Moon Boots, and they crowded around a baby in a cot on the table. A bored-looking man was sitting on the steps of a trailer smoking a cigarette; his muscles bulged from behind his armpits like fins. The girl talking to him (in Russian, angular sounds and fast) had the body of a thin eleven-year-old. In the sewing room, the *Schneiderein*, the sewing lady, peered at the point of a sewing machine and the girl behind her grumbled and closed her lips in a sullen stare as she looked at the pile of shirts to be washed. All the ring-boys hitched up the tails of their red and gold coats and sat on the benches; they pretend they have never tried to glimpse inside the girls' dressing rooms. The dust was settling on the sawdust in the ring, dry ice floated in the air, the public were waiting, and in the dressing room two of the chorus girls pulled off their Versace jeans, complained of their weight and longed for a holiday.

I liked the sounds at Roncalli and they often matched my nerves as I sat in the dressing room trying to arrange my hair. I rode in the *haute école* act, and wore a stern tail coat with brass buttons and my hair scraped back. Outside, in the small tent behind the big top, a tall, dark blue, two-poled tent lined with dressing rooms, the artists and workers came and went, their feet scuffling in the sawdust or snapping on the wooden boards. Something hummed and banged from the tent, the music changed again, somebody called for the time, somebody else replied in German, and in the dressing room the Russian girl shuffled her feet on the lino floor. If it was raining the tent seemed to hiss, like hairspray hissing out of its can, coat-hangers grated along the rail, and on première nights double bunches of flowers lay on the dressing-room table, twice jealous flowers – the girls practically fought for the prettiest bouquet – twice reflected and our made-up tired faces twice reflected too.

The myth and the reality of the circus coexist as usual. It is still surreal, surprising. The trombonist in the twelve-piece band is a nuclear physicist, and the man who sells the *bratwurst* to the public is a Polish jeweller. Kai in the Sky hangs by his legs from the top of the tent and juggles upwards, reversing gravity, and there is a man who places a long pole on his forehead and carries a woman perched at the top, hoisting her high in the air so that she can retrieve a lost helium balloon. The doctors have warned him that the work will kill him, but he carries on anyway and the band call him the Unicorn. There is still the unearthly picturesque of circus life – in the daytime the metal frame in the roof of the tent lifts a few feet to release the hot air and close human smells that thicken the atmosphere, and sometimes the blue balloon of the woman at the top of the pole drifts out and into the blue German skies and away above Bonn or Heidelburg or Munich. It is still monotonous, still something painful that by artifice appears beautiful. To make the horse do its work you have to apply maximum pressure with the legs. So sit still and smile, look relaxed, while you are squeezing until the muscles in your legs burn as if they were on fire. To the audience, the horse and you are a pretty equestrian type of ballet, weightless, effortless, mythical and not concerned with day-to-day problems and normal pain. I still think that the circus is one of the hardest lives available. At Roncalli I see that the best artists are those who have given over their whole lives to the circus. I see that an artist is someone who has worked out a complete number for themselves. They are not simply participating in a circus. They are creating and inventing it by their work. I am riding someone else's horse. I am not an artist I am a prop. An artist is someone whose life corresponds to the moment of their act and does not go in other directions. I saw that there was only one freedom in the circus – and that was the freedom experienced by a true artist while working in the ring. All the rest of circus life is confinement.

There was no slackness of professionality among the artists at Roncalli. There I met people more dedicated to their work than I have met anywhere else, and will never meet people more dedicated to their art. Joseph Bouglione had dark skin and transparent blue eyes. He walked with his toes out and he had an extreme lightness of step, as if he were walking down a staircase as he moved. Thirty-eight, with the face and body of a twenty-year-old, Joseph seemed supremely happy when he was in the ring. The ring was his world and he was master of it. The finale of the show lasted for about twenty-five minutes. There would be a series of staged curtain calls in which the entire company would reappear through the curtains in a series of explosions of activity – juggling, tumbling, dancing. We waltzed with a member of the audience and fireworks were let off in the ring. Joseph would invisibly direct the finale, running at the curtains at the very end of the show and throwing a somersault into the air to land among the artists and ballet grouped in the blue sparkly box at the entrance to the ring split seconds before the curtains dropped and the finale ended. He did an act on wire. He said that the thickness of the wire increased with his age – he worked on a twelve-millimetre wire now, whereas when he was younger the wire was eight-millimetres, thin enough to cut him in half if he slipped on completion of the forward somersault. A forward somersault to land on a wire that would slice through flesh as sure as wire through cheese. He styled his act on *Riverdance*, jumped through a flaming hoop and wore a pin-sharp, gleaming black suit. He made his own props. He had a precisely engineered practice wire set up at the back of the tent and he would run up and down it every day, his arms held out from his shoulders, balancing his body like wings. He polished the wire every day. They said his caravan was so tidy because every night he washed the floor with bleach and colour-coded his clothes. The cables around the caravan were laid in perfect straight lines and the hosepipes arranged in coils. He hosed the shiny aluminium exterior walls every day. Along the top of the windscreen of his white van there was a sticker reading Bouglione – Le Professional du Cirque. He did not disappoint this assertion, and it seemed to me that the precision of his life was the precision of his weight on the wire. If the caravan looked dirty he would slip in the air. Like the other artists on the show, he did not drink or smoke. Nicole, the girl with whom I shared a dressing room, dragged lip-gloss across her lips like varnish and looked at her pretend double in the mirror. She tossed back her hair and told me that none of the artists in the circus drank or smoked, apart from the Russian. She said that the Russian artists were always different.

But the Russian artist's professionalism was not in question. My friend in the orchestra, Czuba, a Hungarian who played the saxophone, said that they were the most professional of all the artists he had seen working in Roncalli. 'It is their big chance to escape life in Russia.' One of the Russians wore a red costume covered in huge red rubber spikes. The orchestra called him All Dick but the act was brilliant and perhaps the *pièce-de-résistance* of the show. It was a traditional form – wire-walking, combined with juggling – worked and reworked into an eerie, sexual, futuristic piece. The traditional circus people hated this number and the audience – affluent German middle-class readers of broadsheet newspapers, attuned to the avant garde, expecting something new – loved it. These were lives lived to the extreme – it would be impossible to be more of a circus artist than Red Spiky (as I always thought of him) or Joseph: they were immersed in their art. By this sacrifice flesh was somehow transformed in the ring: by going to the limits of human behaviour – a forward somersault to land on a cable eight millimetres thick, climbing a ladder balanced on a wire, juggling question marks – they seemed to overrule the limits of the normal human universe and become other than human. It was not a believable fantasy about themselves that the audience saw, it was unbelievable fantasy.

I was working for the great Yasmin Smart, the granddaughter of Billy Smart, a glorious old-fashioned equestrienne, funny, bawdy, sexy, a girls' comic-book heroine, a St Trinian's ringleader, and a modern icon of female strength and independence.

Her husband had left her and the horses and, without flinching, Yasmin took her ten stallions out on the road for the 1998 season. Smitten men would give her plaited leather bridles and ring her up begging for a dinner date. She said that they said they wanted to talk. She laughed and crumpled up her face. 'I don't want to talk all the time, want to laugh and have jokes.' She had short black hair and dark eyes, a big appetite for food, a head for drinking, an eye for strangers, a way with words; she is a restless, ambiguous mover among all classes. She was the champion arm-wrestler of the circus world. One evening all the artists were having dinner in a restaurant. The owner challenged one of the boys to an arm-wrestle, and beat him. Yasmin challenged the owner, and suggested that if she won the bill for the meal would be waived. He accepted and she beat him. Not that she was overtly macho, she had just developed strong shoulders from working with horses all her life. In the daytime she would walk off to town in dark glasses and a caramel-coloured coat, her two Scottie dogs on leads, a svelte anonymous European.

We went to the fairground one evening after the show, a huge funfair in Düsseldorf. There had been a million people through the gates on the first day, and as we arrived they were taking people away on stretchers. The rides were massive – it was more a mobile Alton Towers than a cheery little funfair of the sort you see in market towns in England. There were twenty-foot-high walls of fluorescent toys to be won, mini streets of bars, *faux*-Parisian street scenes, discos, plastic wood-effect funnels of water, soaring and dipping above our heads, and a slow, stately Big Wheel with glass boxes, pale faces pressed to the glass in rotating observation of the Düsseldorf night lights. As we left the fair we saw Yasmin leaning against one of the bars, around the back, chatting and drinking with an old fairground man. That was typical, though: she seemed to know people wherever she went. Everyone who met Yasmin fell in love with her. That was one of the reasons for her success. The majority of women who have horse acts do so with the support of a family circus. Although she had grown up on her grandfather's circus and had learned her trade there, Yasmin had trained and worked the horses independent of family. In any case she is the only Smart still working in the ring. She is known right across Europe for her act, which is a classical Liberty routine in which eight Arab stallions work free – 'at liberty' around her. She wears long evening dresses and dances to jazz music as she works. She has star quality, can switch on the lights for the public, project dazzling pleasure, privately, publicly, to every member of the audience. 'Yasmin smiled right at me,' a friend of mine said. He had been sitting about half-way back, in the darkness beyond the ringside seats, where to the artist the audience are faded into black shapes, individuals invisible. She could not have seen him in this darkness and, in any case, Yasmin is very short-sighted. She is brilliant at making the horses work – they kneel down for her, stand on their back legs, weave figures-of-eight, paw the air – but better than this is her ability to communicate with every single member of the audience, shining, beaming, right into their eyes. She makes them all feel that she has worked especially for them. But again, like Joseph, like Red Spiky, her life is all that, all circus.

'Do you like working?' I asked her, referring specifically to the time in the ring. She said she did, she said that she liked the feeling of it – which is exactly the point. All that sacrifice, all that work, practice, practice, practice, thousands of hours of practice, for the feeling of it. There, in the middle of the ring, surrounded by lights and music and people and applause, laughs, admiration, amazement, is the place where freedom can be experienced.

I learned from Joseph a lesson about sharpness, about precise self-reliance, from Red Spiky a lesson about following a creative impulse, however unorthodox, from Yasmin a lesson about projection and glamour and the merits of avoiding self-deprecation. They are a vain and egotistical bunch, but they have to be, for their careers depend on self-invention.

An illusion of happiness, but great too, with the lights in my eyes and the sound of the band from their glorious wedding cake bandstand. As the big black horse knelt down and the applause lifted from the audience, for that little moment life was not prosaic, but I was only ever vicariously experiencing the feeling of being a circus artist. I am not a circus artist and I guess that living among Joseph and Yasmin and the professionals on that show showed me that I did not want to go the distance, sacrifice my life for this specific art. I had a different life to lead. Perhaps the whole of my circus career has been this: a search for authenticity. But it occurs to me that this might be a characteristic of human experience known to all: a search for a place where we can stay and know that we belong.

Bibliography

Bell, Betty Boyd *Circus* (Putnam, New York, 1931)

Blyton, Enid *Enid Blyton's Circus Book* (Latimer House, 1949)

Casey, Juanita *The Circus* (Dolmen Press, 1974)

Conrad, Joseph *Heart of Darkness*

Croft Cooke, R. (ed.) *The Circus Book* (Sampson-Lowe Marston & Co Ltd, London, 1948)

Demoriane, Hermione *The Tightrope Walker* (Secker and Warburg, London, 1989)

Dickens, Charles *Hard Times*

Eipper, Paul *Circus-men, Beasts and Joys of the Road* (1931)

Eliot, T.S. *Portrait of a Lady* (Faber & Faber, London)

Jenkins, A. *Circus Through the Ages* (Children's Educational Books, 1972)

Josipovici, Gabriel (ed.) 'A Hunger Artist', 'First Sorrow' and 'The Wish To Be A Red Indian' from *Franz Kafka Collected Stories* (Everyman Library, 1993)

Kober, A.H. *Circus Nights and Circus Days* (Sampson-Lowe Marston & Co, London, 1931)

Laing, Jan *The Belle in the Top Hat* (T. Werner Laurie, 1955)

Mayo, Eileen and Payne, Wyndham *The Circus Book* (P. R. Gawthorn, London)

Seago, Edward *Circus Company* (Putnam, London, 1935)

Seuss, Dr *If I Ran The Circus* (HarperCollins, London)

Stainer, Sylvia and Lijsen H.J. *Classical Circus Equitation* (A. Allen and Co, London, 1993)

Toll, Robert C. *On With The Show* (Oxford University Press, 1976)

Walton, O.F. *A Peep Behind the Scenes* (Lutterworth Press, London)

Wykes, Alan *Circus! An Investigation Into What Makes the Sawdust Fly* (Jupiter Books, London, 1977)

The author gratefully acknowledges permission to quote
from the following:

Classical Circus Equitation by Sylvia Stanier and H.J. Lijsen.
Copyright © 1993, Sylvia Stanier and H.J. Lijsen.
Reprinted by permission of J.A. Allen & Co Ltd.

If I Ran The Circus by Dr Seuss. Copyright © 1956,
Dr Seuss Enterprises, L.P. All rights reserved.
Reprinted by permission of International Creative Management, Inc.

The Tightrope Walker by Hermione Demoriane. Copyright © 1989,
Hermione Demoriane. Reprinted by permission.

Falling by Colin Thubron. Copyright © 1989, Colin Thubron.
Reprinted by permission of William Heinemann.

'A Hunger Artist', 'First Sorrow' and 'The Wish To Be A Red Indian' from
Franz Kafka Collected Stories, ed. Gabriel Josipovici. Copyright © 1993,
Gabriel Josipovici. Reprinted by permission of Random House Inc. USA.

'Portrait of a Lady', from *Collected Poems 1909–1962* by T.S. Eliot.
Reprinted by permission of Faber & Faber Ltd.

On With The Show by Robert C. Toll. Copyright © 1976, Oxford University
Press, Inc. Reprinted by permission of Oxford University Press, Inc.

The Power Of Love Words by Jennifer Rush and Mary Susan Applegate.
Music by Candy de Rouge and Gunther Mende. Copyright © 1985, EMI
Songs Musikverlag GMBH, Germany. Reproduced by permission of EMI
Songs Ltd, London WC2H 0EA.

Who Do You Think You Are Words and music by Paul Wilson,
Andy Watkins and The Spice Girls. Copyright © BMG Music Publishing
Ltd/Windswept Pacific Music Publishing Ltd. All rights reserved.
Reprinted by permission.

Delilah Words and music by Les Reed and Barry Mason. Copyright © 1967,
Les Reed and Barry Mason. Reproduced by permission of Donna Music Ltd,
London WC2H 0EA.

Every effort has been made to trace the copyright holders and to clear
reprint permissions for *A Peep Behind The Scenes* by O. F. Walton.

If notified, the publisher will be pleased to rectify any omission
in future editions.